"No one involved in the current debates over civil society—and there can only be a few serious scholars who are not—will want to miss John Ehrenberg's trenchant and thrill packed (well, for us theorists anyway) biography of this amazing idea. A major contribution to the history of political theory by one of the brightest stars in the critical galaxy!"
—Bertell Ollman, New York University and author of *Dialectical Investigations*

"An absorbing study of a seminal idea in the history of political theory . . . This is a beautifully written work with an important critical perspective. It makes a genuine scholarly contribution."
—Stephen Eric Bronner, Rutgers University

Civil Society

The Critical History of an Idea

John Ehrenberg

NEW YORK UNIVERSITY PRESS

New York and London

NEW YORK UNIVERSITY PRESS
New York and London

Library of Congress Cataloging-in-Publication Data
Ehrenberg, John, 1944–
Civil society : the critical history of an idea / John
Ehrenberg.
p.   cm.
Includes bibliographical references and index.
ISBN 0-8147-2208-3 (cloth : alk. paper)
ISBN 0-8147-2207-5 (pbk. : alk. paper)
1. Civil society—History.   I. Title.
JC336 .E35 1999
301'.09—ddc21   98-40140
                       CIP

New York University Press books are printed on acid-free paper,
and their binding materials are chosen for strength and durability.

Manufactured in the United States of America
10 9 8 7 6 5 4 3

Contents

Acknowledgments

This book would never have seen the light of day if my wife Kathleen hadn't urged me to write something "relevant." This is often difficult for political theorists, but my students' desire to navigate a complex world also provided early motivation and continuous support. I have also been helped by the interest, encouragement, and assistance of many friends and colleagues, among whom Stephen Bronner, Mark Naison, and Bertell Ollman deserve special mention. Finally, I want to thank Cecelia Cancellaro for getting me in—and Eric Zinner and Niko Pfund for getting me out.

Introduction

For three days toward the end of April 1997, the President's Summit for America's Future focused national attention on a succession of speeches, workshops, and exhibits in Philadelphia. President Clinton gathered George Bush, Jimmy Carter, Nancy Reagan, Colin Powell, thirty governors, dozens of corporate executives, and Oprah Winfrey to urge Americans to volunteer for community service. "The campaign, which General Powell is heading, seeks to mobilize volunteers and corporate money to help two million children by the year 2000," reported the *New York Times*. "It hopes to compensate for a retreating federal government—much of the retreating done under Mr. Bush and Mr. Clinton—by providing children with mentors, safe places after school, health care, job skills and a chance to perform community service themselves." Articulating a central theme of his administration, the President called on volunteers to tutor children, paint schools, revitalize communities, and strengthen habits of good citizenship and public service.

The Philadelphia summit's emphasis on local action and voluntary associations captured an important moment in a period marked by rapid economic change, sweeping attacks on the welfare state, and general withdrawal from political engagement. It articulated a distinctively American way of thinking about "civil society," a notion that has figured prominently in academic and political discourse for most of the past decade. In the absence of noble public goals, admired leaders, or compelling issues, many observers have charted an alarming erosion of civic spirit and a corresponding decline in the quality of public life. An increasingly distressed literature has alerted the country to the damage done by cheapened standards of behavior, rude political speech, "road rage," and offensive jokes. Experts worry that an overworked, disengaged, acquisitive, and self-absorbed population has allowed its moral connections, social engagements, and political participation to atrophy. Their concern is not limited to bad manners but has spilled over into political affairs and generated many suggestions about how public life could be improved in a period marked by fraying communities, widespread apathy, and unprecedented levels of contempt for politics. The American Political Science Association, for example, has organized a "Civic Education Project for the Next Century" to support research and stimulate teaching about "civic trust, civic engagement, and civic education." In an effort to combat rampant cynicism and anger about public affairs, the project seeks to reinvigorate a particularly American orientation toward "the civic work of ordinary people who, located in diverse, plural communities, work on behalf of their communities and seek eagerly for common goods, both heroic and mundane." Driven by an uneasy sense of decline and animated by a deep suspicion of the state, a growing body of contemporary work hopes that civil society can revitalize public life.

But the view that local voluntary activity sustains democracy is only one way of understanding civil society. Ironically, those who brought this notion to the center of contemporary political life conceptualized it in very different terms. In the early 1980s, a remarkably broad series of civic forums, independent trade unions, and social movements began to carve out areas of free political activity in the Eastern European countries of "actual existing socialism." Their leaders talked of "the rebellion of civil society against the state," and when they started coming to power in 1989 the stage was set for an explosion of interest that has been gathering force ever since. Liberal political theory was revived in demands for "law-governed states" that would protect private life and public activity from the intrusive hand of meddling bureaucracies. It was not surprising that Eastern Europeans should conceptualize civil society in terms of limiting state power, or that Americans should express it in the neo-Tocquevillean language of intermediate organization. If civil society meant constitutional republicanism in one area and local volunteerism supported by informal norms of solidarity and mutual aid in another, both bodies of thought sought to theorize it as a democratic sphere of public action that limits the thrust of state power.

As important as such formulations have been, the current literature leaves a great deal unsaid and unexplored. Seemingly new and hastily used concepts sometimes turn out to have revealing and instructive genealogies. Civil society is a very old idea and has long provided a fruitful vantage-point from which to evaluate the central categories of political thought. But many of the lessons that the past offers are obscured by the restricted political environment that conditions much contemporary work. Because its antecedents have not been adequately explored, civil society is often deployed in a thin, undertheorized, and confusing fashion. There is considerably more to this concept than meets the eye, and an explication of tradition can help us evaluate contemporary assumptions about its democratic potential.

This book examines the historical, political, and theoretical evolution of the way civil society has been theorized over two and a half millennia of Western political theory. Broadly speaking, three rather distinct bodies of thought have marked its development, though considerable cross-fertilization has always enriched each tradition. Reflecting its orientation toward broad categories of analysis, classical and medieval thought generally equated civil society with politically organized commonwealths. Whether its final source of authority was secular or religious, civil society made civilization possible because people lived in law-governed associations protected by the coercive power of the state. Such conceptions shaped the way civil society was understood for many centuries. As the forces of modernity began to undermine the embedded economies and universal knowledge of the Middle Ages, the gradual formation of national markets and national states gave rise to a second tradition that began to conceptualize civil society as a civilization made possible by production, individual interest, competition, and need. For some thinkers, the Enlightenment opened unprecedented opportunities for freedom in a secular world of commerce, science, and culture. For others, civil society's disorder, inequality, and conflict falsified its emancipatory potential and required a measure of public supervision. However civil society was perceived, it was clear that the world could no longer be understood as a system of fused commonwealths. Civil society developed in tandem with the centralizing and leveling tendencies of the modern state, and an influential third body of thought conceptualized it as the now-familiar sphere of intermediate association that serves liberty and limits the power of central institutions.

In chapter 1 the origins of civil society can be found in a classical heritage that understood it as a politically organized commonwealth. Reflecting the general dominance of political categories, "civility" described the requirements of citizenship rather than private sensibilities or good manners. Plato's wish to articulate an invariant ethical center for public life drove his attempt to unify dissimilar elements and stimulated his greatest student's powerful critique. Aristotle's civil society was still a political association that improved its citizens, but it was founded on respect for the different spheres and multiple associations in which life is lived. As important as Aristotle's respect for variation and distinction was, however, his civil society was still organized around the face-to-face relations of friends whose leisurely aristocratic benevolence enabled them to discover and articulate the public good.

Cicero and others sought to develop a broader notion of civil society by adding the distinctive Roman recognition of a legally protected private realm, but republican degeneration and imperial collapse brought classical theory to a halt.

Christianity supplied the central categories of political life and theory for the better part of a millennium, beginning with Augustine's devastating critique of classicism's prideful striving for self-reliance. Chapter 2 traces how secular notions of political life succumbed to Christian theories of civil society, which were organized around humanity's fallen condition and depravity, emphasized dependence and hierarchy, and initially denied that the works of human beings could guide moral action. As powerful as it was, such a blanket condemnation of the classical heritage eventually conflicted with the needs of a Church that had to make its way in the world. Augustine's recognition that the state is both the result of and corrective for sin opened the way to more developed notions that did not denigrate the here and now. Thomas Aquinas invested the secular order with a fuller measure of ethical potential than Augustine was willing to admit and revived Aristotle's civil society as an organized political community predicated on the distinct logics of different orders of creation. Since the moral content of human affairs was not erased by revelation, a politically constituted civil society was now essential to human life, expressed man's nature, and served God's purposes. Aquinas took Aristotle's ideas as far as he could within the bounds of Christian orthodoxy, but notions of a civil society constituted by religion would not survive for long. As medieval attempts to theorize a Christian Commonwealth began to crumble under the corrosion of markets and the pressure of kings, Dante Alighieri and Marsiglio of Padua anticipated modern conceptions of a civil society constituted by a single point of secular sovereign power.

Chapter 3 traces the gradual transition to the two modern conceptions of civil society. Centralizing monarchies stimulated distinctly modern theories of power, legitimacy, and sovereignty. The end of classical and medieval attempts to theorize civil society in universal terms was reflected in Niccolò Machiavelli's recognition that Rome's tradition of civic republicanism enabled the empire to turn conflict into stability. But his understandable preoccupation with political decadence made it difficult for him to theorize a sphere of meritorious action outside a purely instrumental understanding of politics. The discovery of the individual was the work of the Reformation, and as Martin Luther drove the conscience inward he left it to princes to organize civil society and choose their subjects' religion. A unified and religiously constituted Christendom yielded to the autonomy of faith, a sharper distinction between the external and internal spheres of life, a new justification of state power, and a civil society that regulated the external relations of a fellowship of equal believers. But not all transitional conceptions were so rooted in theology. The great work of this period, Thomas Hobbes's *Leviathan* announced the appearance of a new calculating individual who had to take account of other self-interested entities. Hobbesian civil society was an artificial creation for the purposes of survival, but a constitutive sovereign power made the benefits of civilization possible. Justice, morality, culture, art, and science depended on the state's ability to shape a civil society that allowed people to go about their business in peace and security. If Hobbes looked backward to the politically organized universal community, he discerned a future marked by the individual pursuit of self-interest.

Modernity came in the form of centralizing nation-states, extensive markets, and political movements for freedom. Civil society was no longer understood as a universal commonwealth but came to mean private property, individual interest, political democracy, the rule of law, and an economic order devoted to prosperity. Chapter 4 begins with John Locke's understanding that a civil society constituted by property, production, and acquisition required a law-governed state to preserve order and protect liberty. Civil society denoted the possibility of people living in conditions of political freedom and economic activity. Adam Ferguson was worried about the disintegrative and divisive effects of the competitive pursuit of self-interest and tried to locate an innate ethical sensibility at civil society's heart. Adam Smith shared Ferguson's awareness of the corrupting effects of commerce, but it was he who articulated the first distinctively bourgeois sense that civil society is a market-organized sphere of production and competition driven by the private strivings of self-interested proprietors. The important role he reserved for the state did not conflict with his simultaneous recognition of civil society as the sphere of moral sentiments, arts, sciences, morality, and all the other benefits of civilized life. Smith's tendency to privilege people's actions in the economy epitomized a powerful strand of liberal thought which assumed that civil society was constituted by the market.

Chapter 5 traces the implications of this first modern conception. Immanuel Kant's separation of essence and appearance led him to regard civil society as a protected sphere that can enable people to make their own decisions in conditions of freedom. A liberal public sphere, fair and equally applied procedures, extensive civil liberties, and legitimate republican institutions would establish a "republic of letters" and turn the pursuit of individual interests toward the public good. But Kant's morality could never find an empirical referent, and G. W. F. Hegel's criticism of Kant's "introversion" led to a theorization of the three ethical moments of the family, civil society, and the state. Hegel's civil society was inhabited by "economic man," was constituted by his private interests—and was a sphere of moral action. A network of social relations standing between the family and the state, it linked self-serving individuals to one another in a mediating sphere of social connections and moral freedom. But Hegel's civil society fails to realize the fullest measure of freedom because it cannot solve the persistent problem of pauperism, and he ended with the reactionary doctrine that Prussia's bureaucratic state could resolve social antagonisms. Karl Marx agreed that civil society was the problem that had to be overcome but rejected Hegel's solution. His conclusion that the state could not be conceptualized apart from economic processes drove him to a theory of social revolution that placed the proletariat at the center of socialist politics and looked to a transformed state to take the lead in democratizing civil society. Marx brings to a close the modern tradition of thought that theorized civil society as a sphere constituted by production, class, and their attendant social and political relations. It was not hostile to the state in principle because its conception of civil society raised the urgent question of how a chaotic sphere of competition could be subjected to public supervision. In so doing it posed the relation between civil society and the state as the fundamental question of modern life and developed a powerful reminder that civil society is not an autonomous sphere of self-contained democratic activity.

Chapter 6 shows how the second major strand of modern theory led in a different direction. It conceptualized civil society in light of conditions in France, where a tradition of centralizing monarchs and a powerful state stimulated notions of community and intermediate organization. Drawing on Aristotle's concept of mixed constitutions and wishing to protect local traditions of aristocratic privilege from central power, Baron de Montesquieu located intermediate bodies at the heart of republican theories of civil society. Jean-Jacques Rousseau mounted a romantic attack on Enlightenment notions of progress, the arts, and sciences but was unwilling to defend the privileges of blood. For him, civil society was a community whose solidarity reconciled the subjectivity of individual interests with the objectivity of the common good. But his indifference to intermediate bodies left him open to Edmund Burke's defense of local traditions against the leveling and centralizing French Revolution. This second strand of modern thought culminated in Alexis de Tocqueville's attempt to understand how American localism and informal norms of voluntary association could limit the thrust of the democratic state in conditions of economic equality and political freedom. His attention to public life outside the state dominates contemporary thinking about civil society even though his initial postulate of American equality exempted him from considering the effects of economic forces on local traditions of self-reliance and voluntary association.

Chapter 7 begins the examination of how civil society is theorized in contemporary political discourse by focusing on the experience of Eastern Europe. The historical trajectory of twentieth-century communism has been shaped by the course of revolutions in underdeveloped societies. A state-driven strategy of industrialization built around the requirements of steel seemed to require the "leading role" of a highly organized party. Committed to central planning, suspicious of the market, and wary of spontaneous social initiatives, the bureaucratized party-states of "actual existing socialism" never developed a credible record of democratic accountability and were unable to accept significant levels of uncontrolled activity. As conformity, pretense, and hypocrisy came to mark Soviet-style socialism, it made sense that dissident intellectuals would theorize civil society in the familiar liberal terms of constitutional republics and limited states. But their conflation of economic regulation with political tyranny and their antistatist understanding of civil society blinded them to the dangers of the market. In the end, almost all of their civic forums, citizen groupings, "flying universities," and social movements were swept away as traditional political structures emerged to apply the iron logic of the market. The once-heady discourse of civil society has long since faded in the region that restored it to the center of contemporary affairs.

The United States has the constitutional limitations on state power that were so attractive to Eastern European dissidents, and chapter 8 chronicles the development of a hegemonic neo-Tocquevillean view among American intellectuals that civil society is a set of informal norms supporting local intermediate associations. Rooted in the traditions of American federalism and informed by James Madison, pluralism's reliance on political culture and interest groups has become the dominant trend of contemporary thought. Its failure to address the structural obstacles preventing some interests from even being articulated, however, also appears in much contemporary theory—particularly in communitarianism's nostalgic and moralizing infatuation with localism. Serving as a counterweight to this trend, however, Hannah Arendt, Richard Sennett, Jürgen Habermas, Herbert Marcuse, and others investigated how a powerful culture industry limits civil society's ability to perform the mediating role demanded by neo-Tocquevillean theory. In different ways each has called attention to the invasion of ever-wider spheres of social life by the totalizing logic of commodification. The easy trust that civil society is the most important contemporary site of democratic activity will be rendered problematic unless its theorists can broaden their field of inquiry and question some of their inherited assumptions.

Chapter 9 raises some of these issues and suggests that localism may not be all that it is made out to be—particularly because heightened levels of economic inequality call Tocqueville's assumptions into question. A foundation has been provided by the path-breaking work of Grant McConnell, Jane Mansbridge, and Sidney Verba and his associates, which suggests that the intermediate organizations so much in favor cannot provide the democratizing effect called for by contemporary theory. An impressive body of theoretical and empirical work suggests that civil society is a badly undertheorized category because it cannot account for some of the most important developments of contemporary life. It is time to move past small thinking and the celebration of local fragmentation to engage the big questions of economic justice and political democracy. If civil society is to play a role in contemporary democratic theory, it needs to be reconceptualized, enriched, and made appropriate to the concrete conditions of the real world. Theorizing civil society in the limited antistatist terms of the current discourse makes it impossible to grasp the emancipatory possibilities of political action. An important tradition of thought can help us grasp the possibilities and limitations of current modes of thinking as we move into a future in which economic justice and political democracy will demand more, not less, of the state.

Civil Society

PART I

The Origins of Civil Society

1

Civil Society and the Classical Heritage

The classical understanding of civil society as a politically organized commonwealth received its first coherent formulation in the cities of ancient Greece. It also revolved around the understanding that men and women lived their lives in separate spheres, and Greek theory considered a wide range of human relations. Love, friendship, teaching, marriage, citizenship, the duties of slaves, the responsibilities of masters, the skills of artisans, and the division of labor—all were studied in their uniqueness and in their connectedness. The observation that people live together in distinct yet related associations stimulated debate about uniqueness and commonality, particularism and universalism. Systematic political theory arose out of these discussions, and political categories framed the first approach to civil society.

Classical thought consistently maintained that political power made civilization possible. The celebrated distinction that the Greeks drew between themselves and barbarians separated those whose membership in a political association enabled them to live in civil society from those who were unable to do so. The broadest and "self-sufficient" level of activity, politics made it possible for men to rise above their immediate circumstances and consciously establish the principles of moral life. If the *idiotes* was the solitary man whose life was constituted by individual drives, the self-governing citizen personified what public action guided by reason could accomplish. "Here," said Pericles in his celebrated testament to Athens, "we do not say that a man who takes no interest in politics is a man who minds his own affairs; we say that he has no business here at all."[1]

The willingness to subordinate one's private interests voluntarily to those of the city was the decisive mark of the citizen-soldier. Pericles knew firsthand how powerful civic spirit could be. "No one of these men weakened because he wanted to go on enjoying his wealth; no one put off the awful day in the hope that he might live to escape his poverty and grow rich. More to be desired than such things, they chose to check the enemy's pride."[2] Forged in the aftermath of the ruinous Peloponnesian War, classical Greek political philosophy insisted that the common good could be discovered through public debate and organized by public action. It followed that civic decay was the inevitable consequence of private calculation and individual interest. Plato first articulated political theory's orientation toward the comprehensive public life of a moral community. In so doing, he revealed some of the strengths—and dangers—of a civil society organized around a common moral project.

The Danger of Private Interest

The son of a prominent Athenian family, Plato tried to counter the political and moral confusion of his day with a philosophical realm of absolute categories supported by a rationalistic approach to knowledge. Born in 428 B.C., the year after Pericles's death, he came to maturity in an environment shaped by Athenian military defeat, economic chaos, political instability, and ethical confusion. His drive to establish the moral principles of government was a direct response to the uncertainty and disorder of his day. The primacy he accorded to political knowledge and power shaped a theory of civil society that owed as much to its unified conception of truth as to its powerful aversion to private interests and separate spheres. Because Plato was unable to theorize the individual, beauty, goodness, or any category of social life apart from the state, his understanding of civil society was ultimately betrayed by the same orientation to universality that gave it life.

Socrates's early debate with Thrasymachus established *The Republic*'s central claim that individual interest can never provide a sufficient foundation for a happy, just, or civilized life. Legitimate power, authority, and knowledge exist only for the welfare of those for whose sake they are exercised. Just as a doctor's craft lies in curing disease and a captain's authority is exercised on behalf of his crew, "no ruler, in so far as he is acting as ruler, will study or enjoin what is for his own interest. All that he says and does will be said and done with a view to what is good and proper for the subject for whom he practices his art."[3] Political power exists to serve the welfare of the city and its citizens. Civil society can be comprehended only in relation to the organizing principles of the state.

Plato knew that people lived in different spheres of association, each of which has its own intrinsic organizing logic. It was important for him to understand each—but only because he wanted to arrive at a comprehensive understanding of the whole. Like the human body or the crew of a ship, civil society is composed of different elements that have different skills and perform different tasks. It rests on human beings' material needs for food, shelter, and clothing; indeed, the division of labor based on natural aptitudes lies at the heart of Plato's theory of justice, politics, and civil society. Guided by the master virtue of reason, justice enables each part to contribute to the welfare of the whole by doing that for which its nature has suited it—whether in family life, friendships, or political affairs. Plato's is a functional theory; the welfare of the soul, of the body, and of the state depend on the balanced harmony that results when each constituent element discharges its proper function. He always investigated these reciprocal relationships, for "without justice men cannot act together at all."[4] Justice and health require understanding the division of labor and the consequent relations of subordination and guidance appropriate to the natural aptitudes of the elements concerned.

For Plato, the task of political theory was to address the twin problems of corruption and decay. He was sure of their source: "Does not the worst evil for a state arise from anything that tends to rend it asunder and destroy its unity, while nothing does it more good than whatever tends to bind it together and make it one?" he asked.[5] The persistent search for unity drove his understanding of the state and civil society and lay behind his famous claim that political disease is caused by the same forces that make individuals sick. If justice is balance and health, then injustice is strife and decay is disorder. All disturbances can be traced to the inability of the state's constituent parts to function according to their natures and to the consequent disruption of the health of the whole. Just as wickedness stems from ignorance, so the corruption afflicting Athens originated in division. If "injustice is like disease and means that this natural order is inverted,"[6] it follows that political theory should seek to identify the source of social and political turmoil. Life was lived in separate spheres, and it was more important than ever to discover the political principles that could organize civil society into a coherent whole.

Unity was as important for the soul as it was for the state. Plato was guided by the Socratic dictum that the happy man will orient himself according to his knowledge of life's ultimate purposes. "The Good" denotes what is worthy of pursuit for its own sake rather than for the sake of any subsidiary or consequent advantages it might bring. In a time of corruption, effective political leadership requires knowledge of unprecedented breadth. Plato's bitter dispute with the Sophists was driven by his conviction that they prostituted knowledge by reducing it to a set of narrow skills for the pursuit of personal advantage. Elevating private interest over the common good encouraged the anarchical forces that were weakening Athens, but the Sophists were only one element of a much larger problem. *The Republic* was organized around Plato's attempt to contain all the centrifugal tendencies that constituted the city's crisis. The unity he sought required that private interests and passions be brought under conscious control. The desire for wealth caused conflict, and Plato's ascetic sense of stability required that all "luxurious excess" be eliminated.[7] The private interests that often animated the actions of both rich and poor could only erode the ties that held civil society together. "The one produces luxury and idleness, the other low standards of conduct and workmanship; and both have a subversive tendency."[8] Nothing was more dangerous to the organic unity that Plato sought than the anarchy caused by different centers of gravity organized around concern for self.

> And this disunion comes about when the words "mine" and "not mine," "another's" and "not another's" are not applied to the same things throughout the community. The best ordered state will be the one in which the largest number of persons use these terms in the same sense, and which accordingly most nearly resembles a single person. When one of us hurts his finger, the whole extent of those bodily connections which are gathered up in the soul and unified by its ruling elements is made aware of it and all share as a whole in the pain of the suffering part; hence we say that the man has a pain in his finger. The same thing is true of the pain or pleasure felt when any other part of the person suffers or is relieved.[9]

Unless it is nipped in the bud, concern for self will spread from the city's leadership to the general population, for "diversity, inequality, and disharmony will beget, as they always must, enmity and civil war. Such, everywhere, is the birth and lineage of civil strife."[10] Plato was certain that ambition, greed, rivalry, and competition are constant threats to civil society because it is difficult to control private appetites with external sanctions in the absence of shared commitments. Force is important, but in the end civil society rests on patterns of thought. Unhealthy states are like diseased souls because their lack of balance orients them toward individual purposes and thus renders them indifferent to the common good. Private strivings stand behind all deviant personalities and political formations because they cripple the master virtue of reason and precipitate psychic breakdown and civil war. The glue that holds together the soul and civil society is supplied by the integrative power of reason, which discerns the single truth that organizes the world.

His suspicion of private passions drove Plato's theory of censorship as well. *The Republic* attacked painting and expelled poetry because they pandered to the emotions, drowned truth in subjectivity, and undermined the guiding faculty of reason. Their appeal to immediate gratification made it impossible to discern the Good by inflaming citizens' private fears, passions, and judgments.[11] Strong, effective leadership could counteract the centrifugal force of diversity because it could root civil society in an ethical totality. Plato's goal was always clear: "For the moment, we are constructing, as we believe, the state which will be happy as a whole, not trying to secure the well-being of a select few."[12] Civil society fused truth, beauty, and goodness with knowledge, power, and the state. Plato's drive to unify all aspects of human experience around an unvarying Good drove him to the first systematic defense of state censorship. Founded on a recognition of diversity and a sophisticated understanding of the division of labor, his civil society ended with a frozen unity and a silent stability.

Such an orientation had important institutional ramifications. Leadership was reserved to "those who, when we look at the whole course of their lives, are found to be full of zeal to do whatever they believe is for the good of the commonwealth and never willing to act against its interest."[13] If absolute ethical knowledge could be located in a few highly trained experts, then democracy stood condemned by its mediocrity, permissiveness, and disorder. At the same time, anyone could become a guardian—even women, a feature of Plato's thinking that often surprises first-time readers. It was a true meritocracy; political leadership represented the self-sacrificing union of power with knowledge. The famous "myth of the cave" made it clear that the philosopher-king had to be forced to assume power against his will. But legitimate political authority required more than training and knowledge.

Plato's communism, reserved for *The Republic's* leadership, was motivated by his conviction that property, the family, and other institutions of private life always tend to establish a pole of particular interest and draw the leaders away from the objective interests of the whole. The guardians would own no private property beyond the barest necessities, have no permanent family attachments, receive their food from their fellow citizens, eat in common, and live the ascetic life of soldiers. If civic corruption began with the pull of individual interest, the guardians could have no private life. Those who organized and defended civil society would not be part of it.

> This manner of life will be their salvation and make them the saviors of the commonwealth. If ever they should come to possess land of their own and houses and money, they will give up their guardianship for the management of their farms and households and become tyrants at enmity with their fellow citizens instead of allies. And so they will pass all their lives in hating and being hated, plotting and being plotted against, in much greater fear of their enemies at home than of any foreign foe, and fast heading for the destruction that will soon overwhelm their country with themselves.[14]

For all his emphasis on unity, Plato knew that civil society coordinates the activities of people with different skills and aptitudes. An understanding of the division of labor lies at the center of his political and psychological theories and informs his epistemology as well. But diversity, different spheres, and the division of labor only identified the problem. That which comes into being and passes away does not constitute the truth. The indeterminate, changing, and mortal world of sensible things is the outward manifestation of the eternal and unchanging Forms, knowledge of which is the key to peace and justice. Civil society can live up to its ethical potential only if it is organized on the same invariant basis as the Forms. Most people might be content to live among the shadows of the cave, but leadership requires understanding that moral potential cannot be reduced to pleasure. Politics is not about coordinating particular self-serving activities or resolving conflicts of interest, but rather in setting the conditions in which individuals are oriented toward the general and the universal can be discerned in the particular, for

> the law is not concerned to make any one class specially happy, but to ensure the welfare of the commonwealth as a whole. By persuasion or constraint it will unite the citizens in harmony, making them share whatever benefits each class can contribute to the common good; and its purpose in forming men of that spirit was not that each should be left to go his own way, but that they should be instrumental in binding the community into one.[15]

Plato tried to provide a counterweight for the centrifugal pull of different interests with a public philosophy that would ground politics in moral wisdom and the good life. But *The Republic*'s breadth turned out to be the cure that killed the patient. People move in different spheres and civil society is a composite of different functions, but this seemed to make it all the more important that Plato provide an invariant center for public life. His drive toward unity rested on a single Good, which effectively erased his great insight that a coherent public life composed of different elements required an integrative moral purpose. His insistence that civil society could be held together by political power assumed that social organization was defined within a set of distinctly political boundaries. It was left to his greatest student to develop a more nuanced conception of civil society, even as he agreed that politics was "the master science of the Good."

The Mixed Polity

Born in 384 B.C., Aristotle spent twenty years as a student in Plato's Academy but seems to have concluded rather early that it was impossible to conceptually unify all aspects of Being. Every intellectual synthesis is necessarily incomplete because different realms of thought and life are governed by their own particular logics. As important as this insight would be for classical theories of civil society, it was easier for Aristotle to proclaim than to implement. Living in the final years of an independent Athenian city-state, one of humanity's most encyclopedic intellectuals remained attached to a relatively limited aristocratic view of public life and was never able to accommodate his thinking to the comparatively vast scope of a Macedonian world empire.

The very first paragraph of his *Politics* established Aristotle's understanding that people live in multiple spheres—and his equally powerful assertion that politics is the most comprehensive of these spheres. Less finished levels of organization have their own logic but can be fully comprehended only in relation to the more complete levels to which they contribute. His classic view that all subsidiary affiliations find their culmination in the state framed his orientation toward civil society as the politically organized community:

> Observation shows us, first, that every polis or state is a species of association, and, secondly, that all associations are instituted for the purpose of attaining some good—for all men do all their acts with a view to achieving something which is, in their view, a good. We may therefore hold . . . that all associations aim at some good; and we may also hold that the particular association which is the most sovereign of all, and includes all the rest, will pursue this aim most, and will thus be directed to the most sovereign of all goods. This most sovereign and inclusive association is the polis, as it is called, or the political association.[16]

Aristotle shared Plato's understanding that human bonds are rooted in material need and that the division of labor rests at the heart of civil society. Since it was the basic productive unit of the ancient world, the household was the foundation of Aristotle's state. Several families, in turn, comprised a village. Both spheres of organization were partly constituted by the particular ends or purposes around which they were organized. At the same time, they could be comprehended only in terms of the more complete totality of which they were a part. But Aristotle spent relatively little time analyzing these subsidiary spheres, and it soon became clear that his real interest was the city. Human beings have to eat before they can do anything else, but their ultimate purpose cannot be reduced to food.

Aristotle's teleological method led him to regard the polis as the most inclusive and sovereign of all human associations because it aims at the most inclusive and sovereign of all human ends. The family and the village exist for the sake of "mere life," but the polis exists for the sake of the "good life" and is the full and self-sufficient consummation of human moral development.[17] If the state was preceded by the family and the village in time, it is prior to them in nature because their moral potentiality is consummated in it.[18] The self-sufficient moral life of the polis is the endpoint implied in all less complete forms of organization. "Man is thus intended to be a part of a political whole, and there is therefore an immanent impulse in all men towards an association of this order," Aristotle asserted. "Man, when perfected, is the best of animals; but if he is isolated from law and justice he is the worst of all."[19]

Humans can realize their unique capacity for ethical life through political deliberation and public action, but the state is not the only sphere in which this faculty can be expressed. If Plato had sought to tightly organize all spheres of civil society, Aristotle was far more prepared to admit the intrinsic if limited potential of subsidiary levels of organization. The household and village are spheres of moral action, but their range is restricted because they are constituted by necessity, private strivings, and inequality. Necessary but insufficient conditions for the fully moral life of the self-sufficient person, subordinate spheres of activity cannot provide moral freedom and autonomy by themselves. But they help set the conditions for the full realization of human potential and thus share in the ethical content of the polis.

Plato could never have agreed with Aristotle's contention that the household was constituted by three sets of legitimate moral relations: master and slave, husband and wife, and parents and children. The art of household management, *oikonomia* was a contradictory network of private necessity and mutual dependency that served a moral purpose and contributed to the fuller measure of human development in the city. Aristotle's description of it as the art of managing slaves and exercising marital and paternal authority expressed the classical view of the family as the domain of free Athenian males. But this did not erase its standing as a moral association. The authority exercised in the family contributed to the moral development of those on whose behalf it was directed. Even though it was structured by relations of necessity and inequality, the household served the moral purposes of its members and hence contributed to the welfare of the city.

Its important role in Greek economic life notwithstanding, slavery for Aristotle was neither a racial category nor a factor of production but rather a system of household service.[20] Slaves and masters were bound together in a network of mutual dependency that reached deeper than the domestic incompetence or laziness of the rich. Slaves contributed to the development of masters by releasing them from domestic labor; masters contributed to the development of slaves by providing them with the moral guidance and rational deliberation they could not furnish for themselves. Aristotle saw slavery as a relationship between naturally ruling elements and naturally ruled elements, to the benefit and for the preservation of both. Everything depended on both parties recognizing and accepting the role they played. "The part and the whole, like the body and the soul, have an identical interest; and the slave is part of the master, in the sense of being a living but separate part of his body. There is thus a community of interest, and a relation of friendship, between master and slave, when both of them naturally merit the position in which they stand. But the reverse is true and there is a conflict of interest and enmity, when matters are otherwise and slavery rests merely on legal sanction and superior *power*."[21]

Aristotle also conceived marital and parental authority as relations of necessity and inequality that link people in mutually beneficial relations and hence serve a real, if limited, moral purpose. The moral superiority of the husband over the wife and of parents over children ultimately served the development of all. Even so, the ethical potential of the household was limited. Since it existed for the sake of supporting life, nothing could issue from "household maintenance" beyond itself. Limited by the conditions of a natural economy, the private sphere was oriented toward the production of subsistence and was not involved in sale or exchange. "It is impossible to live without means of subsistence," Aristotle noted, and if the family was a productive unit it followed that exchange played little or no role in household relations because everything was held in common, production was for use, and hardly any surplus was generated.[22] Exchange became a factor only in the village. Initially, it took the form of simple barter, but it soon became possible to accumulate more than was needed for subsistence. The consequences were extremely troubling, and Aristotle shared Plato's concern that individual accumulation and private profit could subvert civil society.

Markets have been part of human life for a long time but have come to dominate social affairs only recently. A complicated set of expectations and institutions have shaped human social organization for many thousands of years, and these have been primarily noneconomic in character. Norms of reciprocity, redistribution, solidarity, and dependence organized the production and distribution of life's necessities in precapitalist societies. Markets played a restricted role and were not sufficiently developed to organize social life on their own. There was neither the possibility nor the need for extensive trade and hence no possibility of asserting the existence of distinctly economic motives. An independent set of economic institutions could not arise in such conditions, and it was difficult to theorize economic activity apart from the historic practices and institutions of a community whose most basic organization was understood in noneconomic terms.

The economy was "embedded" in social organization in that economic affairs were not distinguished from other relations and economic activity was not carried on for purely "economic" reasons. Humans provided for their basic needs through religious and kinship institutions that could not be understood primarily, or even largely, as "economic" in character. Economic affairs were fundamental to organized subsistence societies, of course, but they would not acquire their apparent independence and visibility until capitalism gave rise to a distinctly modern disposition to pursue economic gain for its own sake. Until then, neither the material development of civil society nor the associated corpus of theoretical work about it permitted a sharp distinction between "economic" and other institutions or values.[23] This is why classical theories of civil society understood it as a commonwealth organized by political power.

Barter between distant centers tends to generate increasingly extensive relations of exchange that soon require money, and Aristotle knew how corrosive this could be. Once money makes possible the exchange of commodities over long distances and the accumulation of wealth, retail trade for profit becomes unavoidable. Acquiring money replaces satisfying needs as the purpose of exchange, and Aristotle's suspicion of commerce and trade was based on his fear that there were no natural limits to the amount of money that could be accumulated.[24] The pursuit of wealth for its own sake would become the goal of "economic" activity that threatened to break free from the constraints of a premarket moral order. This fear is what drove Aristotle's famous and influential condemnation of usury and profit. The art of household management was properly limited by the immediate needs of the family, but the pursuit of wealth encouraged people to stray from "natural" arts of acquisition and forms of wealth derived directly from nature and oriented to the needs of the household. Commerce and trade separated the acquisition of wealth from its moral purpose of providing subsistence. "It is the business of nature to furnish subsistence for each being brought into the world," but the pursuit of wealth distorted the moral potential of human activity because it threatened to subordinate all virtues to its own imperative:

> Because enjoyment depends on the possession of a superfluity, men address themselves to the art which produces the superfluity necessary to enjoyment; and if they cannot get what they want by the use of that art—i.e. the art of acquisition—they attempt to do so by other means, using each and every capacity in a way not consonant with its nature. The proper function of courage, for example, is not to produce money but to give confidence. The same is true of military and medical ability: neither has the function of producing money: the one has the function of producing victory, and the other that of producing health. But those of whom we are speaking turn all such capacities into forms of the art of acquisition, as though to make money were the one aim and everything else must contribute to that aim.[25]

Aristotle's suspicion of commerce was fed by an additional concern. All acquisition from exchange—and this included profit as well as usury—is unnatural because it is made "at the expense of other men."[26] Money came into being as a means of exchange; it was not meant to be a store of value, and its acquisition severs the appropriate relationship between activity and reward. It makes a just distribution of wealth impossible and elevates private desire to a dangerous position of command. Money is morally dangerous because it overwhelms other spheres of activity and subjects them to a foreign totalizing logic.

Aristotle's denunciation of economic activity for gain and his defense of production for use expressed the core of Greek political thought. The tendency to divorce economic motives from the social relations in which they were embedded could be remedied only by insisting on the morally redemptive character of politics. Unlike commerce and trade, politics does not deny the logic of subordinate spheres. Aristotle's teleology allowed him to theorize politics as the moral consummation of all the partial levels of human activity.

As ready as he was to take account of diverse loyalties and manifold associations, Aristotle was not prepared to take things too far. The elevation of private interest that lay at the heart of exchange, money, profit, and usury would destroy the increasingly fragile equilibrium on which he rested his hopes for the moral and deliberative public life of the commonwealth. His household was a sphere of slavery, patriarchy, and parental authority constituted by relations of domination and inequality. But it served a moral purpose insofar as it was concerned with the welfare of human beings. Even if it could not be as inclusive a sphere of moral action as the polis, its moral standing was derived from its teleological connection to a more comprehensive association. These considerations precipitated Aristotle's important critique of Plato's theory of the state—a critique that led to a new way of conceptualizing civil society.

Aristotle was convinced that Plato's drive to impose unity on civil society would destroy the very possibility of political association. The polis is not like the elements that comprise it. Individuals and households are unitary moral phenomena, but "the polis is composed of a *number* of men; it is also composed of different *kinds* of men, for similars cannot bring it into existence."[27] Plato's failure to understand this came from Socrates and had profoundly destructive results:

> The object which Socrates assumes as his premiss is contained in the principle that "the greatest possible unity of the whole polis is the supreme good." Yet it is obvious that a polis which goes on and on, and becomes more and more of a unity, will eventually cease to be a polis at all. A polis by its nature is some sort of aggregation: i.e. it has the quality of including a large number of its members. If it becomes more of a unit, it will first become a household instead of a polis, and then an individual instead of a household; for we should all call the household more of a unit than the polis, and the individual more of a unit than the household. It follows that, even if we could, we ought not to achieve this object; it would be the destruction of the polis.[28]

The polis is the only category within which the public life of citizens outside the family can be comprehended, but Plato failed to understand what makes it so special. People move in different spheres and cannot be expected to agree uniformly about what is theirs and not theirs. The individual and the household might rest on a high degree of material and moral unity, but the polis "necessarily requires a difference of capacities among its members, which enables them to serve as complements to one another, and to attain a higher and better life by the mutual exchange of their different services." Plato did not pursue the implications of his insight that the state rests on the division of labor, for "a real unity, such as a polis, must be made up of elements which differ in kind."[29]

Plato denied private property and family life to *The Republic*'s guardians because he feared that *any* expression of particular interest would limit the leadership's ability to organize civil society. Aristotle was as suspicious as his teacher of the pursuit of gain for its own sake, but he was convinced that no public purpose would be served by eliminating private life altogether. A modest measure of ownership could strengthen civil society if it could be put to public use. "When everyone has his own separate sphere of interest," he suggested in terms that would have horrified Plato, "there will not be the same ground for quarrels; and the amount of interest will increase, because each man will feel that he is applying himself to what is his own."[30] Private concerns are not, in and of themselves, fatally corrosive of public life. An "excess of self-love" is the problem, and the solution is not to eliminate the natural human desire for privacy but to civilize it through education and turn it toward the public good. Plato had gone too far. "It is true that unity is to some extent necessary, alike in a household and a polis; but total unity is not. There is a point at which a polis, by advancing in unity, will cease to be a polis: there is another point, short of that, at which it may still remain a polis, but will none the less come near to losing its essence, and will thus be a worse polis."[31]

So Aristotle's mixed state was based on the unitary household, just as the public rested on the private and the general was rooted in the particular. If the family was a private realm of necessity, it made possible the free public life of the deliberating and acting citizen. Its incomplete measure of freedom served freedom as the insufficiency of the part served the sufficiency of the whole. Just as inequality constituted the family, so equality made it possible to achieve honor, excellence, and glory in public. It follows that all groups of people who live together do not necessarily constitute a polis. Citizens are the basic elements of civil society and the state, but they will differ from one another because of their roots in the private sphere of necessity and particularity. If Plato regarded difference as a source of weakness, Aristotle saw it as a source of strength. The solidarity of civil society can only be one of diversity. "A polis or state belongs to the order of 'compounds,' in the same way as all other things which form a single 'whole,' but a 'whole' composed, none the less, of a number of different parts."[32]

If the polis is a unity of unlike elements, it follows that there is no single excellence common to all citizens. Plato had conflated state and individual, public and private, politics and psychology on the foundation of the Socratic dictum that "virtue" is an undifferentiated unity that will always generate a determinate course of action. Aristotle's suggestion that there are different virtues appropriate to different situations struck at the heart of Plato's notion of civil society and theory of the state. Aristotle's famous definition of the citizen emphasized conscious public activity and moral self-determination: "The citizen in the strict sense is best defined by the one criterion, 'a man who shares in the administration of justice and the holding of office.'"[33] The citizen lives according to rules that he makes for the welfare of the community as a whole. The purpose of the polis is living well, not just living; the state exists in order to promote goodness and is the only association of its kind. Citizenship is a moral category and is determined by more than birth, residence, and common obedience to law.

Civil society may be composed of unlike elements that move in spheres appropriate to their nature, but Aristotle was as aware as Plato of the dangers of private judgment and interest, even if he was willing to recognize them as the basis of unity and public life. People come together for a variety of reasons, but it is possible to rank them and arrive at a method of classifying different kinds of associations. Necessity forces us to live in households, but the search for "the good life" draws us to politics and is the commonality that Plato sought to impose mechanically; it is "the chief end, both for the community as a whole and for each of us individually."[34] The distinction Aristotle drew between healthy and perverted constitutions was between those directed toward the common good and those directed toward the welfare of their ruling authority. But how can "the common good" be discovered?

People enter into all sorts of different associations, but a universal standard can be derived because the common good is more than the sum of all private interests and can be objectively determined. "Those constitutions which consider the common interest are *right* constitutions, judged by the standards of absolute justice. Those constitutions which consider only the personal interest of the rulers are all *wrong* constitutions, or *perversions* of the right forms."[35] The standards of "absolute justice" are accessible to most people if they use their reason, and this insight enabled Aristotle to arrive at his celebrated classification of states. If the common good links the three healthy forms of monarchy, aristocracy, and "polity," private interest and class advantage is common to the perversions: "Tyranny is government by a single person directed to the interest of that person; Oligarchy is directed to the interest of the well-to-do; Democracy is directed to the interest of the poorer classes. None of the three is directed to the advantage of the whole body of citizens."[36] Plato's notion that injustice was strife occasioned by concern for self found its institutional expression in Aristotle's scheme of political classification. Ever the reformer, Aristotle sought a constitutional framework that could support civicness.

All civil societies are composed of different families, classes, occupations, circumstances of birth, and orders of merit. Anticipating Baron de Montesquieu and James Madison, Aristotle went beyond Plato and suggested that mixed constitutions could be strong only if they recognized the plurality inherent in social life. "A properly mixed 'polity' should look as if it contained both democratic and oligarchical elements—and as if it contained neither. It should owe its stability to its intrinsic strength, and not to external support; and its intrinsic strength should be derived from the fact, not that a majority are in favor of its continuance . . . but rather that there is no single section in all the state which would favor a change to a different constitution."[37] A strong and durable polity would be based on the middle class and its property and would combine the wisdom of aristocracy with the strength of democracy. Only moderation could tame excess and turn diversity into strength through a mixed constitution.

"In all states," Aristotle said, "there may be distinguished three parts, or classes, of the citizen-body—the very rich; the very poor; and the middle class which forms the mean. Now it is admitted, as a general principle, that moderation and the mean are always best. We may therefore conclude that in the ownership of all gifts of fortune a middle condition will be the best."[38] The rich and the poor are likely to be driven by their greed, fear, and insecurity. The rich know only how to rule and the poor only how to obey, but the middle class is likely to have fewer enemies than either of its associates. Amenable to reason, discipline, and moderation, it is likely to be less violent, ambitious, or covetous than other classes. A healthy state requires citizens who know how to rule and obey at the same time, and this knowledge is most appropriate to those whose moderate economic station makes it possible for peers and friends to practice the disinterested politics of virtue. "A state aims at being, as far as it can be, a society composed of equals and peers [who, as such, can be friends and associates]; and the middle class, more than any other, has this sort of composition. It follows that a state which is based on the middle class is bound to be the best constituted in respect of the elements [i.e. equals and peers] of which, on our view, a state is naturally composed."[39] A healthy state is a mixed polity based on the middle class and combining rich and poor.

Such polities are less prone to sedition and revolution because they can protect the greedy rich and the grasping poor from one another. Quarrels among the notables should be suppressed, tax burdens should be constantly adjusted, and the constitution should be enforced. But great care must be taken to avoid the root cause of political degeneration. "The most important rule of all, in all types of constitution, is that provision should be made—not only by law, but also by the general system of economy—to prevent the magistrates from being able to use their office for their own gain."[40] Healthy political structures protect different classes from one another and guard against degenerate forms based on particularity, suspicion, privilege, greed, and violence.

Plato failed to understand that private interest is a permanent part of the human condition. People form different associations because they seek some advantage for themselves or because they have to provide for life's necessities. Aristotle knew that even narrow communities aim at some good for their members. "But all these communities seem to be encompassed by the community that is the state; for the political community does not aim at the advantage of the moment, but what is advantageous for the whole of life."[41] Aristotle's recognition of multiplicity carried him beyond Plato. Civil society was the politically constituted community that organized separate spheres of life in the state and, in the process, permitted them to express the full measure of their limited ethical potential. Plato's mechanical desire for unity drove him to suppress the consequences of the division of labor, which nevertheless sat at the heart of his theory of the state. Aristotle tried to organize different spheres in the common life of the polis. Both men agreed that membership in a political society encompassed a life of collective involvement and that the state expressed the common moral life of the community. Politics was the "master science of the Good" because it moderated the impact of individual interest with the generality of common concerns.

Aristotle's understanding of a differentiated civil society was considerably more sophisticated than that of Plato, but his theory of citizenship was heavily influenced by the aristocratic sensibilities of his youth. The free man in the polis engages in debate and deliberation with his friends and peers. A network of face-to-face public interactions is a morally uplifting and personally fulfilling environment. A benevolent and dispassionate orientation toward the public good will permit men who have enough property and leisure time to attend to public matters free of corrupting material considerations. Such a view could not survive the passing of Athens's aristocratic republicanism, even if its echoes can be found in contemporary theories of civil society.

Civil Society and the Res Publica

It is one of the more prophetic coincidences of history that Aristotle died just as the independent Greek city-states were disappearing. His optimism about humanity's capacity for self-government soon yielded to the pervasive skepticism about politics that characterized Hellenistic thought. The Greek sense that human beings could create the conditions of their own moral life was soon in full retreat. As the overarching framework for public action dissolved, a new sense that private affairs offered protection from a threatening outside world often assumed a religious coloration. Doctrines of self-sufficiency and individual well-being provided the foundations for theories of individual autonomy, moral equality, and personal rectitude. Addressing themselves to a disintegrating world, the Cynics, Epicureans, and early Stoics drove Aristotle's politicized notion of "the good life" inward.

All of these thinkers were convinced that the classical search for recognition, honor, and glory could not constitute civil society in the absence of autonomous ethical action rooted in private notions of honor and integrity. Late Stoicism would develop the norms of self-control, kindness, devotion to duty, and public service that came to play such an important part in Roman thought. When married to universal reason's ability to discover the law of nature, it would become a secular religion suited to the requirements of a bureaucratic world empire. In the immediate aftermath of the collapse of the Macedonian Empire, however, Hellenistic doctrines of personal salvation developed independently of political forms and action.

The attack on the political community was initially expressed as a philosophy of resignation, self-reliance, and retreat. Self-sufficiency and authenticity replaced citizenship and public action. Epicurus declared that blind nature cannot guide human conduct and dismissed ancient religions and political formations as the arbitrary products of convention. Humans can lead a "natural" life only if they rid themselves of accumulated superstitions, assumptions, and gods. The individual desire for happiness is the only dependable anchor in a chaotic and indifferent universe. It requires, first, that pain be avoided. Since irritation and distress flow from the unavoidable connections we are forced to have with others, disengagement and withdrawal became the prerequisites of a moral life now defined as autonomy and authenticity. Civil society and politics are no longer the source of ethical development and the self is not disclosed in public activity. Humans have an inner life that is independent of political associations and determinations. We are on our own.

Civil society is composed of isolated atoms whose capricious interactions provide no natural basis for association. All public entanglements are strictly conventional and can be justified only if they mitigate pain and remove some of the barriers to happiness. Since there are no objective standards by which felicity can be determined, Hellenistic civil society was seen as an artifice whose maintenance of public order would facilitate the private search for individual well-being. An indifferent universe requires that individuals take care of themselves. In a radical restatement of Aristotle's notion of self-sufficiency, Epictetus declared that freedom is a condition of the soul that understands what it cannot do and has learned how to reduce its social connections to the barest minimum. The true self lies within and must be sought in private. The best way to avoid pain is to avoid the social entanglements and personal dependencies that cause it. "We must free ourselves," advised Epicurus, "from the prison of affairs and politics."

Such a pessimistic doctrine of withdrawal could not serve the ideological needs of a confident and expanding Rome, and late Stoicism began to assert a correspondence between the rational universe and the requirements of a moral life. "Living according to nature" no longer meant detachment but signified that human beings shared in the same divine reason that orders the universe. The fire that lights the world lives as a spark in each individual and allows one to achieve one's proper ends, for reason directs everything toward self-fulfillment. If the Epicureans and Cynics had sought perfection by withdrawing from the world, some Stoics would identify with nature while others retreated into an ethic of private edification. Even Seneca modified the earlier hostility to social connections in his recognition that privacy required a public life and that civil society could be strengthened by withdrawal.

We must retire more within ourselves, for intercourse with those of different disposition throws into disorder that which is well arranged, awakens low, ignoble passions, and causes that to ulcerate which is still weak in the mind and not yet entirely healed. These things must be mingled and alternated, namely, solitude and society. The former will cause us to have a desire for men, the latter for ourselves, and the one will be a remedy for the other: solitude will heal our hatred of the crowd, and the crowd will heal our hatred of solitude.[42]

Seneca's individualism did not necessarily conflict with a more politicized understanding that a universal world-state constituted by reason can counter the divisiveness of self-interest and overcome the narrowness of the here and now. It also laid the basis for the first systematic view of human solidarity and universal brotherhood. All Stoics agreed that human beings are rational creatures made for social life. The whole universe is a civic community in which everything alive shares in a harmonious unity organized by reason. Human commonality could now be expressed as brotherhood in reason and common membership in a universal civil society that would wash away artificial social distinctions. "If the power of thought is universal among mankind," asserted the Stoic emperor Marcus Aurelius,

so likewise is the possession of reason, making us rational creatures. It follows, therefore, that this reason speaks no less universally to us all with its "thou shalt" or "thou shalt not." So then there is a world-law; which in turn means that we are all fellow-citizens and share a common citizenship, and that the world is a single city. Is there any other common citizenship that can be claimed by all humanity? And it is from this world-polity that mind, reason, and law themselves derive. If not, whence else?[43]

The late Stoic ideal of a universal civil society organized by reason presumed a much wider moral equality than had been possible in the restricted environment of the city-state. For all Aristotle's erudition, his theory of citizenship had never included women, slaves, children, resident aliens, or people living outside Athens. Hellenistic theories of natural law could fix one's place in the universal order of things. Self-interest is a mortal enemy of reason, Marcus Aurelius declared, and universal animating principles can transcend the limitations of mortality by fixing attention on the single source shared by all products of creation.[44] Stoicism tried to develop an integrated notion of a unified world-community that was built on subordinate affiliations and transcended their limitations. "My own nature is a rational and civic one," observed Marcus Aurelius; "I have a city and I have a country; as Marcus I have Rome, and as a human being I have the universe; and consequently, what is beneficial to these communities is the sole good for me."[45]

If the Stoics recognized that people lived in a wide variety of associations, surely the most compelling of them was Rome itself. As the Republic entered into the protracted crisis that marked its decline, a permanent civil war accompanied an endless series of foreign confrontations. Class conflict, slave rebellions, mutinies, assassinations, constant conspiracies, and intensifying economic exploitation sapped the strength of republican institutions as powerful warlords organized private armies to support their ambitions. Street fighting, periodic riots, widening inequality, unprecedented urban squalor, and a numbing crisis of agriculture sparked demands for public works, democratic government, land reform, and other measures to alleviate the misery of the poor. As the aristocracy shattered into an unstable mass of competing and suspicious cliques, Rome became a predatory war machine run by and for a narrow oligarchy.

Born in 106 B.C., Marcus Tullius Cicero tried desperately to arrest the final collapse of the Republic and witnessed the rise and fall of Julius Caesar. Philosophically skeptical, attracted to the Stoic ideal of self-sufficient wisdom, and embodying the conservative republican aristocracy's orientation to disinterested public service, he greatly enriched classical conceptions of civil society. Hostile to corrupt aristocrats and grasping popular movements, he defended the authority of the Senate and resisted all calls for social, economic, and political reforms. Politically active throughout his life, he tried to embody the Stoic republican virtues of generosity, far-sightedness, honesty, and dedication to the public good in a succession of high offices, powerful speeches, and influential writings.

Rooting justice in the Stoic conception of nature rather than in Epicurean utility, Cicero declared it the foundation of organized human life and law. Natural-law theory always tended to identify civil society with the benefits of civilization, and Cicero's was no exception. He shared Lucretius's conviction that the fatal malady of prerepublican Rome was the endless and lawless competition for power and glory, which reduced politics to assassination, forgery, theft, and war. Private judgment, ambition, appetite, and desire had come close to destroying civilized life then and were threatening the Republic now. The *res publica* was the "people's possession" and denoted the *populus* considered as a whole—"an assemblage of people in large numbers associated in an agreement with respect to justice and a partnership for the common good."[46] Civil society was an organization of political power that made civilization possible. Justice was its basic organizing principle. If Plato's civil society rested on the division of labor and Aristotle's was constituted by different natural and moral capacities, Cicero's was based on the universal human capacity to share in the right reason that is consonant with nature, exists independently of human history, and orders the universe. The chaos inherent in a world of particular interests and private judgments could be overcome by organizing civil society according to the principles of reason.[47] Cicero echoed Socrates's words to Crito and Pericles's speech to the citizens of Athens as he declared that

> our country has not given us birth and education without expecting to receive some sustenance, as it were, from us in return; nor has it been merely to serve our convenience that she has granted to our leisure a safe refuge and for our moments of repose a calm retreat: on the contrary, she has given us these advantages so that she may appropriate to her own use the greater and more important part of our courage, our talents, and our wisdom, leaving to us for our own private uses only so much as may be left after his needs have been satisfied.[48]

Cicero's attempt to arrest the lawless slide into chaos led him to declare that civil society originates in a "social spirit" that nature has implanted in humans. Animated by this innate sociability and informed by reason, people are drawn to associate with one another. But sentiment alone is not enough to establish a durable social bond—institutions are also necessary. Private property can protect citizens against tyranny and the state against corruption. Security of possession is an indispensable condition of public life because it protects aristocratic autonomy and liberty. Cicero was bitterly opposed to any agrarian law aiming at expropriating and sharing the wealth, but he also wanted to protect the poor against the predatory and uncontrollable rich. There is a "natural" limit to wealth beyond which it can serve no socially useful purpose, he declared. The only justification for private property is that it be used,[49] and he echoed Aristotle's misgivings about purely economic motives when he warned that "great-heartedness and heroism, and courtesy, and justice, and generosity, are far more in conformity with nature than self-indulgence, or wealth, or even life itself. But to despise this latter category of things, to attach no importance to them in comparison with the common good, really does need a heroic and lofty heart."[50]

Cicero's defense of property illustrated his characteristically Roman respect for privacy. At the same time, he shared the classic suspicion that separate spheres could be dangerous. The pursuit of one's interests at the expense of another tends to erode the fabric of organized life. Like Aristotle, he feared that it would open the door to corruption and disaster because it severs the principle of utility from its moral and political foundation and threatens to make it an independent force. Economic forces always press to subordinate other spheres of life to the logic of individual advantage and can never be understood as an autonomous sphere of activity with its own rules. The rational principle that organizes nature generates moral rules that restrain individualism and make civil society possible. Private interests are inevitable in social man, but

> to take something away from someone else—to profit from another's loss—is more unnatural than death, or destitution, or pain, or any other physical or external blow. To begin with, this strikes at the root of human society and fellowship. For if we each of us propose to rob or injure one another for our personal gain, then we are clearly going to demolish what is more emphatically nature's creation than anything else in the whole world: namely, the link that unites every human being with every other. Just imagine if each of our limbs had its own consciousness and saw advantage for itself in appropriating the nearest limb's strength! Of course the whole body would inevitably collapse and die. In precisely the same way, a general seizure and appropriation of other people's property would cause the collapse of the human community, the brotherhood of man.[51]

Cicero's protest against both rapacious exploitation and economic redistribution underscored the importance of political institutions. As important as reason and right thinking were, ancient republican ideals and moral exhortations alone would not convince individuals to forego a measure of self-interest in the name of the common good. It was clear to him that "everyone ought to have the same purpose: to identify the interest of each with the interest of all. Once men grab for themselves, human society will completely collapse." However, formal institutional measures were necessary.[52]

A mixed constitution could give political expression to economic differences while mitigating their disintegrative political potential. The propensity of the magistrate, the aristocracy, and the commons to encroach on the liberties of each other could be limited through appropriate institutional safeguards, which would create a balanced and flexible equilibrium of class forces. The enormous influence that Cicero exerted on the Enlightenment's constitutionalism was expressed in his warning that "unless there is in the State an even balance of rights, duties, and functions, so that the magistrates have enough power, the counsels of the eminent citizens enough influence, and the people enough liberty, this kind of government cannot be safe from revolution."[53] A mixed constitution would avoid tyranny and mob rule by providing institutional expression to the principles of monarchy, aristocracy, and democracy. Drawing on Aristotle's moderate aristocratic constitutionalism, Cicero sought a political arrangement that would balance the interests of the propertied few with those of the propertyless many. Decay and corruption could be arrested if economic conflicts could be prevented from assuming a political form.

Cicero's mixed constitution did not hold the interests of all classes in equal balance. Reflecting his conservative politics and the importance of property in his conception of civil society, he located the Senate at the heart of state power. Cicero knew that the Senate, balanced by the "people's tribunes," represented the interests of the aristocracy, and he trusted that it could prevent the further degeneration of the Republic. Machiavelli, Montesquieu, and Madison would be heavily influenced by his desire to organize civil society around the inherited property and political wisdom that could enable those of moderate wealth to protect the very rich and the very poor from one another. Proportionate equality reflected Cicero's view that individual interests are not of equal worth while recognizing that stability requires the protection of all. In the end, his civil society depended on a set of political arrangements that fused elements of monarchy, aristocracy, and democracy. It would reflect the distribution of economic power and make it possible for unequal classes to live in peace at the same time, for

> just as in the music of harps and flutes or in the voices of singers a certain harmony of the different tones must be preserved, the interruption or violation of which is intolerable to trained ears, and as this perfect agreement and harmony is produced by the proportionate blending of unlike tones, so also is a State made harmonious by agreement among dissimilar elements, brought about by a fair and reasonable blending together of the upper, middle, and lower classes, just as if they were musical tones. What the musicians call harmony in song is concord in a State, the strongest and best bond of permanent union in any commonwealth; and such concord can never be brought about without the aid of justice.[54]

By making justice independent of the private judgments of individuals and locating it at the center of the "people's business," Cicero enriched the classic tradition of conceptualizing civil society in political terms. More than a convention of self-interested people who seek to avoid the painful consequences of living alone, civil society is a natural institution and its political expression is the most inclusive and important association to which individuals belong. Its foundation will always be justice informed by reason understood as the common good, and all legitimate state formations are founded upon this first principle. Political corruption means that civil society has ceased to exist. "For what is a State except an association or partnership in justice?"[55]

Cicero's attempt to preserve the Republic, safeguard aristocratic property, and strengthen senatorial authority ultimately failed because the constant military campaigns and domestic instability of an expanding empire led in the direction of centralized leadership. Julius Caesar proved to be the gravedigger of the Republic, and the assassinations of both men within a year of one another signaled the passage to Empire as it redefined the Roman sense of civil society. The *pax Augusta* temporarily ended foreign wars of conquest, held the aristocracy and its Senate in check, and tried to separate politics from interest through a bureaucratized legal system. The notion of the *res publica*, the "common good" implied in the Roman idea of the commonwealth, had signified a civil society of peasants and soldiers who protected the Republic and reaped most of its benefits. But imperial expansion transformed Rome into a vast cosmopolitan city in which a bloc of magnates and financiers confronted an ocean of proletarians, subjects, and slaves. The rights and liberties of the commons had always been the foundation of the city's greatness, and if it was hoped that *imperium* would organize political life on the basis of natural reason and equity, it also concentrated enormous power in Augustus's hands. The Republic had attempted to establish a system of checks and balances in which all social classes would be represented by particular institutions and the military would be neutralized. Augustus's evident desire to limit the Senate's prerogatives and the growing importance of his Praetorian Guard would prove more damaging over the long run than the immediate problems they were designed to solve.

Even so, the Roman order claimed to represent a finality and universality to which alternative systems of private and public life could not pretend. Amid the wreckage of empires founded on tyranny and exploitation, it claimed to stand for the rational and genuinely "political" ties that transcended boundaries of class, religion, and nationality. The legal apparatus that began to take shape during Augustus's reign initially defined the rights and privileges of Roman citizenship, but as time went on and political power became concentrated it gave expression to a legally recognized private realm that stood alongside the public orientation of the polis and the Republic. The Roman notion of the *res publica* soon implied the existence of a *res privata* as a correlative sphere. Constituted by family and property and protected by a network of rights, it marked the area of intimate associations and particular interests. Private law regulated the relations between individuals, provided legal expression to the family and property, governed the inheritance of property, and established a legally recognized zone of private life that was profoundly important to later understandings of civil society. The individual was now separated into a private person and a public citizen. Religion gradually became a private matter, even as it continued to be an affair of state. So long as citizens rendered appropriate worship to Rome's gods in public, they were increasingly free to worship any gods they desired in private. It was said that Roman public law stopped at the citizen's doorstep. If the Republic literally belonged to "the people," then private rights, property, family, and religion came to constitute a measure of citizenship. The public law that defined common interests, specified civic duties, and regulated the relations between citizens and the state addressed itself to criminal affairs, public institutions, and state officials. If the state was the "property" of the citizens, however, the *populus* consisted of the male citizen heads of households. The Romans were no more able than the Greeks to escape their limitations, but they contributed a profoundly important view of civil society as a sphere of reason, justice, participation, and rights that sought a universal understanding of citizenship even as it recognized a powerful private center of gravity.

Plato's vision of a political leader who would unite knowledge with power seemed to find its realization in the imperial claim that the divine emperor embodied the state and the people at the same time. Even if the Augustan system was ultimately unable to protect Rome from internal decay and external threat, it did continue the classical effort to rescue humankind from barbarism and secure for it the possibility of a politically organized civilization. The transition from polis to republic to empire described a man-made civil society where reason and civilization would be safe. It was exactly this hope against which the Fathers of the Church, and Saint Augustine most importantly, set themselves.

2

Civil Society and the Christian Commonwealth

The collapse of Roman civilization, which Edward Gibbon attributed to the triumph of barbarism and Christianity, weakened the classical understanding of civil society as a politically organized community. Its disintegration introduced a dualism into Western thought that made it impossible for hundreds of years to theorize politics as the sphere of humanity's highest values. While the Eastern Empire endured with a centralized state backed by the Byzantine Church and centered in Constantinople, the Germanic conquerors made personal and tribal custom the basis of political life in the West. Given the economic and political decentralization of the Dark Ages, no consolidated political organs would develop in the West for some time. The region slowly reorganized itself as a structure of tribally based territorial kingdoms rather than as a reconstituted Universal Empire, which now existed only in memory.

Christianity supplied the West with whatever social and ideological unity it had during the millennium following the fall of Rome. It did so by providing the basis for a common spiritual fellowship and by articulating a relatively consistent theory of the state and civil society as a Christian Commonwealth. Religion had been subordinated to the requirements of the political order in Greece and Rome, but it assumed a stronger independent standing for much of the Middle Ages. Whatever legitimacy state structures had was provided by religion and theology wielded by an increasingly centralized Church. Even so, the period's tendency to theorize politics in religious terms resulted in notions of a fused community that made it impossible to understand civil society apart from classical political categories. But the effort to articulate a unified theory of human affairs could not last forever. The end of medieval Europe's attempt to organize its politics on a spiritual basis came when corrosive markets, stronger kings, opportunistic princes, and more assertive local bodies made it impossible for theology to provide the overarching framework within which philosophy, science, politics, and other activities were conducted. By the end of the period, a more purely political conception of the state was beginning to emerge, accompanied by an equally secular conception of civil society now organized in economic terms.

The transition from the theories of the classical world to those of the Middle Ages can be summarized as the passage from an ideal of self-sufficiency to a recognition of dependence. Greek thinkers proposed that ethics and politics resulted from the rational action of enlightened men who aimed at a life of moral autonomy and public recognition. Virtue was not a revealed truth, and external demands did not set the standard for human belief or conduct. People were fully capable of organizing civil society in accordance with moral principles they developed for themselves. Aristotle's sense that citizenship combined reasoned deliberation, prudent legislation, and voluntary obedience was the culmination of this point of view.

Early Christianity had been relatively indifferent to matters of state, regarding them as passing concerns that would be quickly washed away. But as it became clear that Christians would have to wait for the coming of God's Kingdom, ecclesiastical authorities were compelled to make their peace with the world. The lengthy process by which the Church came to terms with the Empire also saw it develop a justification of coercive political power and a set of guidelines for its use that would locate the Church at the center of civil society. The doctrine of Original Sin would lead many Church Fathers to conclude that the state was a God-given consequence of humanity's fallen nature. Under the guidance of the Church, the state could play an important role in Universal History by correcting human error. If the Greeks concluded that politics is natural to human beings, the Church located it alongside war, slavery, and property as a purely conventional result of failure. The late Roman notion of the sacred monarchy, one of the last attempts to reconstruct the imperial order with the aid of notions derived from the pagan East, was definitively abandoned.

But this did not signal a return to the humanism of the Greek polis and Roman Republic, which had recognized religion as one of several requirements of organized civil societies. Now, a large area of human life was placed outside the *res publica*, for the injunction to "render unto Caesar" also implied that much had to be rendered unto God. The fusion of Church and state that followed Constantine's conversion transformed the political community into as partial an institution as it had been under the pagan emperors, except that it now openly proclaimed itself to be a Christian state.

Caesaropapism gave renewed legitimacy to political institutions. Power could now be used for spiritual and temporal purposes. Keeping the peace, defending the Church, and enforcing theological orthodoxy became affairs of state. Power was freely brought to bear against the heresies that populated the world of the early Church, and an energetic Christianity gradually became the vital principle of political cohesion. Thinkers soon turned to the elaboration of a specifically Christian theory of civil society, along with a critique of the Greco-Roman past.

The Church regarded classicism as a pagan error precisely because it looked outside for its creative and moving principle. The conviction that humans could organize a fully moral life with their own resources was a dangerous illusion and a prideful error. Just as the necessity for individual choice sits at the heart of Augustine's theology of the Fall and the accompanying doctrine of Original Sin, so the early Church identified the Trinity as the creative and moving principle to which fallen humanity owes ultimate obedience. The only impediment to human understanding consists in the barriers we impose on ourselves through deliberate blindness and stubborn refusal. Augustine knew a good deal about both, and his deep skepticism about the work of humanity drove his theology of the redemptive power of grace and established him as the most important theologian of the early Church.

Pride, Faith, and the State

Augustine began writing *The City of God* in A.D. 413, three years after Rome was sacked by Alaric and his Goths. Addressing himself to the Eternal City's sophisticated intelligentsia, he denied the popular claim that her recent disasters came from neglecting the ancient rites. Christianity was not responsible for the fall of Rome, he insisted; if anything, the weakness of the newly Christianized Empire resulted from her toleration of paganism, heresy, and immorality. Augustine's defense of the Church soon broadened into the first systematic Christian theory of history and civil society. He provided a running commentary on scriptural narratives and linked the rise, progress, and destiny of the Church in the world to the creation, fall, and redemption of humankind. In the process, he mounted a powerful attack on the secular claim that one could discover in nature and reason the moral rules for the conduct of human life and defended Christianity against the pagan charge that it was little more than an Eastern superstition. The humanistic veneration of science and reason yielded to the unrelenting emphasis on faith and grace that constitutes mature Augustinianism.

A pervasive sense of human weakness rests at the center of Augustine's understanding of civil society. Humankind is too depraved to draw moral values for itself. All durable standards of truth, beauty, goodness, and meaning are derived from the mysterious working of the Holy Spirit. History is the record of God's presence in human affairs and its meaning is to be found, not in any product of the human mind, but in the revelation of Christ. The Greeks and Romans had thought that speech, deliberation, and action in a politically organized civil society established the grounds for human happiness. Augustine now proposed faith, Scripture, and the Church. Only Christian principles could constitute the foundation for the conduct of politics and the organization of civil society.

But there was still something valuable to be learned from the history of Rome, for God had made her into a mighty empire for a reason. An all-embracing and obsessive love of praise had driven her citizens' enormous accomplishments. "Glory they most ardently loved; for it they wished to live, for it they did not hesitate to die. Every other desire was repressed by the strength of their passion for that one thing," Augustine observed. "That eagerness for praise and desire for glory, then, was that which accomplished those many wonderful things, laudable, doubtless, and glorious according to human judgement."[1] Manichean, neo-Platonist, sinner, convert, bishop, theologian, controversialist, and judge, Augustine had thought long and hard about matters of spirit and flesh. He had a healthy respect for the Empire's accomplishments. But the same search for glory that drove Rome to unheard-of heights of power was the Achilles heel that brought down the Empire.

Pagan worldliness stood in stark contrast to the possibilities opened up by the presence of Christ in human history. Since the fall of Adam, the human race has been divided into two great "cities," spiritual embodiments of the two powers that have contended for supremacy in God's creation since the fall of the angels. Belief and unbelief are locked in timeless struggle and are intermingled throughout the world. They are not completely expressed by any particular institution but are represented in the world by parallel hierarchies of loyalty. One city serves the Devil and his demons, while the other serves God and the angels. One city represents the instability and conflict that accompany the affairs of the flesh, while the other represents the unity and peace that come from God. One city embodies the divisions and particularities of human desires, while the other embodies the oneness and universality of God's love. Inextricably mixed in both secular affairs and the Church, these two realms constitute distinct and related spheres of human action. The City of Man and the City of God are condemned to coexist until the end of the world. Their relationship constitutes all human societies and comprehends the whole of human history.

> Accordingly, two cities have been formed by two loves: the earthly by the love of self, even to the contempt of God; the heavenly by the love of God, even to the contempt of self. The former, in a word, glories in itself, the latter in the Lord. For the one seeks glory from men; but the greatest glory of the other is God, the witness of conscience. The one lifts up its head in its own glory; the other says to God, "Thou art my glory, and the lifter up of mine head." In the one, the princes and the nations it subdues are ruled by the love of ruling; in the other, the princes and the subjects serve one another in love, the latter obeying, while the former take thought for all. The one delights in its own strength, represented in the persons of its rulers; the other says to its God, "I will love Thee, O Lord, my strength."[2]

Augustine knew that Rome was dying, but he was convinced that her history taught eternal lessons. Both the City of Man and Rome originated in a fratricide whose roots lie deep within fallen humanity. The twin crimes of Cain and Romulus cannot be understood apart from the jealousy, lust for possessions, and drive to dominate that characterize all human beings. Constituted and defined by egoism, pride, and willfulness, the *civitas terrena* is rooted in murder and disorder. Its principal spheres—household, city, empire—can never be the grounding of moral life.[3] The best we can do is try to arrange as harmonious an interplay between their conflicting demands as possible.[4] The City of Man is the realm of perpetual struggle, conflict, and war.

If the classical tradition had established that civil society depends on justice, Augustine's denial that any permanent good could result from the work of human beings struck at the heart of Greek and Roman optimism. Rome was never a true republic because, Cicero's hopes notwithstanding, it was never founded on justice. Its prideful drive for glory and dominion made it unable to realize that all good comes from God. Augustine's claims were dramatic indeed. Where proper worship is absent there can be no true people, commonwealth, or civil society. "I grant," he said, "there was a republic of a certain kind, and certainly much better administered by the more ancient Romans than by their modern representatives. But the fact is, true justice has no existence save in that republic whose founder and ruler is Christ, if at least any choose to call this a republic; and indeed we cannot deny that it is the people's weal."[5] How can people be capable of justice if they serve impure demons and wicked spirits?[6] Augustine used Cicero against the classical tradition. "For how," he asked, "can there be right where there is no justice?"

> Justice being taken away, then, what are kingdoms but great robberies? For what are robberies themselves, but little kingdoms? The band itself is made up of men; it is ruled by the authority of a prince, it is knit together by the pact of the confederacy; the booty is divided by the law agreed on. . . . Indeed, that was an apt and true reply which was given to Alexander the Great by a pirate who had been seized. For when that king had asked the man what he meant by keeping hostile possession of the sea, he answered with bold pride, "What thou meanest by seizing the whole earth; but because I do it with a petty ship, I am called a robber, whilst thou who dost it with a great fleet are styled emperor."[7]

Augustine's famous equation of states with bands of robbers and emperors with pirates derived from his more fundamental critique of the classical tradition. Humans will never be able to organize peaceful and moral social relations by themselves. The most important "goods" of the earthly city will always be conditional and elusive because of the unbalanced appetites that drive the discordant wills in society. No human being can be exempted from the physical needs of the flesh, but the fallen members of the earthly city regard these needs as sufficient in themselves. Human pride makes the affairs of the world into a closed system, which it mistakenly imagines can be attained by human effort.

Division and strife will always mark the earthly city, for Cain's envy and Romulus's pride represent the twin evils into which unaided humans must inevitably fall.[8] To live for the flesh is to take the part for the whole, but it is difficult for humans to acknowledge our need for and dependence on God. The crimes that lie at the heart of political life explain humanity's history of conflict. The Romans organized the greatest empire in history, but even vast wealth and foreign conquest could not relieve it of pervasive division and malady. A destructive scramble for wealth and power, constant insecurity and mutual fear, civil war, rebellion, sedition, and servitude mark human life. The institutions of the earthly city have no sustained moral content. Redemption can come only with the "love of God to the contempt of self," which the presence of Christian faith and the Roman Church made possible for the first time in history.

Augustine endlessly taught that the failure of pagan classicism lay in its prideful inability to acknowledge that God is the only source of justice. The glory and honor valued by the Greeks and Romans depended on the praise and admiration of other men, and this infected classical notions of civil society with the fatal germ of pride. Aristotle's comprehensive moral project of a politically organized and self-governing civil society had faded from view. "For there is nothing so social by nature, so unsocial by its corruption, as this race."[9]

People's inclinations are disastrous and they are always prone to error. So sweet is sin to fallen humanity that there is no way to combat it without powerful external pressure. The fraternity and concord that prevailed in Eden have been shattered, and the natural law that regulated civil society has all but disappeared from the heart. In a world populated by sinful people, coercion is an essential condition of moral action.

Augustine was preoccupied by a pervasive sense of the need for restraint, and he looked for a mechanism that could defend a fatally flawed civil society from the constant threat of disintegration. Purely spiritual pressure cannot keep humans from sin, for its source lies deep in our very nature. Even our greatest achievements have been possible only because a "strait-jacket" of unremitting harshness has kept us from our own worst desires. Since most people are unredeemed and will remain so until the end of the world, some institutional structure must introduce a measure of peace, order, and stability into the conflict and chaos that would otherwise make life impossible. Augustine shared Plato's appreciation of balance and agreed that "the blessedness of a community and of an individual flow from the same source: for a community is nothing else than a harmonious collection of individuals."[10] The state was a restricted sphere with a narrow range of motion and a diminished set of responsibilities.

The central features of civil society—among them war, property, slavery, and the state—are caused by and serve as remedies for sin. All are structured by an inequality among human beings that is not a feature of the natural order, since God intended for rational man to have dominion over the irrational beasts and not over his own kind. But sin introduced hierarchy into human history and simultaneously made it possible for the institutions of civil society to have a remedial influence.[11] Augustine transformed classical civil society, which had served the Greeks and Romans as the arena of public debate and moral action, into a coercive mechanism that serves God's purposes by punishing error and hopefully reducing sin. Even if civil society cannot touch the heart, it can force depraved and fratricidal man to act *as if* he cares about his brothers.

The peace that the state maintains makes it possible for humans to live and work together, but it is a peace founded on violence and fear rather than on a shared commitment to a common moral project. "To be innocent, we must not only do harm to no man but also restrain him from sin or punish his sin, so that either the man himself who is punished may profit from his experience, or others be warned by his example."[12] The state exists to protect institutions that have no independent moral standing but are necessary for civilized human life. Its primary task is helping the Church exercise its teaching, converting, and saving ministry. In reconciling the state to the Church and explaining how inequality and violence could serve God's purposes, Augustine crafted the first comprehensive Christian theory of obligation and offered kings the support of an increasingly powerful ecclesiastical apparatus. In demonstrating how state violence in the service of Christ could be used to deter humans from error, he was also the first philosopher of the Inquisition.

But even if a political organization is dedicated to Christian ends, headed by Christian princes, organized by Christian law, and administered in a Christian manner, it can never substitute for the redemptive power of grace. The political order is peripheral at best. If it serves God's purposes, it does so indirectly by punishing sin and defending the Church. Born of sin, the state is an instrument for regulating the "exterior" person but cannot touch the deep springs of weakness that lead to error. State coercion can reduce sin by instilling fear, but the roots of a fully moral life lie elsewhere.

A realist about state power, Augustine delegated to the Church ultimate responsibility for civil society, which provided a measure of safety in a world ruled by the chaos unleashed by demonic power. Such a view was common enough in the early years of organized Christianity, but Augustine's unique contribution was to make the Church the heart of a new universal community. His views took shape in the context of his important struggle against the Donatist heresy.

Echoing a tendency as old as the earliest Christian communities, the Donatists viewed the message of Jesus as a radical alternative to the corruption surrounding them. The Church has to be pure in its relation to God and to the world. Its rites are a precise and invariant code of rules that establish the correct relationship between humanity and God. As the only body in the world in which the Spirit lives, it has to be an unblemished example of holy innocence, ritual purity, and meritorious suffering. The sacraments link humanity and God and must be administered by intermediaries who have proven their righteousness.

Augustine countered that the Spirit exists independently of the quality of its human agents. The sacraments rest on Christ's promises and ordinances, and the Church's rites do not depend on the inner state of those who deliver or receive them. The Donatists' notion that the Church is a collection of the Chosen who have to preserve their identity against the temptations of an unclean world was too sectarian, passive, and defensive and would make a Universal Church impossible. Christianity cannot isolate itself from the world and rest content with guarding a static alliance between itself and God. Humans must not interpose willful caution between their history and the imperative demands of a purposeful universe. It is no longer sufficient that the Church defend itself. More is at stake than the purity of isolated Christian communities, and Truth now has a powerful ally in the state. A universal Christian civil society will expand until it encompasses the whole world. Augustine's famous saying, "Love, and do what thou wilt," justified the use of state compulsion in defense of the Church and announced that the entry of Christ into human history had changed everything.

The "true Church" is the body of Christ, while the tangible Church that lives in the imperfect City of Man is a shadow of perfection. The Christian is fated to coexist with evil, and the Church is his only dependable defense against sin. If the Donatists regarded it as a refuge from the world, Augustine believed that its destiny was to become coextensive with human society as a whole. In alliance with the state, it could serve God's purpose by absorbing, transforming, and directing the bonds that join human beings whose essential connection has been lost to sin. It was a microcosm of God's desire to reunite a divided and estranged humanity, which he had initially fashioned from one man. Augustine's civil society organized by the Church replaced Aristotle's polis and Cicero's republic. Faith and grace supplanted reason and public action.

Such a conception of a Christian Commonwealth tended to break down the barriers between the sacred and the profane, between the spiritual sanctions exercised by the Church and the coercive ones administered by the emperor. Gone was the old attitude of antipathy to the state, an inappropriate remnant of the Age of Persecution. The Donatists claimed immunity from the civil obligations of an inherently evil political apparatus, but Augustine laid the basis for later theories of divine right when he demanded that rulers serve God *as kings* because the state is a natural necessity backed by divine power. As hostile as he was to the classical tradition of self-reliance, Augustine preserved a truncated moment of its nod to secular authority. But he was a theologian above all, and his orientation toward the state was part of a coherent worldview organized around the power of faith and the meaning of revelation. Fallen humanity needed more than spiritual sanctions to keep it from evil, and the Church would have to call on the state for assistance against schismatics, heretics, pagans, and Jews.

Augustine always adhered to the standard Christian emphasis on free will and agreed that the final act of faith must be uncoerced and spontaneous. But God's purposes could be served by coercive procedures that people might not want or freely choose for themselves. The corrective process of teaching, learning, and disciplining could be imposed on the individual, even against his or her will, so as to prepare the soul for Christ and the Church. People need the whip of fear and the shackle of constraint in their battle with sin. After all, the Old Testament God had not hesitated to visit a series of calamities and disasters on his Chosen People in order to turn them from their prideful errors. If coercion had played an essential role in the history of Israel, it could be equally important to the progress of the Church. At all times it would be administered by the state. The Church's hands must be clean.

The sophisticated pagan skeptics of the late Empire could never accept Christianity's exorbitant claim to be the only path to salvation, universal knowledge, and truth. Such an assertion made no sense to them, and the great Porphyry had objected that it was deeply contrary to human nature. Polytheisms are generally more tolerant than monotheisms because they are disposed to recognize that different civilizations have distinct histories and gods. But Augustine regarded Christianity as the natural and true religion of the entire human race, the only way to reestablish the relationship between God and humanity that had been ruptured by sin. *The City of God* was now an outline of Universal History. An independent civil society was out of the question. The general collapse of the human race means that we cannot raise ourselves up by our own efforts. God alone decides our fate, and only the Church can explain how justice is served by the suffering of innocent babies. As well run as the Roman Republic and Empire had been, true justice could not exist there. It has no existence except in that republic whose founder and ruler is Christ. The Universal Church will organize the Universal Community and safeguard its universal knowledge.

Since, then, the supreme good of the city of God is perfect and eternal peace, not such as mortals pass into and out of by birth and death, but the peace of freedom from all evil, in which the immortals ever abide, who can deny that that future life is most blessed, or that, in comparison with it, this life which now we live is most wretched, be it filled with all blessings of body and soul and external things? And yet, if any man uses this life with a reference to that other which he ardently loves and confidently hopes for, he may well be called even now blessed, though not in reality so much as in hope. But the actual possession of the happiness of this life, without the hope of what is beyond, is but a false happiness and profound misery. For the true blessings of the soul are not now enjoyed; for that is no true wisdom which does not direct all its prudent observations, manly actions, virtuous self-restraint, and just arrangements, to that end in which God shall be all and all in a secure eternity and perfect peace.[13]

Augustine never articulated a comprehensive theory of the relationship between Church and state, but he deepened Paul's political accommodationism and laid the foundations for a profoundly important Christian theory of political obligation and civil society. His lip service to free will notwithstanding, Augustine's relentless insistence that all human works carry the stain of Original Sin proved a serious burden for later theologians because it systematically denigrated the here and now. If the love of God enters humans through the undeserved action of the Holy Spirit, there is little room for genuinely free human response to the gift of grace. If God alone is the source of every human movement toward good, then our works always stand in the shadow of sin. We can order our temporal affairs in the profane world only because God provides us with the opportunity to train and discipline the soul. The life of Christ and the gift of the Church, Augustine repeatedly declared, do not do away with civil society but fulfill and complete it. Human history is the dialectic of good and evil, the love of God and the love of humanity. It is now possible for Church and state to unite and contribute to the salvation of fallen humanity. The grace of God has made it possible to use power in the defense of truth and for redemption. Such a view came to rest in a theory of civil society that destroyed the very category it proposed to make whole. For all his criticism of paganism, Augustine shared Plato's problem even as he laid the foundation of a distinctly Christian theory of civil society.

The Christian Commonwealth

Augustine's attempt to turn Caesaropapism's fusion of state and Church to the service of God had to be refined because the Christianization of the Empire was accompanied by its disintegration. The slow development of Christendom as a single Church-state encouraged early medieval thinkers to develop an overarching structure within whose boundaries they could comprehend the relations between different peoples and different spheres. The division of labor between the official ecclesiastical structure of the Church (the *Sacerdotium*) and the secular officials of Empire and Kingdom (*Imperium* and *Regnum*) described shifting lines of authority between the complementary spheres of a single Christian Commonwealth.

The theory of the "two swords," developed by Patristic writers and solidified after the fifth century by Pope Gelasius I, implied a dual organization and control of civil society in the interests of the two great classes of values whose conservation was central to God's relationship with humanity. Each was said to correspond to the two large bodies of human needs, and it was Gelasius himself who described "the two powers by which this world is chiefly ruled" as those of pope and emperor. Spiritual interests and matters of salvation were properly the affair of the Church, while temporal matters of order, peace, and justice were the province of civil government. The Gelasian doctrine of the "two swords" described a pair of independent but intertwined spheres of human affairs administered by twin Christian hierarchies whose separate jurisdictions merged in a single purpose. The state existed to give order to public affairs. The Church existed to provide moral guidance to all its members. Each power was to be supreme within its own sphere, although it was generally assumed that in case of a clash the spiritual power of the Church should prevail.

The notion of a universal Christian Commonwealth was the dominant legacy the Church Fathers and Augustine passed on to the Middle Ages. The Gelasian attempt to delineate different spheres of ecclesiastical and political authority established the standard agenda that political philosophers would follow for hundreds of years, although its own vagueness and a series of unavoidable contradictions between Church and state could not prevent serious clashes from breaking out. If Gelasianism implied a certain differentiation between Church and State, it also presupposed a single Christian civil society. All ecclesiastical philosophy of the High Middle Ages sought to integrate, organize, unify, systematize, and reconcile. Politics, economics, science, ethics, and art remained under the controlling influence of theology, and no independent developments in these areas would be possible until the Reformation and the Renaissance broke the unity of medieval Christian thought.

In the short run, the dominant tendency was toward a fusion of Church and state, symbolized by Charlemagne's famous coronation at the hands of Pope Leo in 800. The central claim of most medieval political and ethical theory was that a single Christian ideal could be applied to the manifold conditions of life. This generated its characteristic drive to treat every form of human organization both as an organic unity in its own right and as a manifestation of a single higher purpose whose ultimate meaning could be explained only by the Church. The defining premise was that of a uniform whole that expressed the compound and articulated character of God's creation. The universal order of all things presupposes a divinely instituted harmony that pervades the whole and every part of it. The universe is an integrated and articulated organism, every part of which shares in its essential nature and is a replica of the universal whole. Every human individual and association is a microcosm in which the macrocosm is expressed. All created things are simultaneously themselves and images of God.

The essence of God is a unity that existed before plurality and created order out of chaos. All existence is ordered in grades, each rank receiving meaning from above and transmitting it below. Every thing in the universe occupies its assigned place, and every link between these things corresponds to a divine decree. Differentiated inequality marks the created world, and both existence and merit issue from above in a "great chain of being."[14]

Since the universe is hierarchical, harmony and justice on earth require that humanity understand its place in God's creation. The medieval notion of a uniform and articulated social organism necessitated a theory of membership that assigned to each individual his proper place and task within a larger unity he did not create. A single uniform organism implies an integrated union of the like and unlike, a balance of contrasts and differences in rank, estate, profession, and political power. Every individual, group, guild, or estate occupies a definite place within an order that stretches from the lowliest individual to the supreme single whole. If faith was not enough, meaning could be explained by a Church whose authority was always backed by the sword.

Augustine transmitted to the Middle Ages the Greek idea that every created part has its own definite place in a universal order of things while also expressing its own order, constitution, and end. This hierarchical view of a compound universe reflected the character of medieval society and ultimately provided a powerful defense of the existing order. Its complex array of ranks, estates, guilds, and professions could be explained only by locating it in a larger structure of a divinely created universe. Medieval political thought gave rise to an involved corporate theory of intermediate bodies but located them all within the oneness of God. The continuing drive to think in terms of the most comprehensive levels of association made it impossible to develop a theory of civil society that could stand independent of theology. The Greeks had tried to organize everything around the polis; medieval writers centered their thinking around God's organization of the cosmos.[15] Their similar commitment to a comprehensive theory of social life was at least as important as their differing accounts of its character. Medieval theory's preoccupation with unity and order was rooted in its attempt to justify aristocratic power amid the decentralization, differentiation, and corporatism of medieval society.

An acceptance of hierarchy did not preclude considerable local activity, and complicated networks of social interaction involved a wide range of people throughout the period. Personal status, class conflict, custom, hierarchy, and voluntary cooperation structured the debates about the rights and duties of collectivities that were a permanent feature of medieval affairs. A decentralized and rural social order provided limited opportunities for general political activity, but medieval society was structured by different levels of conflict and cooperation within and between a variety of groups. Such a society was thoroughly penetrated by Christian norms, and complicated horizontal forces helped shape overlapping relations in a social order that shared a single religious orientation.[16] The development of medieval society was partly constituted by a tug of war between its centralizing and fragmenting tendencies.

On one hand, the increasing power of the Roman papacy and an accompanying series of twelfth-century theological innovations began to consolidate the unity of the medieval Church and facilitated its role in forging a unified Christian civil society. Three specifically medieval dogmas—the universal episcopate of the pope, the superiority of the spiritual power over the temporal, and the impartation of grace through the seven sacraments—expressed the Church's claim to independence from and superiority to the state. An ecclesiastically organized civilization marked the ascendancy of the papal Universal Church's claim to incarnate the morally uniform principle of an entire social order.[17] The consolidation of the Church was paralleled by similar developments in the political sphere, and it would not be long before kings began to challenge Church claims of absolute supremacy.

If centralization and claims to universality marked one important aspect of medieval life, powerful economic forces were also fragmenting social organization and driving toward a collection of small, self-sufficient agricultural communities. Periodic collapses of trade and commerce contradicted the increasingly insistent claims of centralized ecclesiastical and secular bureaucracies. Kings tended to see themselves as sitting on top of a pyramid of personal loyalties rather than being a monarch of the Roman or Byzantine variety. The only agent of solidarity was the general sense that everyone belonged to a Christian Commonwealth, but there were many ways of expressing what this meant.

The period's decentralized agricultural economy could never generate an integral theory of the state that stood apart from theology. Rural life fostered networks of personal relationships, strengthened sentiments of local solidarity in the organization of social life, and developed a powerful ethic of personal dependence and mutual help. Patriarchal authority and subordination, comradeship and mutual contact, and loyalty and respect helped structure social life in the absence of powerful markets and centralizing states. No secular central power could organize social life on a widespread basis, no claims of temporal sovereignty could challenge those of the Church for some time, and no formal body of public law could compete with the claims of priests and bishops. Religious influence and values penetrated every nook and cranny of medieval life. Independent organizations or ideals that could claim loyalty apart from or in opposition to the Church did not exist in sufficient strength to generate viable centers of autonomous theory or practice.[18] The controversies of the period were not really between Church and state as two distinct powers but rather between two branches of one and the same Christian civil society. The thoroughgoing conflation of religion and politics allowed for little more than structured disputes about how a unified Christian social order should be organized and whose authority should govern its separate spheres. Under the circumstances, it was impossible to generate a theory of civil society that could stand outside the strictures of the Church.

The organization of medieval society also made it difficult to theorize a civil society independent of the Church. Even as they contested with each other for leadership of Christendom, the centralizing Church and state had to deal with their local particularisms. Popes were always engaged with bishops who were anxious to preserve their centers of power against the intrusive claims of the Roman authorities, and kings were always constrained by the demands of local princes, autonomous guilds, and independent towns.

The political influence of local authority was strong throughout the Middle Ages. Talk of a unified Christian body politic coexisted with a complicated and often incoherent structure of local privilege and custom. Even as the papacy and the secular monarchs pressed hard for administrative coherence and centralization, they had to consult and compromise with their dependent populations and local bodies. Corporate organizations were forming in both *Sacerdotium* and *Regnum*. Monastic chapters, Church orders, trading guilds, communal and civic councils, universities, and corporations proliferated within medieval society, and they always tried to protect their hard-won autonomy. Their success in doing so formed a powerful if temporary barrier to further centralization. In the Church, there was little contradiction between the pope's roles as feudal overlord and public head of the ecclesiastical community. In the state, there was little contradiction between the king's roles as feudal overlord and public head of the political community. Sovereignty was complicated and dispersed; each baron, corporation, or order was sovereign in his sphere, even if popes and kings struggled over who was going to guide the community as a whole.

The famous eleventh-century contest between Pope Gregory VII and Holy Roman Emperor Henry IV helped define many of the issues that preoccupied medieval thinkers. Strengthened by the great Cluny reform movement's demand for a spiritual church that was independent of secular authorities, Pope Nicholas II had established a College of Cardinals in 1059 and invested it with exclusive authority to elect subsequent popes. Although secular rulers continued to have considerable indirect influence in Church affairs, Nicholas's successor, Alexander II, was the first pope elected solely by the new body.

It was Alexander's successor, Gregory VII, who translated longstanding Church demands for independence into the famous "investiture controversy." Strongly influenced by Cluny's strict view of clerical life while he had been Cardinal Hildebrand, Gregory broadened its program of moral regeneration and papal centralization. His demand for "freedom for the Church" required the end of lay investiture—that is, the selection and appointment of church officials by secular authority. From now on, he declared in 1075, any layperson who presumed to invest bishops and abbots with the symbols of authority faced excommunication. Immediately Henry IV in the Holy Roman Empire, William the Conqueror in England, and Philip I in France protested.

The strongest reaction came from Germany, particularly dependent on churchmen for the administrative tasks of government and competing with the papal states for control of northern Italy. Gregory's decree had raised the question of the proper role of a Christian monarch in a unified Christian civil society. Did the king have ultimate jurisdiction over all his subjects, or did some of them answer to a papacy whose creation of the College of Cardinals had announced its independence of the kings? Henry now found himself ordered by the pope to secularize the empire—but anyone could see that Gregory's edict was only a first step toward the ultimate assumption of authority over all of Christendom by a resurgent papacy.

An increasingly bitter exchange of letters ensued. Gregory accused Henry of lack of respect for the Church and informed him that disobeying the pope was disobeying God. The territorial princes, eager to see the emperor weakened, supported Rome. Henry responded by declaring Gregory deposed in a famous letter that began "Henry King not by usurpation, but by the pious ordination of God, to Hildebrand, not now Pope, but false monk." In ironic opposition to the princes, the German bishops were brought together at Worms and proclaimed their support for Henry and independence from Rome. Gregory answered by excommunicating them and the emperor and releasing Henry's subjects from their vows of allegiance. By Christmas 1076 the clergy was supporting the emperor and the great nobles were siding with the pope.

The ensuing revolt of the princes forced Henry to come to terms with Gregory. In the most dramatic event of the High Middle Ages, he traveled to the pope's castle retreat at Canossa and stood barefoot in the snow for three days in January 1077. Gregory's absolution marked the high point of papal power, but the investiture controversy dragged on for another fifty years until the Concordat of Worms allowed for papal investiture of bishops in the presence of lay rulers. If members of the clergy now received their office and attendant power exclusively from ecclesiastical authorities, kings were still free to influence them with grants of land and other worldly goods. Papal authority was strengthened somewhat, but the Concordat's major effect was to adjust the relationship between the secular and religious branches of a unified Christian civil society in a way that strengthened local princes and accelerated the division and weakness of the empire.

In the short run, Gregory's victory over Henry encouraged Rome to assert its exclusive jurisdiction over Christendom. As the Church continued to centralize its organization and theology, the papal party effectively abandoned the Gelasian compromise and demanded that all political arrangements be regarded as part and parcel of ecclesiastical organization. God may have willed the separation of the two spheres and sanctioned the secular state, but it is only by the mediation of the Church that the temporal power possesses divine sanction and mandate. Rooted in sin and defined by violence, the state needs the hallowing authority of the Church. The general theory of the Gregorian Church was that the emperor and all other secular rulers derive their offices mediately from God but immediately from the pope, who acts as God's regent because he was given both swords by Jesus through Peter. The pope retains the temporal sword but gives it over to kings and princes on condition that they use it in the service and under the direction of the Church. The legitimacy that the Church imparts requires the subordination of the state to the ecclesiastical order in all respects and at all times.

Faced with the claims of an aggressive papacy, the imperial party tended to rest content with traditional Gelasianism and argued that the Church and state were parallel and coordinate bodies. William of Occam, Marsilius of Padua, and other thinkers would later claim an independent standing for temporal power that does not depend on the sanction of the pope. Both *Imperium* and *Sacerdotium*, on this reading, derive directly from God and do not depend on the Church. Other theorists conceded a certain measure of independence to the Church but remained content to demand that it limit itself to purely spiritual matters. In the end, most acknowledged that the supremacy of the spiritual over the temporal meant that the Church would predominate in most cases of serious conflict with a Christian king.

But monarchical and papal centralization forced medieval theorists to move away from the simple Patristic and Augustinian claim that the state was little more than a coercive remedy for sin. This made possible a more sophisticated understanding of an increasingly complex civil society. The profoundly important recovery of Aristotle in the thirteenth century made it possible to regard politics as something more than the unfortunate reminder of error that exists only because of the debased nature of the human race. For the first time since the fall of Rome, it became possible to suspect that political society might be a positive—if limited—good in its own right. The exclusive focus on a unified religious-political Commonwealth slowly yielded to a consideration of the ethical possibilities afforded by secular political activity in a Christian civil society.

The work of Thomas Aquinas is one of the turning points in this formidable project. By the time he arrived in Paris to study with the great scholar Albertus Magnus in 1245, the influx of Arabian-Aristotelian science was arousing a sharp reaction within the Church. Christian believers were confronted with the rigorous demands of scientific rationalism. At the same time, the increasing importance of urban centers and the slow spread of markets were pressing against the traditional contempt for the world that had dominated so much Christian thinking since Augustine. Aquinas's effort to create a comprehensive Christian theology demanded that reason be made the companion of revelation and that natural law be integrated into Catholic morality. All human institutions and spheres of activity were subordinated to a Christian standard of life that suffused a graded and hierarchical civil society. Different ranks served one another in a structure held together by an absolute and binding law of reason derived from nature. Thomas's theory of a universal Christian civilization married a recognition of the manifold differences immanent in God's creation to an Aristotelian hierarchy of ends that stressed progress toward a divine ideal and tended to downplay the Augustinian implications of the Fall. The uniform theory that resulted did not suppose that the Church had different foundations from other institutions of the world, but Thomas considered separate problems from the standpoint of a single set of fundamental ethical principles. Christian civil society was now an organism composed of different groups and estates within and outside of the Church, all united in their common love of God and driven by their shared goal of fulfillment expressed as salvation.

The effort to find a place for reason clearly implied that the moral standing of human affairs was not erased by revelation. The existence of higher values does not deny that subordinate spheres have a determinate part to play and may be organized by forms of understanding appropriate to them. Neither sin nor salvation obliterates human works. Aquinas followed Aristotle in deriving the state from human nature, and in doing so he derived a powerful justification for civil society. No longer an institution appointed by God as a response to and remedy for sin, it is an expression of human nature and serves God in a directly positive sense. Within the limits of a Christian worldview, Aquinas was ready to attempt a reconciliation between the classical and Christian notions of the political community. He agreed with Aristotle that the polity is the highest and most comprehensive of all associations formed by human reason:

> Now since human reason has to order not only the things that are used by man but also men themselves, who are ruled by reason, it proceeds in either case from the simple to the complex: in the case of the things used by man when, for example, it builds a ship out of wood and a house out of wood and stones: in the case of men themselves when, for example, it orders many men so as to form a certain society. And since among these societies there are various degrees and orders, the highest is that of the city, which is ordered to the

satisfaction of all the needs of human life. Hence of all the human societies this one is the most perfect. And because the things used by man are ordered to man as to their end, which is superior to the means, that whole which is the city is therefore necessarily superior to all the other wholes that may be known and constituted by human reason.[19]

At its highest level—the level from which it derived its ultimate meaning—civil society was expressed as Aristotle's comprehensive political life of the "city." The political order is the highest form of human association because it is the work of reason, aims at the satisfaction of human needs, and makes possible a life lived well. Aquinas's important recognition of plurality and difference was always contained within the boundaries of his Christianized Aristotelianism. His rescue of reason from Augustine enabled him to restore politics to a theoretical prominence it had not occupied for centuries. Since the city is "the most important of the things that can be constituted by human reason, for all the other human societies are ordered to it," political science is the most noble and important of all the practical sciences and must direct the others "inasmuch as it is concerned with the highest and perfect good in human affairs."[20] It follows that the many subsidiary forms of human association that dotted the medieval landscape culminated in the polity, for

> the whole is naturally prior to the parts of matter, even though the parts are prior in the order of generation. But individual men are related to the whole city as are the parts of man to man. For, just as a hand or a foot cannot exist without a man, so too one man cannot live self-sufficiently by himself when separated from the city.
>
> Now if it should happen that someone is unable to participate in civil society because of his depravity, he is worse than a man and is, as it were, a beast. If, on the other hand, he does not need anyone and is, as it were, self-sufficient, he is better than a man, for he is, as it were, a god. It remains true, therefore, from what has been said, that the city is by nature prior to one man.[21]

Aquinas opened up the possibility that politics could serve general moral purposes. Social and political life, he asserted, is fundamental to the human condition *as such* and can no longer be understood as unfortunate consequences of the Fall. It followed that civil society—the combination of Aristotle's organized political commonwealth and a wider Christian Commonwealth—is natural to humans. *Even if humanity had never sinned,* there would be some need for coordinated activity directed toward the common

good. Just as "it is natural for man to live in the society of many, it is necessary that there exist among men some means by which the group may be
governed. For where there are many men together and each one is looking
after his own interest, the multitude would be broken up and scattered unless there were also an agency to take care of what appertains to the common weal."[22] Humans are given reason by God to guide our actions, and it
is our reason, not our sin, that leads us to live with others in a political association.[23]

Far from reflecting God's disappointment and serving as an instrument
for divine wrath, civil society is a necessary condition for freedom. Sin explains slavery, injustice, war, penal law, and the other strictly punitive features of temporal life. But it cannot explain the political community, which
is rooted in human nature and serves ends higher than those served by coercion. Even a pagan or non-Christian state has a certain ethical content, a
position that Augustine's denunciation of such states as the work of sin
made impossible. Political Thomism moved politics away from Augustine's
unitary notion of a Church-ordered economy of redemption. To the extent
that it was now a function of human nature, politics was part of the economy of creation; it would have been necessary even if we had not sinned
and made redemption necessary. If the Augustinian tradition held that civil
society was entirely conventional and necessarily bound up with the
Church, Thomas's conception of it as a Christian Commonwealth's political
order allowed it a limited independence.

But he was a theologian and in the end could not get too close to Aristotle. The Thomistic state may be more than Augustine's partial remedy for
sin, but it had to be subsumed to God's plan for the human race as revealed
by the Church. All stages of human history and all forms of human social
organization depend on humanity's relationship to God if they are to fulfill
their potential. The ultimate meaning of any human institution is to be
found in its conformity to God's universal moral law. Thomas tried to liberate reason from the requirements of faith, but he ended by making it the
faculty that allows humans a limited ability to understand and participate
in the workings of God's eternal law. His important differences with Augustine could not obscure their fundamental agreement that human beings'
own efforts cannot be a sufficient condition for the good life. There might
be many states and spheres of human activity, but there was only one
Church. Thomas was working within well-understood limits, and in the
end he had to regard civil society as part of a hierarchy that is ultimately
subordinate to the Church. The full revival of the classical heritage would

have to wait for theorists who were willing to confront Church authority directly from the outside.

Early Fractures

Aquinas's incomplete compromise notwithstanding, the tendency to transform the *Regnum* from a branch of the Christian Commonwealth into the autonomous corporate body of the state continued. It had always found a powerful antagonist in the papacy's claims that it should supervise the entire Commonwealth, but the tides of history were beginning to turn against Rome. Dante Alighieri took an important step toward a conception of civil society that did not depend on the authority of the Church, but it was Marsilius of Padua's claim that all the interests of the community could be contained within the boundaries of the secular state that directly anticipated modern theories of civil society.

Dante worked within the limits of Gelasianism's two spheres, but his immediate concern was restoring a civic peace that had been disrupted by Church meddling in Italian affairs and papal claims of ecclesiastical immunity from state authority. He held these encroachments on the proper duties of the political sphere responsible for undermining the balance that had defined the contours of a reasonably peaceful civil society. Dante looked to a powerful unitary monarchy to represent God's universal empire and assume exclusive responsibility for temporal affairs. Only a sovereign who has everything can institute justice, for he will not be tempted to turn the state toward his own private purposes.

His Gelasianism notwithstanding, Dante was interested in considerably more than the standard debate about Church and state. People pursue many goals and live in a variety of associations, but they need peace to live a decent life at any level. Only a single government can help us realize the ethical potential of all our subsidiary temporal associations.[24] The world-government Dante sought "must be understood in the sense that it governs mankind on the basis of what all have in common and that by a common law it leads all toward peace."[25] Only a single directing will can make sense of the diversity of human goals. The monarch serves God because only he can "hold the human race subject to a single system of approvals and disapprovals."[26]

Since emperor and pope represent irreducible and "different species of power," it follows that the emperor's temporal authority comes directly from God rather than through the mediation of the Church.[27] The head of state is independent of the Church, for "the authority for temporal world-government must come directly, without intermediary, from the universal Fount of authority, which, though it flows pure from a single spring, spills over into many channels out of the abundance of its goodness."[28] But Dante knew the limits of his argument. As much as he desired to establish a single comprehensive political structure with no temporal superior, his Universal Empire could not comprehend every detail of human life. Different associations have their own characteristics and require their own laws. The king rules over individuals, households, cities, and states, but each has its own nature and purpose and must be organized accordingly. If "mankind can be ruled by a single supreme ruler or world-governor," it is no less true that "not every little regulation for every city could come directly from the world-government, for even municipal regulations are sometimes defective and need amendment. . . . Nations, states, and cities have their own internal concerns which require special laws."[29]

Dante's effort to derive a single integrating principle that could comprehend plurality led to his theory of world-government, a "function for the whole of mankind as an organized multitude which can not be achieved by any single man, or family, or neighborhood, or city, or state."[30] But this anticipation of the future applied only to worldly matters. The temporal and religious spheres would have to coexist. Humans aspire to two beatitudes—one on earth and the other in heaven. The former is accessible through the moral and intellectual virtues and is the province of secular power, while the latter comes through theology and is rightfully the province of ecclesiastical authority. In true Gelasian fashion, Dante believed that the two parallel lines of organization ultimately answer to God but not to one another.[31] Temporal affairs could be contained within the single overarching framework of the state. Religious matters were the affair of the Church.

Dante had powerful antagonists, for the Gelasian settlement was coming under increasing pressure from Rome throughout the thirteenth century. Popes such as Innocent III and Innocent IV continued to exalt papal power and claim jurisdiction over an ever-widening area of secular life, but Boniface VIII's celebrated *Unam Sanctum* of 1302 advanced the most extravagant argument for papal authority. Responding to the efforts of Edward I of England and Philip the Fair of France to tax ecclesiastical estates, Boniface proclaimed that the Church cannot be limited by the state in any respect. The most extreme medieval assertion of papal supremacy, *Unam Sanctum* asserted that there is no salvation outside the Roman Church and that "every human creature" was "subject to the Roman pontiff." Boniface accepted the two spheres in theory but insisted that, if the temporal sword is wielded by the State, it can be legitimate only in subordination to the judgment of the Church. The spiritual power is the judge of the temporal and can be judged only by God. Civil society is the creation of the Church.

Boniface's formulation represented the high point of the medieval ecclesiastical polity and had been directly influenced by Giles of Rome. Written in 1301, *On Ecclesiastical Power* admitted the existence of the two powers and acknowledged that the Church should not wield the sword. But even if the state organizes the affairs of the world, the Church has unlimited and ultimate jurisdiction over all things on earth because it is the final guardian of the meaning of Christ's life.[32] The Church was claiming the full measure of power and jurisdiction over all areas of civil society. It was clear to Giles and Boniface that "earthly power and rule must obey and serve the spiritual power and rule . . . because it is more particular, and because it disposes and prepares the materials, and because this earthly power does not come so close to what is best or attain it so perfectly as the other."[33] The temporal power serves the spiritual as the lower serves the higher and the particular serves the universal. If the Greeks and Romans worked with a politicized notion of the universal and thought of civil society as a politically organized community, Giles's medieval Christian Commonwealth rested on a religious and ecclesiastical vision.

In the end, these theoretical disputes were decided as they often are: by political power and the sword. Philip responded to Boniface's extravagant claim by sending soldiers to arrest him. Boniface's subsequent death threw the dispute back to the College of Cardinals, which responded to heavy French pressure by electing a pope who promptly removed his court to Avignon and began the century-long "Babylonian Captivity" of the Church. The papacy's claims also aroused serious theoretical objections, and the Dominican John of Paris countered with a defense of the emperor's independent power. The Church may be a universal and catholic community, but autonomous political associations existed before Christ. They are rooted in human nature, which was created by God and is endowed with an autonomous moral standing. Civil society is a natural community, has always been a quality of settled peoples, and is essential to human well-being. Government does not derive its authority from, and need not answer to, the Church. It follows that ecclesiastical organization cannot serve a model for the state. All priests may be subject to a single master in the pope, but the diversity in human affairs and the existence of private property explains why people live under a variety of political forms.[34] John was willing to accept a portion of Boniface's claims but was not prepared to take them to the pope's conclusion. Spiritual authority may be higher than that of the state because of the higher goal at which it aims, but this does not mean that one power answers to another on earth. "If the priest is superior to the ruler in dignity and absolutely speaking, nevertheless it is not necessary that he be superior to him in all things."[35] Even if the Christian king of France is subject to the spiritual power of the pope because he is a Christian, this does not mean that he is subject to the pope's temporal power because he is a king.

No matter how coherent these arguments sounded, the medieval relationship between Church and state was always fluid. Much of the ambiguity was a function of the ever-shifting relationship between the two spheres, but the inherent uncertainties of the theories themselves also played an important role. Gelasianism was the bedrock of all the arguments of the period, but it never pretended to solve the problem of boundaries between the two spheres of what everyone continued to recognize as a single Christian civil society. At best it provided a general framework within which Church and state could debate their responsibilities, powers, and relationships. The argument was eventually settled in favor of the national states because of economic and political developments rather than a newfound theoretical clarity.

It was Marsilius of Padua who anticipated the end of the entire medieval tradition. Like Dante and others, he began by blaming the papacy for northern Italy's widespread corruption, factionalism, and violence. Indeed, the *Defensor Pacis* attempted to address the familiar evil of papal encroachments in the spiritual and temporal spheres and trace their disastrous consequences for civic peace. But Marsilius went beyond Dante's concern with the requirements of universal order. He began with the most basic human needs and looked to the state to organize civil society so humans could live with one another in peace. This orientation enabled him to mount the most effective argument against Rome that the Middle Ages produced.

Politically organized associations more extensive than the family, "civil communities" cannot become the perfect and self-sufficient communities that God intended without peace.[36] Humans live two sorts of "good lives"—the temporal and earthly and the eternal and heavenly. Civil society is the home of the first and comprises the entire extent of our life on earth.[37] Originally brought into existence for the sake of life, it is constituted by the adjudication of disputes, restraint and punishment of wrongdoers, protection of what is common, and promotion of the worship and honor of God.[38] The life of the Church is contained in and defined by the political institutions of a secular civil society.

The core of Rome's position was the pope's claim to be the ultimate guardian of the divinely ordained ends that govern human life. But Marsilius denied that external ends had any connection to political organization and insisted that they be replaced by more immediate concerns in shaping the affairs of the world. Civil society originates in the fundamental principle of human association, "that all men desire sufficiency of life and avoid the opposite."[39] The requirements of stability and reason were the only criteria by which the affairs of the world could be ordered, and this meant that the Church was just another institution. Where traditional medieval theory thought of two spheres whose relationships had to be theorized, Marsilius saw a single sphere that subordinated the priestly function of civil society to the political requirements of the state. The priesthood is nothing more or less than an element of civil society. Since his goal was to limit the Church claims that had proven so disruptive to peace, Marsilius went on to develop a theory of republican government that recognized that "men came together to the civil community in order to attain what was beneficial and to avoid the opposite. Those matters, therefore, which can affect the benefit and harm of all ought to be known and heard by all, in order that they may be able to attain the beneficial and to avoid the opposite."[40]

Marsilius recast the entire debate between the traditional spheres of the Christian Commonwealth by exploding the religious content of the category. His goals were broader than defending the prerogatives of the temporal sphere from Church interference. Before he subordinated Church to state, papal lawyers seemed to have the upper hand in their disputes with the defenders of secular government. If the salvation of humanity's immortal soul ranked higher than material matters and Augustine's Church represented God's intervention in human history, it was difficult for imperial apologists to defend state prerogatives against papal claims of *plenitudo potestatis* in a Church-organized Christian civil society. Marsilius's denial that there was any connection between the work of the state and that of the Church broke the medieval synthesis of a united Christendom of spirit and flesh. The priesthood can concern itself with divine matters and administer the sacraments as it chooses, but where matters touch on people's outward acts legitimate power belongs exclusively to the government. The state is the sovereign source of law, it defines and constitutes the Church, and it is to be obeyed because it is itself the expression of justice. Its responsibilities are far more extensive than those of a conventional concentration of coercive power.

Marsilius's work anticipated the end of Gelasianism and of the ecclesiastical civil society it tried to organize. In overturning the traditional notion of the two spheres and the two powers necessary to govern the Christian Commonwealth, it ruptured the central category within which Dante and John of Paris had tried to construct an opposition to papal claims of earthly power. A new logic of undivided sovereignty began to form against the traditional medieval understanding of a theologically constituted sphere with dual responsibilities. Marsilius's theory of the state anticipated the fully secular theories of sovereignty whose appearance would bring the Middle Ages to a close. If civil society is composed of different spheres and tranquility requires that they be able to perform their activities in accordance with reason and their own natures, the papacy could no longer claim the power to organize public life. The spiritual truths proclaimed and guarded by the Church have no compelling force apart from the state's organizing and coercive power.

Marsilius's insistence that the Church be treated as a subsidiary organ of the state marked the beginning of the Christian Commonwealth's lengthy theoretical crisis. Augustine's state had been responsible for regulating the external human being of flesh and cupidity, but the important work of ministering to fallen humanity's inner sin and weakness had been reserved to the Church. Marsilius reversed the order of priorities and dealt a massive blow to medieval theories of universal knowledge and universal commonwealths. Sovereignty soon came to be located at a single secular point, and the state started to claim final authority over all intermediate corporations and individuals inhabiting a given geographical area. As the medieval notion of a theologically centered civil society came under pressure from developing markets and political structures, modern theories of sovereignty would redefine the state as the community that knows no superior. As the universal political and religious foundations of the first tradition of theory dissolved, a new set of categories developed within which modern civil society could be theorized.

3

Civil Society and the Transition to Modernity

Transitional periods are never easy, and the passage to modernity was no exception. The disintegration of medieval religious, political, and economic life produced such chaos and instability that it became impossible to conceptualize a coherent theory of civil society. The old categories were plainly inadequate but new ones were not in place; civil society could no longer be understood as a universal political or religious commonwealth, but modern economic and political structures were still in their infancy. The growing power of national markets and national states had been eroding feudalism's hierarchical structure of grades, ranks, and statuses for some time before the devastating attacks of the Renaissance and Reformation. Understanding politics as the coercive arm of Christian civil society had generated a powerful principle of legitimacy, but the Christian Commonwealth was succumbing to Italian political chaos and German religious turmoil.[1] Its universal fabric could not accommodate itself to the autonomous political centers that were being prepared by the growth of markets, and sooner or later it was bound to collapse.

Niccolò Machiavelli's preoccupation with political corruption led him to the civic virtues that had nourished Roman power, but his debt to the past made him unable to theorize civil society outside of familiar republican categories. Nevertheless, his thoroughly secular approach to politics anticipated a distinctly modern understanding of state and society. The Vatican might still quote Innocent III or Boniface VIII in support of its claim to world dominion or even refer back to Gelasius to buttress more limited assertions, but the relentless erosion of the old order was clear to all. Machiavelli's secular economy of power and the Reformation's liberated conscience anticipated a civil society organized around private interests. Thomas Hobbes announced the birth of a new calculating individual operating in a civil society organized by state power. It was not long before the medieval attempt to understand *Sacerdotium* and *Regnum* as complementary jurisdictions within a single Christian Commonwealth was in ruins.

Machiavelli incorporated elements of earlier attempts to achieve virtue and balance without the intervention of a timeless moral agent. The papal centralism whose consequences he deplored was matched by an equally rapid consolidation of royal absolutism throughout Western Europe. In both Church and state, the concentration of power came at the expense of the complex array of intermediate orders, monasteries, parliaments, cities, guilds, and estates that marked the landscape of late feudalism. Almost everywhere the medieval structure of corporations and representation was decaying and collapsing. More extensive markets, developed patterns of exchange, improved communications, and far-reaching means of transportation began to undermine the local monopolies that had supported medieval corporatism and federalism. The control of trade gradually escaped from local bodies and flowed toward the centralized royal bureaucracies that were arising to nurture and feed off it. A commercial bourgeoisie began to take shape, and its initial tendency was to ally itself with the concentrated royal power that protected it from its aristocratic antagonists and depended on it for tax revenue and loans. Monarchies learned how to exploit national resources, expand trade, wage war, and conduct foreign relations. Their bureaucracies moved to outflank or demolish intermediate institutions as they leveled the political field and extended their range of action.[2]

The consequences of this centralization were enormous. Political power had been widely dispersed during the late Middle Ages but was being consolidated in the hands of the king. The *Sacerdotium* gradually vanished and papal supremacy came to mark a Church that was transformed from the organizer of Christendom into a junior partner of the state as religion began its slow retreat into the realm of private devotion. Absolute monarchies became the characteristic form of political organization throughout Western Europe, and the notion of a single point of secular sovereign power became a centerpiece of political thought.

Benefiting from its proximity to the Mediterranean, northern Italy was distinguished by advanced trading and commercial forces. But the rapid development of modern economic relations would not find political expression there until well into the nineteenth century. While unified monarchies developed rapidly in France, Spain, and England, Italy suffered from a particularly debilitating combination of economic and cultural development and political backwardness. Like Dante, Marsilius of Padua, and many educated Italians of his day, Machiavelli blamed this on pervasive political corruption and a meddling Church that was too weak to unify the country on its own but strong enough to prevent anyone else from doing so.

Machiavelli was acutely aware that the Church's ancient claims could no longer provide a framework for political activity. Statecraft occupied an empty field that could no longer be organized by a general principle of legitimacy. Murder, deception, violence, and selfishness provided the only springs of action, and the "prince" stood alone with his strength, skill, and ambition. Raw power was the most important element of politics. Machiavelli looked to a creative prince and ancient traditions of Roman civicness to clear away archaic institutions and set the conditions for civil society.

Whether analyzing a principality or a republic, Machiavelli was interested in the rise and decline of states and in the organizing potential of political power. He knew that important spheres of human activity stood outside of politics, but he regarded a renovated and strengthened state as the prerequisite to civilized life. Private matters of religion, family, economics, and morality were of interest to him only to the extent that they affected the ability of political figures to hold civil society together. This explains why he conceptualized the state as an organized political force that is supreme in its own territory; seeks maximum power in its relations with other states; and strives to control, regulate, and organize subsidiary spheres of life after its own interests. *The Prince* proposed to examine the nature of power and the conditions of political activity in a chaotic environment where a principality had to be "a work of art."[3] But republics enjoyed a greater measure of stability and legitimacy than principalities, and *The Discourses* looked beyond the short-term political aims of leaders to ask how power could help preserve the civilized life of cities. Born of collapse and failure, Machiavelli's emphasis on politics anticipated some elements of modern theories of civil society even as it was rooted in ancient categories that were plainly inadequate to the tasks at hand.

Virtue and Power

The Prince was perfectly suited to an unorganized environment composed of conflicting wills and animated by different interests. If rulers lacked legitimacy and true citizenship was impossible, only power could hold human affairs together. Anticipating the new monarchs of Church and state, Machiavelli regarded the political innovator as the only force that could restore some integrity to public life in a profoundly corrupt age. As important as politics was to him, he did pay some attention to private affairs—but he was interested in them only as they affected the prince's ability to move freely. He knew that a durable political order rests on the goodwill of the population and requires respect for people's habits and for the foundations of the existing social order. The prince "must change neither their laws nor their taxes," be careful not to take liberties with women, and try to rule conquered cities through their own citizens and institutions. Before anything else, it is essential that he never forget the most important element of his subjects' private attachments, for "above all a prince must abstain from the property of others; because men sooner forget the death of their father than the loss of their patrimony."[4] Political skill might enable the prince to prevail against his rivals in the short run, but nothing can substitute for the "strong roots and ramifications" that can bring together the most effective combination of power and glory.[5] Success will quickly fade if it is not backed by popular support and organized through political institutions. Machiavelli made it clear that "if it is a prince who builds his power on the people, one who can command and is a man of courage, who does not despair in adversity, who does not fail to take precautions, and who wins general allegiance by his personal qualities and the institutions he establishes, he will never be let down by the people; and he will be found to have established his power securely."[6] A wise prince will establish institutions that can protect lives and property, respect different spheres of social organization, and help his subjects pursue their livelihoods:

> A prince should also show his esteem for talent, actively encouraging able men, and honoring those who excel in their profession. Then he must encourage his citizens so that they can go peaceably about their business, whether it be trade or agriculture or any other human occupation. One man should not be afraid of improving his possessions, lest they be taken away from him, or another deterred by high taxes from starting a new business. Rather, the prince should be ready to reward men who want to do these things and those who endeavor in any way to increase the prosperity of their city or their state. As well as this, at suitable times of the year he should entertain the people with shows and festivities. And since every city is divided into guilds or family groups, he should pay attention to these, meet them from time to time, and give an example of courtesy and munificence, while all the time, nonetheless, fully maintaining the dignity of this position, because this should never be wanting in anything.[7]

Like Dante and Marsilius, Machiavelli was driven by his desire for security. Like them, he turned to politics to provide it. As important as it was to support a degree of autonomous social activity, everything depended on the political prescience and wisdom of the prince. In a corrupt environment, only the creative use of political power could substitute for the public spirit that had once made Rome great. *The Prince* provided practical advice for leadership in a corrupt age, but Machiavelli's heart was always with republican Rome. He looked for a more solid foundation of political health than the prince's activity and hoped that he had found it in Rome's mixed constitution and popular government. Under the right circumstances, a vibrant civic life can support freedom, stability, and prudent politics. If citizens can put the common interest above their own, they can save themselves and each other from private corruption. Convinced that his times needed lessons in political virtue, Machiavelli wrote *The Discourses* because of "the natural desire I have always had to labor, regardless of anything, on that which I believe to be for the common benefit of all."[8]

Rome had been riven by class conflict, but the republic's free institutions and differentiated civil society made it possible to turn class division to the service of unity. Those who attributed Rome's fall to persistent conflicts between aristocrats and plebs were mistakenly blaming the most important source of her strength. Machiavelli's interpretation of history taught him the important lesson that "in every republic there are two different dispositions, that of the populace and that of the upper class and that all legislation favorable to liberty is brought about by the clash between them."[9] Social conflict cannot be eliminated, but it can be civilized with appropriate institutions, a vigorous public life, and creative leadership.[10] States fail when social conflict degenerates into political strife. But Machiavelli was confident that such conflict could support liberty if political institutions could resolve the inevitable disputes that arise from class struggle or strivings for personal advantage. The key to Rome's greatness was its ability to respond to conflict with laws and institutions that facilitated the political representation of different classes, preserved their liberty and that of the city as a whole, and thus enlisted widespread civil support for the city's leadership. Properly organized, politics could organize civil society. The appointment of the popular tribunes, a result of rebellion against the aristocracy's predatory attempt to reduce the free plebs to servitude, was a perfect illustration of how a mixed constitution could shape political virtue from civic strife.

> It was in this way that tribunes of the plebs came to be appointed, and
> their appointment did much to stabilize the form of government in this re-
> public, for in its government all three estates now had a share. And so favored
> was it by fortune that, though the transition from Monarchy to Aristocracy

and thence to Democracy, took place by the very stages and for the very reasons laid down earlier in this discourse, none the less the granting of authority to the aristocracy did not abolish altogether the royal estate, nor was the authority of the aristocracy wholly removed when the populace was granted a share in it. On the contrary, the blending of these estates made a perfect commonwealth; and . . . it was friction between the plebs and the senate that brought this perfection about.[11]

All states have a normal tendency to decay, and any Florentine could see how easily political corruption accompanied cultural brilliance. Here again Rome offered a cautionary tale. Her strength enabled her to acquire a vast empire. But success brought wealth and introduced corruption into the life of a republic known for its prudence and virtue. For Machiavelli, this made free institutions and wise leadership more important than ever.[12] A healthy political structure could accommodate the interests of different social spheres and retain the capacity for quick and decisive action. The key was mixing the one, the few, and the many through a mixed constitution that combined the principles of monarchy, aristocracy, and democracy. Mixed government could preserve the flexibility that Machiavelli regarded as essential in difficult times.[13] But it is not easy to maintain equilibrium during times of intense class conflict, and the Agrarian Laws showed how destructive factional activity could be. Rome's great lesson—the wise use of political power as an instrument for mitigating economic conflict—was ignored in this case, and the results were fatal.

Plebeian pressure had led to the creation of the tribunate, but the plebs immediately began quarreling with the nobles and demanding a share of their honors and property. Machiavelli was convinced that the same political measures that had protected the Republic betrayed it by making matters worse. "This grew into a disease, which led to the dispute about the Agrarian Law and in the end caused the destruction of the republic."[14] Passed under the pressure of plebeian greed, the law limited the amount of land that could be owned and required that all war booty be divided among the plebs. Its onesidedness and evident partisanship struck so directly at the interests of the nobility that "it seemed to them that, in opposing the law, they were acting in the public interest."[15] Existing institutions could not temper the partisanship of the plebs or the nobles, and before long the Republic was doomed. The Agrarian Law made inevitable that which it had been designed to prevent. "For by that time the power of its adversaries was twice as great, and, as a result, the mutual hatred existent between the plebs and the senate was so intense that it led to armed conflict and bloodshed, in which neither moderation nor respect for civic customs was shown. So that, the public magistrates being unable to find a remedy and none of the factions having any longer any confidence in them, recourse was had to private remedies, and each party began to look out for some chief to head and defend it."[16] The plebs made Marius their consul and the nobility turned to Sulla; permanent civil war allowed Caesar to take control of the Marian faction while Pompey became the head of Sulla's. Eventually Caesar triumphed, became Rome's first tyrant, and "the city never again recovered its liberties."[17]

Enmity between the plebs and the nobles had once been the condition of Roman freedom, but the Agrarian Laws demonstrated how self-serving factionalism made it difficult for political institutions to help a republic adapt to changing circumstances. So long as the plebs had been willing to accept their poverty because they enjoyed political representation, "virtue was sought out no matter in whose house it dwelt. This way of life made riches less desirable."[18] But the combination of unremitting pressure from the nobility, heightened plebeian insecurity, and the failure of public institutions proved fatal. "Composite bodies" such as mixed states and religious institutions can survive and prosper with wise leadership and a favorable environment, but protracted economic conflict weakens their ability to organize a healthy civil society. Rome taught Machiavelli that the deadliest political disease is unbounded private interest, and that faction is its carrier.

Machiavelli's study of history convinced him that Florence was threatened by the same dangers that had doomed Rome.[19] Politics is the solution to corruption, for only citizenship can move people away from the concern with self that had brought down the greatest of ancient civilizations. But weakened political institutions can lead to more harm than good. Uncontrolled private interest threatened Florence as it had destroyed Rome. History demonstrates "that men never do good unless necessity drives them to do it; but when they are too free to choose and can do just as they please, confusion and disorder become everywhere rampant. Hence it is said that hunger and poverty make men industrious, and that laws make them good. There is no need of legislation so long as things work well without it, but, when such good customs break down, legislation forthwith becomes necessary."[20]

This is why Machiavelli looked to political power to organize civil society in a time of decay. Italy was torn apart and normal life was impossible in an environment of predatory wars and economic collapse. The virile orientation to the public good that had strengthened Rome had been overwhelmed by Christian effeminacy and the unscrupulous amorality of illegitimate power. No civil society could stand on its own at such a time, but Roman history offered the important lesson that all depends on politics.

> It is easy to see how this affection of peoples for self-government comes about, for experience shows that cities have never increased either in dominion or wealth, unless they have been independent. It is truly remarkable to observe the greatness which Athens attained in the space of a hundred years after it had been liberated from the tyranny of Pisistratus. But most marvelous of all is it to observe the greatness which Rome attained after freeing itself from its kings. The reason is easy to understand; for it is not the well-being of individuals that makes cities great, but the well-being of the community; and it is beyond question that it is only in republics that the common good is looked to properly in that all that promotes it is carried out; and, however much this or that private person may be the loser on this account, there are so many who benefit thereby that the common good can be realized in spite of those few who suffer in consequence.[21]

In the end, Machiavelli's greatness lay in his having achieved a thoroughly secular and modern point of view from which to assess human life. He rehabilitated an autonomous political sphere because he hoped it could organize civil society and spare Italy further decay. As important as his classical emphasis on political power was, however, he was partly constrained by categories inherited from the past. Times had changed. As attractive as it was, civic republicanism could not resuscitate civil society on its own. More was required, but it would have to wait for the dust to settle from a far more devastating blow that shattered the notion of a religiously constituted universal Christendom.

Civil Society and the Liberated Conscience

The German Reformation revolved around Martin Luther's articulation of a central role for inner experience that would severely limit the impact of the clergy's outward ministrations. Its defense of an unassailable sphere of private life would also have a profound effect on modern notions of civil society. Indeed, it was Luther's early struggles against uncertainty and doubt that led him to embrace Paul's words that "the just shall live by faith" and answered his agonized question of why God would redeem the worthless. As it became a central element in his disputations with Rome, justification by faith would seek to downplay institutions, good works in the world, and the "church visible" as active elements in religious belief or determinate conditions for salvation. "The Word of God cannot be received and cherished by any works whatever but only by faith. Therefore it is clear that, as the soul needs only the Word of God for its life and righteousness, so it is justified by faith alone and not any works; for if it could be justified by anything else, it would not need the Word, and consequently it would not need faith."[22] God cannot be placated by external acts. Works do not touch the freedom or righteousness of the soul. Christ and Scripture provide the only legitimate mediations between the believer and the Holy Spirit. Such a position put Luther squarely at odds with a Church that regarded grace as an objective reality given through its sacraments, the gift through which humanity was presented as blameless and acceptable in the eyes of God. Luther's assertion that the meaning of Scripture could be directly grasped by the average person struck at the heart of all ecclesiastical claims. The fullness of faith cannot be bound by externals, he insisted; "much is ascribed to faith, namely, that it alone can fulfill the law and justify without works."[23] The church was a unity of equal believers in faith, and Luther turned his back on a Christendom that depended on ecclesiastical hierarchy and authority.

As the Reformation gathered strength, however, Luther was compelled to take account of political matters. What made him so important to modern theories of civil society was the way he conceptualized the autonomous conscience and specified the responsibilities of the state in a unified *corpus christianum* that still drew some of its inspiration from the past. Directing himself against papal claims to worldly power and authority, Luther wanted the Church to preach the gospel, administer the sacraments, and tend to the soul, while the magistracy concerned itself with the affairs of the body. The single and undivided rule of God would be administered through spiritual and temporal governments. This view was common throughout the Middle Ages, but Luther's theology of the free Christian conscience took him toward a modern view of civil society. Reinforced by his early dependence on the German princes, his theological critique of Rome produced a powerful argument for a strengthened state and an autonomous understanding of Christian life in the world.

Grace could not be encountered as the result of some sort of transaction in which human beings satisfied God by means of external acts. Neither popes, sacraments, laws, nor priests were necessary for salvation. Cult, ritual, and ceremonial acts of external obedience were not acceptable substitutes for integrity of heart and mind. The conscience was now the seat of faith; "neither pope, nor bishop, nor any one else, has the right to impose so much as a single syllable of obligation upon a Christian man without his consent."[24] Luther directly challenged the most basic claims of the sacramental Church and denied that people could—or needed to—justify themselves to God through works. Humans could not overcome their estrangement from God by their own actions. More was needed.

Luther's emphasis on conscience and faith did not eclipse the ancient Christian teaching that one must live one's life for the sake of others. It was a matter of priorities. By themselves, good works have no effect on salvation. They have meaning only because they follow from faith; the good person will do good works, and the evil person will do evil works. Only faith can turn good works toward the glory of God rather than the wickedness of individual advantage.[25] "We do not, therefore, reject good works; on the contrary, we cherish and teach them as much as possible. We do not condemn them for their own sake but on account of this godless addition to them and the perverse idea that righteousness is to be sought through them; for that makes them appear good outwardly, when in fact they are not good."[26]

Luther initially hoped that the Church would reform itself, but it soon became clear that it could never accept the reduced role of works implied by his doctrine of faith. Driven by the implications of his theology, his notions of separate spheres of responsibility, and the political reality of the times, he turned to secular power to heal the Church.[27] He was not the first reformer to do so, and he followed an old tradition when he called on the princes to end papal indulgences, the abuse of excommunication, masses for the dead, and other well-established practices against which he was beginning to turn his considerable polemical skill. The universities needed to be reformed, the doctrines of the schoolmen replaced by Scripture, and the German people freed from Roman extortion. He knew that matters of faith were not the responsibility of the princes. Only a General Council of the Church could address theological questions, but in its absence their responsibility for their subjects' welfare obliged princes to lead the moral reform of the Church.

It was not long before Luther encountered the three core positions that protected all "Romanist" claims: the superiority of spiritual power to secular power, papal authority to interpret Scripture, and papal superiority to a General Council of the Church. He set out to demolish each of these three "walls" in turn, and in so doing he explained the temporal responsibilities of princes and made his distinctive contribution to modern conceptions of civil society.

Rome's assertions that spiritual affairs are superior to temporal matters in God's order of creation had supported ecclesiastical claims to organize civil society for centuries. Luther denied all of them and helped establish the theological basis for separating church and state, a vital step toward a modern theory of civil society. Christians have different tasks in the world, but all are equally members of the church, he declared. A social division of labor does not imply a hierarchy of dignity or of salvation. All who have been baptized are equal members of the Christian community; "there is, at bottom, really no other difference between laymen, priests, princes, bishops, or, in Romanist terminology, between religious and secular, than that of office or occupation, and not that of Christian status."[28] All Christians—priests, blacksmiths, farmers, bishops, shoemakers, and princes alike—have a responsibility to one another and to the community as a whole. A differentiated civil society does not touch the equality of believers. The secular order is crucial to the spiritual. Different areas of responsibility carry no implications of differences in moral worth.

It was particularly important for Luther that princes understand their duties with respect to the Church visible, for "secular Christian authorities should exercise their office freely and unhindered and without fear, whether it be pope, bishop, or priest with whom they are dealing."[29] If religious authorities were incapable of saving the Church, then Christian princes would have to step forward. Even if the conscience could not be touched by externals, God and the apostles made all Christians—including the church—subject to the sword.[30]

If princes are as responsible for the health of the Church as other Christians, then papal claims of ultimate authority in the interpretation of Scripture cannot be sustained. The keys were given to the entire Christian community and Luther's notion that the church is a "priesthood of all believers" conformed to the requirements of a community composed of free, equal and autonomous consciences. For "each and all of us are priests because we all have the one faith, the one gospel, one and the same sacrament; why then should we not be entitled to taste or test, and to judge what is right or wrong in the faith?"[31]

Rome's third "wall"—the superiority of the pope to a General Council of the Church—could not stand if the first two fell. Princes and emperors had convened councils in the past, Luther observed, including Constantine's organization of the most important of all, the Council of Nicaea. Popes can contradict Scripture and the Church can become infected by Satan. When this happens, they must be judged by all believers in a General Council. Princes are equal to other Christians, but the sword gives them a special responsibility to protect the Church. "No one is so able to do this as the secular authorities, especially since they are also fellow Christians, fellow priests, similarly religious, and of similar authority in all respects. They should exercise their office and do their work without let or hindrance where it is necessary or advantageous to do so, for God has given them authority over every one."[32] The limitations Luther imposed on ecclesiastical organization located power in a state whose proper mission was to purify and defend religion against the danger that threatened from Rome. Princes were granted considerable responsibility for the welfare of civil society, now defined as the external relations of equal believers united in faith.

As the Reformation gathered momentum and his appeals to the princes widened in scope, Luther tended to blur the line between their secular and religious responsibilities. He wanted them to defend Germany against papal thievery, allow priests to marry, abolish masses for the dead, control interdicts and excommunications, end festival days and begging, force nobles and the rich to wear less ostentatious clothing, reform the universities, overthrow canon law, control commerce and trade, and expel the pope from political influence in Germany.[33] Drafted during the eventful summer of 1520, Luther's appeal to the German princes politicized what had been a relatively contained theological dispute and helped stimulate a wave of national resentment against Rome. It was during this period that he invested the secular arm with considerable responsibility, explaining that "it is the part of those in authority to see to the good of their subjects."[34] The autonomy of the Christian conscience now made the political sphere responsible for the health of civil society; it followed that "the pope should withdraw from temporal affairs" and "let temporal lords rule land and people, while he himself preaches and prays."[35] Princes had been given the sword in order to curb evil, punish the wicked, and protect the good. The health of civil society demanded that they exercise it.

But his plea to the princes did not mean that Luther was prepared to extend the equality of the priesthood of all believers into civil society. All Christians might be equal in the eyes of God, but this does not require that they be equal on earth. The Peasant Rising of 1524–5 forced him to distinguish between the freedom of the soul and that of the body as he condemned plebeian attempts to establish social equality through political means. He criticized the excesses of both landlords and peasants and urged them to settle their differences peacefully, but he made it clear that the worldly kingdom cannot exist without inequality. The equality of souls does not require the equality of bodies. This led Luther to reject peasant appeals for support against the nobility with the observation that they were

> making Christian liberty an utterly carnal thing. Did not Abraham and other patriarchs have slaves? Read what St. Paul teaches about servants, who, at that time, were all slaves. Therefore this article is dead against the gospel. It is a piece of robbery by which every man takes from his lord the body, which has become his lord's property. For a slave can be a Christian, and have Christian liberty, in the same way that a prisoner or a sick man is a Christian, and yet not free. This article would make all men equal, and turn the spiritual kingdom of Christ into a worldly, external kingdom; and that is impossible. For a worldly kingdom cannot stand unless there is in it an inequality of persons, so that some are free, some imprisoned, some lords, some subjects, etc.[36]

Luther's claim that freedom was entirely a matter of conscience had fateful consequences. His dependence on the princes and faithfulness to the Pauline tradition of political accommodationism drove his assertion that subjects always owe their rulers the duty of obedience except where faith is directly compromised or an unjust war is waged. "Christians should be subject to the governing authorities and be ready to do every good work, not that they shall in this way be justified, since they already are righteous through faith, but that in the liberty of the Spirit they shall by so doing serve others and the authorities themselves and obey their will freely and out of love."[37] Obedience to constituted authority has nothing to do with salvation. The Christian should do what the secular power commands not because it is necessary for salvation or righteousness, but because it is important to show respect to rulers who maintain order and sustain faith. Obedience may be costly in the world, but one's future depends on the integrity of one's conscience. Faith would always enable a Christian to protect his soul no matter how difficult external circumstances might be. "Although tyrants do violence or injustice in making their demands, yet it will do no harm as long as they demand nothing contrary to God."[38] The sword exists to punish the wicked and protect the upright. If it is used in the service of evil, that is God's affair.

Luther sought to avoid the obvious difficulties of this position by claiming that true Christians will spontaneously do everything the law demands and hence will not require the sting of coercion. State power is not necessary for those who are ruled by the Holy Spirit rather than the sword, so indifference can ease the impact of state violence. "And if all the world were composed of real Christians, that is, true believers, no prince, king, lord, sword, or law would be needed. For what were the use of them, since Christians have in their hearts the Holy Spirit, who instructs them and causes them to wrong no one, to love every one, willingly and cheerfully to suffer injustice and even death from every one. Where every wrong is suffered and every right is done, no quarrel, strife, trial, judge, penalty, law or sword is needed."[39] Christians do not have to be coerced to live a life for the sake of their neighbors. Their desire to do so is carried in their faith and written in their conscience.

But the children of God are compelled to live alongside the children of the world, and Luther's justification of state power really hinges on the presence of non-Christians rather than on an Augustinian view of human beings as creatures of sin. The world has many non-Christians and false Christians. Luther knew as well as Rome that the progress of religious reform in Germany depended on the princes. His awareness of this explains his declaration that God created the state to supplement the commonwealth of Christians. "For this reason the two kingdoms must be sharply distinguished, and both be permitted to remain; the one to produce piety, the other to bring about external peace and prevent evil deeds; neither is sufficient in the world without the other."[40] Luther's intense hostility to papal claims of temporal power was driven by a notion of a civil society in which coercion would compel obedience to the law from those lacking in faith. "For this reason God has ordained the two governments; the spiritual, which by the holy Spirit under Christ makes Christians and pious people, and the secular, which restrains the unchristian and wicked so that they must needs keep the peace outwardly, even against their will."[41] Augustine's sword still exists for the sake of the non-Christian. The Christian needs little more than the Gospel but will obey the state because its coercive power is made necessary by the moral weakness of others. "In this way, then, things are well balanced, and you satisfy at the same time God's kingdom inwardly and the kingdom of the world outwardly, at the same time suffer evil and injustice and yet punish evil and injustice, at the same time do not resist evil and yet resist it. For in the one case you consider yourself and what is yours, in the other you consider your neighbor and what is his."[42] The famous Lutheran distinction between the inner world of the free Christian conscience and the outer world of inequality and coercion would generate a political quietism whose twentieth-century consequences would be profound indeed.

But it also made possible a theory of civil society and the state that was not intimately tied up with the welfare of the Church. Luther agreed with Paul that Christians can serve God in their consciences and satisfy the world with their bodies. Christians' compassion for the non-Christians in their midst drove his theory of obligation, but obedience served the godly as well. Christians are a minority in the world and need the protection of secular authority against the powerful and the wicked. Political power preserves order, protects property, executes the laws, looks after the poor, punishes evil, and makes civil society possible. "Therefore, should you see that there is a lack of hangmen, beadles, judges, lords, or princes, and find that you are qualified, you should offer your services and seek the place, that necessary government may by no means be despised and become inefficient or perish. For the world cannot and dare not dispense with it."[43] The Christian might need the state for the sake of the non-Christian, but Luther thought it indispensable to a life of faith and works as well.

Luther's emphasis was always clear. Two spheres coexist in temporal affairs, the sphere of God under Christ and the sphere of the world under the state. Each has its own laws and regulations. God establishes and sanctifies earthly authority because no kingdom can exist without law and coercion. But the scope of acceptable state activity is limited to protecting life, property, and other requirements of earthly life. "For over the soul God can and will let no one rule but Himself."[44] Belief and faith cannot be the subject of law, and the temporal power cannot presume to legislate on behalf of the soul. Luther's separation between public and private located affairs of conscience outside affairs of state; "every man is responsible for his own faith, and he must see to it for himself that he believes rightly."[45] The church has no business with politics, and the state has no business with the soul. Neither has to exist at the expense of the other, for a healthy conscience and a vigorous state support one another. "Since, then, belief or unbelief is a matter of every one's conscience, and since this is no lessening of the secular power, the latter should be content and attend to its own affairs and permit men to believe one thing or another, as they are able and willing, and constrain no one by force."[46] Even the suppression of heresy is the affair of bishops rather than princes. The state has legitimate authority over the external interactions of people with one another. The private sphere of faith and belief lies outside its purview.[47]

An important step toward a secular theory of civil society was made possible by Luther's insistence on the autonomy of individual conscience. The "priesthood of all believers" was perfectly compatible with an autonomous civil society and a coercive political order so long as it was defined in terms of individual conscience and the equality of all souls before God. If the household, political life, and church affairs constitute the three "orders of creation" of Christian existence, they need the political order because civil society cannot generate the power, domination, and authority necessary to the life of fallen humanity. The state protects equal Christian souls who are united in faith but live in an impure world. If Luther located conscience at the center of Christian life, he also reserved great power to the state, which sustained a civil society necessary for life but was impotent in matters of faith.

Luther's expulsion of politics from religion served to fortify it in the state, and his stress on the inwardness of religious experience provided a theological gloss to princely power. Civil society was a sphere of conflict and discord. It needed temporal rulers to maintain order. Christian liberty was now an inward matter of faith. In the end, however, the ebb and flow of the Reformation made matters of religious choice the province of individual belief and the will of the prince. In politics, obedience was the order of the day. In resting civil society on the coercive power of princes and the innermost voice of individual Christians, Luther drew paradoxical conclusions from his attempt to isolate faith from the tribulations of the world.

Luther's Christians did not have to sanctify civil society through their own efforts. Although his separation of conscience from the world pointed toward the future, important elements of his thinking still moved in medieval channels. The subjective requirements of conscience drove a good deal of his understanding of a civil society shaped by the requirements of religious war. Hobbes would effect a decisive break with the past by entirely removing God from a civil society that now rested on a single point of political sovereignty, made civil war forever impossible, and protected the interests of a new sort of calculating individual.

Sovereignty, Interest, and Civil Society

The 1651 appearance of *Leviathan* was Hobbes's momentous demonstration that civil society cannot exist in the absence of state power. His rigorous effort to reveal the "heart," "nerves," and "joints" of the body politic concluded that they had to be integrated into a single source of dominion if civil society was to be organized and domestic peace established. Only an "artificial man" animated by the "artificial soul" of sovereignty could bring the blessings of civilization to individuals whose collective dangers resulted from their equality and their desires. Alarmed at the English Revolution, Hobbes sought refuge in a state that was coterminous with and constitutive of a civil society conceived in modern terms as a sphere of self-interested activity.

The outline of Hobbes's general theory is familiar enough. The pervasive insecurity to which civil society offered a remedy was the unavoidable result of man's perpetual desire for power in the interest of self-protection. Driven by insecurity, man's hunger to accumulate power—"his present means, to obtain some future apparent good"[48]—chases him from one object to another, for attaining something is only a spur to attaining something else. A new calculating individual defines his private goals for himself in the absence of a "greatest good" to which all men will voluntarily orient themselves. Whether this unending desire to accumulate more arose from Hobbes's insight into the deepest roots of human nature or from the influence of a developing capitalist society,[49] he asserted that man is motivated by "a general inclination of all mankind, a perpetual and restless desire of power after power, that ceaseth only in death. And the cause of this, is not always that a man hopes for a more intensive delight, than he has already attained to, or that he cannot be content with a moderate power: but because he cannot assure the power and means to live well, which he hath present, without the acquisition of more."[50] The need to accumulate more and more power is intrinsic to the human condition and marks all human action in the prepolitical and presocial condition that Hobbes, following the conventions of his day, called the "natural condition" of humankind.

When married to Hobbes's assumption of human equality, this "desire of power after power" poses the threat of endless war unless it can be brought under control. The great paradox of human life is that our simple desire for security and our equal vulnerability to one another come together to produce an intolerable situation. In Hobbes's theory, nature replaces sin and depravity as the cause of humankind's ruin and the turn toward the state. Equality, insecurity, and interest cause the war and competition that define our natural condition.[51] Where people desire the same objects and "there is no power able to over-awe them all," equal insecurity, equal capacities, and equal desires produce permanent warfare. It is clear, said Hobbes, "that during the time men live without a common power to keep them all in awe, they are in that condition which is called war; and such a war, as is of every man, against every man."[52] The absence of a single coercive political authority forces people to rely upon their own reason, judgment, and strength as they pursue their interests in competition with everyone else. Hobbes's famous description of the consequences of this asocial and suspicious self-reliance bears repeating:

> In such condition, there is no place for industry; because the fruit thereof is uncertain: and consequently no culture of the earth; no navigation, nor use of the commodities that may be imported by sea; no commodious building; no instruments of moving, and removing, such things as require much force; no knowledge of the face of the earth; no account of time; no arts; no letters; no society; and which is worst of all, continual fear, and danger of violent death; and the life of man, solitary, poor, nasty, brutish, and short.[53]

Civil society is impossible without a "common power," and the anarchy of humankind's natural condition soon makes life itself impossible. The deep paradox is that each individual's necessary reliance on private reason quickly leads to an intolerable situation for everyone. "And consequently it is a Precept, or general rule of reason, *That every man, ought to endeavor Peace, as far as he has hope of obtaining it; and when he cannot obtain it, that he may seek, and use, all helps, and advantages of War.* The first branch of which Rule containeth the first, and Fundamental Law of Nature; which is, *to seek Peace, and follow it.*"[54] Rational self-interest is the spring of individual action and collective survival. It stands at the center of human life in the state of nature, allows us to derive the "first law of nature," and requires civil society. The passage from barbarism to civilization brings industry, agriculture, navigation, science, morality, and culture into human history.

But people cannot live in peace unless they are all willing to renounce their "right to all things" and be content with a limited degree of liberty. Such renunciation results from a calculation that the benefits of peace will outweigh the loss people incur when they no longer depend on their own wits or are the final judges in matters that involve them. Hobbes's socialized reason replaced Christendom, authority, custom, the divine right of kings, raw power, and tradition as the basis of obligation. Civil society is impossible unless promises can be kept and agreements respected. If people can safely anticipate that others will control themselves, they can all live with a measure of assurance that they will be safe. Only a single sovereign authority makes it possible to pursue justice and protect property; "before the names of just, and unjust can have place, there must be some coercive power, to compel men equally to the performance of their covenants, by the terror of some punishment, greater than the benefit they expect by the breach of their covenant; and to make good that propriety, which by mutual contract men acquire, in recompense of the universal right they abandon: and such power there is none before the erection of a commonwealth."[55]

Above all, Hobbes wanted to avoid the consequences of the unbridled pursuit of "felicity." He knew better than most of his contemporaries that civil society was populated by individuals and their interests. The problem was how to arrange it so people could pursue their interests in conditions of security and peace. Civil society required a set of rules established and enforced by constituted political authority.[56] Hobbes's general standard was a version of the Golden Rule: where there is a number of men, felicity cannot be attained unless each man acts so as not to do to others what he would not want done to him. This means that he must be prepared to surrender his natural right to pursue felicity as if he were the only person in the world. The only way to avoid ruinous anarchical competition and keep individual judgment and interest under control is through a mutual and universal transfer of rights. But Hobbes knew that if a contractual agreement between self-renouncing individuals might address the danger of private reason, it runs counter to some of the most basic human passions—even if it is supported by reason and conditioned by the fear of violent death. Something was needed to stand behind the original covenant—namely, the sword. The decisive core of the state is the power to coerce, and Hobbes's politically organized civil society required compulsion over a wide expanse of human affairs. Man's desire for self-preservation requires a sovereign authority that can establish the minimal conditions of social peace. Civil society is made possible by sovereignty, is constituted by politics, and cannot be formally distinguished from the state.

Hobbes's state of nature and subsequent social contract were hypothetical devices he used for purposes of argument and illustration.[57] But civil society was real and concrete for him. It was composed of palpable, clear, and identifiable individuals who were driven by their entirely understandable desire for the material and cultural benefits of civilization. The renunciation of which he spoke is really a transfer of power, for man's natural drive to accumulate ever-increasing power and his equal vulnerability will quickly nullify all agreements unless they can be enforced. People are equal, insecure, and alone in the state of nature; their drive to protect themselves will always undermine any effort to control disintegration unless it is politically organized and enforced. No voluntary agreements between isolated, fearful, and competitive people can last in the absence of a coercive mechanism that can compel individuals to act as if they trusted each other. The binding cement of civil society is the fear of anarchy, and overcoming it with sovereign power is the political act that constitutes the state and civil society at the same instant.

An important element of Hobbes's civil society looked back to the old-fashioned commonwealth, the formal expression of the ancient fusion of state and society. Established by an act of voluntary and permanent agreement, it is the single expression of a common will organized to make civil society possible by providing safety and security. It is the only instrument people have to protect themselves from the devastating consequences of their original freedom and equality. Civil society makes it possible for a single source of public reason to replace the anarchy of many sources of private reason:

> The only way to erect such a common power, as may be able to defend them from the invasion of foreigners, and the injuries of one another, and thereby to secure them in such sort, as that by their own industry, and by the fruits of the earth, they may nourish themselves and live contentedly; is, to confer all their power and strength upon one man, or upon one assembly of men, that may reduce all their wills, by plurality of voices, unto one will: which is as much to say, to appoint one man, or assembly of men, to bear their person; and every one to own, and acknowledge himself to be author of whatsoever he that so beareth their person, shall act, or cause to be acted, in those things which concern the common peace and safety; and therein to submit their wills, every one to his will, and their judgements, to his judgement. This is more than consent, or concord; it is a real unity of them all, in one and the same person, made by covenant of every man with every man, in such manner, as if every man should say to every man, *I authorize and give up my right of governing myself, to this man, or to this assembly of men, on this condition, that thou give up thy right to him, and authorize all his actions in like manner.* This done, the multitude so united in one person, is called a COMMON-WEALTH, in Latin CIVITAS.[58]

Civil society was established by an act of politics. There is no difference between law and morality, all authority is concentrated in the sovereign, and power constitutes the state and civil society alike. Whether it is composed of one man, a few, or many, the sovereign must have sufficient coercive power to organize civil society as an alternative to the sand-heap of the state of nature. No one can be freed from subjection to the sovereign, for without it society disintegrates and men will be thrown back into the war of all against all. Self-preservation drives all subjects to obey an overwhelming power who makes the rules governing social behavior, organizes the government, decides on all matters of controversy, directs foreign relations, conducts war and peace, and exercises all other prerogatives of sovereignty. In the last instance, the organization of state power is the defining moment of civilized life. *Leviathan* relentlessly attacked Hugo Grotius's and Samuel Pufendorf's social contract theories, which suggested that civil society existed before states were organized. Hobbes's civil society is constituted and held together by state power.

Leviathan did not consider subordinate or intermediate bodies to any significant degree. In political terms, Hobbes was opposed to anything that could weaken sovereign power. The "silence of the law" established a broad sphere of individual activity that he wanted to protect, but he argued that subsidiary organizations exist only at the pleasure of the sovereign. Bodies are "lawful" if they are recognized by the commonwealth and can represent a part of the whole only if the sovereign agrees, but such tolerance can never compromise the state's responsibility for the peace and defense of civil society.[59] He was equally opposed to any suggestions of a mixed constitution or a division of sovereignty. The sovereign must be able to act directly on individuals in all important matters. Civil society is the commonwealth, and it is represented by the sovereign's will. Unless there is a government—a tangible body of people with the power to enforce sovereign will—there is neither state nor society but only a "headless multitude." The sovereign's ability to reward and punish enables civil society to overcome the chaotic and disruptive effect of private strivings. All social authority is concentrated in the "mortal God," for no social body can exist apart from its constituted head. No significant distinction between the state and society existed for Hobbes. The disappearance of the state entailed the disintegration of society. Politics had overcome nature.

Civil society may require a strong state, but Hobbes knew that economics, science, and arts and letters also require respect for the private realm of individual desire and personal welfare. Civil society is a sphere both of collective public life and of self-interest. "The liberty of a subject, lieth therefore only in those things, which in regulating their actions, the sovereign hath permitted,"[60] but the range of private activity turns out to be surprisingly broad. Hobbes identified a recognizable sphere of self-interested activity with which the state need not interfere unless civil order is threatened. John Locke would protect this sphere with a rights-based constitutional order to limit the scope of state action, but the important theoretical distinction between public and private was made by Hobbes. He was unwilling to invest the private sphere with the moral content that would characterize mature liberalism because his theory of the state was necessary for his theory of civil society. No "industry, culture of the earth, navigation, use of commodities, commodious building, knowledge of the face of the earth, account of time, arts, letters or society" was possible before the establishment of sovereign power. But it is equally true that these activities helped define the advantages of civilization that civil society made possible. Hobbes's fusion of state and society was offset by their later separation because of his desire to buttress the many benefits of civil society with the power of a prudent state. The sovereign's overwhelming power exists for the sake of making it possible for solitary, vulnerable, and insecure individuals to live together. Civil society is constituted by state power, but Hobbes left considerable room for private initiative and unregulated activity.

What mattered to him was building a framework that allowed for predictable behavior, and the limits of state power were established by the requirements of stability. Sovereign power exists to ensure internal peace and common defense against external foes. It does not exist to make all men the same but to enable them to pursue their separate desires in an orderly fashion. "For seeing there is no commonwealth in the world, wherein there be rules enough set down, for the regulating of all the actions, and words of men; as being a thing impossible; it followeth necessarily, that in all kinds of actions by the laws permitted, men have the liberty, of doing what their own reasons shall suggest, for the most profitable to themselves."[61] Hobbes's insistence that an indivisible center of state power made civil society possible should not obscure his equally important view that the grounding for any theory of sovereignty is the welfare and safety of the society's individual members. The state's purpose is to protect the integrity of individual property and persons who seek "felicity," and Hobbes often reminded his readers that rational people moved from the state of nature to civil society only because they expected that their private individual interests would be served. Civil society cannot be organized by force alone. The Hobbesian theory of obligation anticipates that obedience to a sovereign authority will generate a larger measure of individual advantage than was possible in the state of nature.

Hobbes's rationalism enabled him to produce a theory of the state without bothering with tradition, revelation, the divine right of kings, canonical interpretation, or other elements of medieval theory's complicated apparatus. Man's "natural condition" of fear and isolation denied the possibility that individuals were naturally sociable. People will not spontaneously respect each others' rights unless it is in their interests to do so. Since any social contract can be exploded if a single person opts out, the performance of covenants will become the norm only if a sovereign power can punish all instances of nonperformance without discrimination or exception. Individuals are socialized to act as if they trust each other by the fear of impartial and universal punishment. Hobbes had not traveled very far from Augustine after all, despite his thoroughly secular theory of sovereignty and accompanying theory of obligation. Yet he moved beyond the common medieval point of view that states should be obeyed because they represented some transcendent set of values. Rights or ethics did not exist prior to the state. The sovereign defined morality.

Hobbes's abandonment of medieval corporatism reduced the state to an instrument whose legitimacy rested on its ability to safeguard individual well-being. The "common good" dropped out of political theory for the moment, replaced by the sum of individual self-interests. The commonwealth was now an "artificial body" composed of a multitude of calculating private individuals whose defining desire is to pursue their interests in conditions of security and peace—a description dramatically conveyed by *Leviathan*'s famous cover. The state protects the individual in the particularity of his private possessions; Hobbes had created a sovereign authority so powerful that civil society could not even exist in its absence, but he had abandoned political theory's ancient preoccupation with shaping human nature and wanted little more than to protect an environment within which individuals could pursue their interests. Hobbes's recognition of individual advantage marked him as a man of the future.

But there were limits beyond which even he was unable to go. The Reformation had given theological shape to the view that the individual is his own judge, advocate, and administrator, but for all his individualism Hobbes was deeply suspicious of private calculation. He certainly wanted to give full rein to individual well-being, but the assumption that truth was a subjective determination filled him with dread. Northern Europe was swarming with bickering Protestant sects that had grown up on the fertile soil of Reformation doctrines of private judgment, individual conscience, and the priesthood of all believers. Hobbes was fearful that this anarchic subjectivism could only undermine the unity he believed essential to peace precisely *because* it was so powerfully connected to self-interest. One of the many popular doctrines he felt "repugnant to civil society" was that "whatever a man does against his conscience, is sin."[62] The sovereign trumped the disintegrative effects of private judgment by establishing authority, meaning, duties, and morality. It was established precisely because the state of nature fell apart when people became judges in their own cases. Political power made reason public and was indispensable to controlling the disastrous effects of the same individual interest it was established to protect.

The passage from the state of nature to civil society represented the abandonment of private reason and individual judgment as the standard of the common good, but Hobbes did not replace them with any integral theory of public welfare or general knowledge. His great achievement was to deduce sovereign political power from the collisions of a mass of unconnected and equal individuals. No long-term connections link the atomized particles comprising civil society beyond their own covenants. What ties do exist result from agreements into which rational and self-interested individuals freely enter. Each member of civil society is driven by his perceived interest. But interest can never be anything more than the public expression of private desire, and Hobbes's orientation toward a political organization of social life anticipated the flowering of the liberal private sphere. Nothing had any general, universal status for Hobbes except the search for security and peace, and the only relation to which he paid any attention was that between sovereign and subject. All instances of private reason were fused into the sovereign, which, since it defines the conditions of peace and stability, must have unlimited power to enforce both—even against the will of individual subjects. The social bond is the surrender of individual autonomy to the will of the sovereign, the only agency through which civil society can speak. But the sovereign's raison d'être is peace and security, and for all his breadth of vision Hobbes anticipated classic liberalism's inability to derive a theory of obligation that went deeper than individual interest. The "poisonous" doctrine "that every private man is judge of good and evil actions" characterized the state of nature precisely because there were no civil laws.[63] The authority of law comes from the sovereign's will; "in the differences of private men, to declare, what is equity, what is justice, and what is moral virtue, and to make them binding, there is need of the ordinances of sovereign power, and punishments to be ordained for such as shall break them," for the reason of the "artificial man"—the commonwealth—replaces that of private persons.[64]

Hobbes was a transitional figure who both looked back to the fused community and anticipated its dissolution. The equal vulnerability of its members stood behind the constant competition that threatened to tear civil society apart. The problem was endemic to civilized life as such. Individual interests can never be fully satisfied, and Hobbes's individual was an "owner" of himself in an atomized civil society rather than a member of a larger community by virtue of being a moral whole. Relations of ownership would come to define not only the content of human social interactions but the nature of man as such. Civil society was an artificial network that existed to protect property and maintain an orderly system of production and exchange. In a universe of disconnected and self-regarding particularities, "the common good" could have no meaning except as the sum of individual desires. Human reason was no longer a capacity that integrated and harmonized. Now it fractured and divided because it had been yoked to the self-interested and competitive pursuit of individual interest. Politics represented coercion pure and simple; while little more than a mechanism for providing security, it also made possible the blessings of civilization. The primacy of the public made possible a theoretically distinct sphere of private concerns, even if such a sphere existed only in embryo. In many ways Hobbes prefigured the specifically bourgeois theory of state and society that would find further articulation in the work of John Locke and would culminate in Adam Smith.

But Hobbes was also working within older categories of thought, the most important example of which was his desire to retain elements of the ancient commonwealth. Medieval theorists had thought in theological terms, but Hobbes was a *political* thinker above all. Despite his recognition of interest and evident desire to respect a measure of spontaneous activity in civil society, politics suffused public life and organized private affairs. Everything was organized by sovereign power, there was no institutionalized distinction between the state and civil society, and Hobbes never developed a coherent theory that could identify a sphere of nonpolitical public activity. State power was directly brought to bear on the individual subject. Mediating institutions played little role in *Leviathan*, and there is little evidence that Hobbes would have shared liberalism's desire to limit public power with a structure of protected rights. Exploitation and coercion were still largely organized "extra-economically," and if Hobbes anticipated the later focus on interest he still believed that only sovereign power stood between civilization and barbarism. Law and morality came from a state against which individuals had no rights.

Hobbes marked both an end and a beginning. European society would begin to fracture soon enough, and the spread of markets would give rise to theories of an autonomous, protected, and self-regulating economic sphere apart from and morally superior to that of the state. Whether thought of as political or religious commonwealths, older notions of universal civil societies would soon be eclipsed by the logic of individual interest. Princely power, civic republicanism, and the liberated conscience could no longer serve as self-sufficient organizing principles of civil society. Hobbes articulated the decisive claim that the definition and pursuit of private goals requires a strong public power to constitute society and protect it at the same time. The rest would wait for Locke and the Scots.

PART II

Civil Society and Modernity

4

The Rise of "Economic Man"

Niccolò Machiavelli broke with the Middle Ages when he subordinated faith to the interests of the prince and the civic republic. Martin Luther's emphasis on the freedom of individual conscience reserved considerable power to political authorities, who were responsible for organizing civil society around the external needs of a community of faith. Much the same was true of Thomas Hobbes's demonstration that civil society existed because of the activity of a single point of sovereign power and that it rested on the advantages that flowed to its individual members. None of these three transitional figures had to rely on celestial forces to apply the general standards that made it possible to identify and pursue particular goals.

If political power mitigated the destructiveness of uncontrolled competition, it also made possible the many benefits of civilization that were not rooted in the immediate struggle for existence. Classical theorists obviously placed far more emphasis on the state's role in organizing civil society than did most medieval thinkers, but both traditions agreed that the essential distinction was between civilization and barbarism. Early modern theorists preserved this element of earlier traditions. For John Locke, civil society made it possible for people to organize a public life of freedom and prosperity for the first time. Echoing the views of many Enlightenment figures, Adam Ferguson's civil society developed ethical sentiments and cultivated virtue in a way that was impossible in "rude" societies. Far more aware of the economic determinations of civil society than most of his colleagues, Adam Smith was confident that it could be organized around individual advantage in such a way that the blessings of civilization would flow to all. Even as they provided the theoretical foundations for modern notions of the individual, science, reason, democracy, and freedom, all three men articulated the characteristically modern claim that the material processes of social life were fast becoming the constitutive forces of civil society.

Rights, Law, and Protected Spheres

Writing in defense of England's Glorious Revolution, John Locke initially targeted not Hobbes but the Court argument that sovereignty was a form of property that could be handed down from monarch to monarch, a position the Stuarts had long used in support of their claims to absolute power. The Crown's position was derived from Robert Filmer's attempt to base political power on paternal authority, but Locke went deeper and argued that the state's unlimited power would undermine the very security it was designed to protect and would make civil society impossible. Hobbes had failed to understand that self-preservation no longer required the commanding political power of a sovereign but could now be identified with the simple protection of property. His purely "political" theory did not grasp that economic forces could organize civil society if allowed to function in conditions of freedom and in the presence of a state with limited powers. As powerful as Hobbes's state appeared to be, said Locke, it could not provide a sufficiently strong foundation for civil society.

Locke's theory of property moved the discussion of civil society to an entirely new level. If citizenship could be based on ownership, rational individuals would have no interest in disorder as long as they were left to go about their business in peace. Some of this was prefigured by Hobbes, but Locke's claim that legitimacy rested on the state's ability to protect a set of prepolitical natural rights took theories of civil society into new territory. Hobbes required obedience if the sovereign kept the peace, but Locke established an economically determined sphere of property, rights, and private desire that could now be theorized apart from the enforcement power of the state.

The earth had originally been given to all humans to enjoy, and Locke began with the familiar position that everyone had a right to draw individual sustenance from what nature had to offer. This natural-law presumption of an original condition of common ownership framed his counterintuitive drive to anchor civil society in a natural right to private property and individual appropriation. "But I shall endeavor to shew," he announced, "how men might come to have a *property* in several parts of that which God gave to mankind in common, and that without any express Compact of all the Commoners."[1]

Locke's explanation is familiar enough. The right to privately appropriate nature's common gifts derived from natural freedom and individual property in one's own person. Private appropriation of that part of nature with which one has mixed one's labor is prior to and independent of organized social life. It is a right of human beings in nature, and Locke organized civil society around its protection because he knew better than Hobbes that property had become a necessary condition of human life. Freedom, labor, exchange, and property were present in the state of nature, and this allowed Locke to derive civil society from a sphere of human action that existed before the state. Natural rights rested at the heart of Locke's antiabsolutist politics and were the source of a new understanding of private property that did not originate in consent.

Locke differed dramatically from Hobbes in describing the state of nature as a condition of "peace, good will, mutual assistance, and preservation." One's natural condition is a state of "perfect freedom" to preserve oneself and "perfect equality" of power to do so. This led to an important conclusion: if human beings were rational, moral, and sociable before they moved to civil society, then Hobbes's absolutist state might not be necessary. It was individual interest that introduced "enmity, malice, violence, and mutual destruction" into an otherwise peaceful state of nature that did not have a common authority to adjudicate private disputes.[2] Civil society and the state became necessary because the rupture of nature's spontaneous "tye" gave every individual the right to punish every other individual.[3] People cannot be expected to be impartial judges in their own case, and this was the famous "inconvenience" that made civil society and the state necessary.[4] Locke's civil society remedied the potentially fatal deficiency of the state of nature by taking executive power out of the hands of self-serving individuals and making it impartial by making it public. People are now social beings who are fully capable of living together without the binding force of Hobbes's sovereign. Their inability to adequately protect their natural rights made civil society necessary, but it did not have to be constituted by "overawing" power.

As important as his break with Hobbes turned out to be, Locke agreed that civil society was formed by political power, "a *Right* of making Laws with Penalties of Death, and consequently all less Penalties, for the Regulating and Preserving of Property, and of employing the force of the Community, in the Execution of such Laws, and in the defence of the Commonwealth from Foreign Injury, and all this only for the Publick Good."[5] Made possible by a political act and constituted by the needs of property, civil society did not create any new rights; it merely registered the transfer to a common authority of the power that individuals had to protect themselves in the state of nature. People formed civil society because the strength of their particular interests made it difficult to organize a common power "for the regulating and preserving of property." The chief end of human association, in civil society as in the state of nature, is the defense of property—the abstract representation of individual freedom. But natural man is rational and the difficulties of the state of nature "makes him willing to quit this Condition, which however free, is full of fears and continual dangers: And 'tis not without reason, that he seeks out, and is willing to joyn in Society with others who are already united, or have a mind to unite for the mutual *Preservation* of their Lives, Liberties and Estates, which I call by the general name, *Property*."[6] Locke gave a more general sweep to the understanding of property than others, but there is no question that he accorded "estates" at least the same level of protection as "lives" or "liberties."

Classic liberalism's important distinction between the state and civil society is present here, but modernity existed only in embryonic form. Like Hobbes, Locke was drawn to the model of a single politically constituted commonwealth. Civil society was made possible by the socialization of "that Power which every Man, having in the state of Nature, has given up into the hands of the Society, and therein to the Governours, whom the Society hath set over it self, with the express or tacit Trust, That it shall be imployed for their good, and the preservation of their Property."[7] The state and civil society are constituted by the same calculus of individual freedom and private choice. Both exist for the sake of private interests; without property, observed Locke, "the common is of no use."[8] The same is true of the state, now conceived as an enforcement mechanism. The basis of human life in nature and civil society is property, and the state is now its protective organ. "The great and *chief end* therefore, of Mens uniting into Common-wealths, and putting themselves under Government, *is the Preservation of their Property.*[9]

Natural law provided a complete and self-sufficient system of rights; the transition to civil society and the state made civilization possible by establishing an enforcement mechanism that could overcome the anarchical pull of individual interest. The state can correct the defect of the state of nature because it is constituted by a common law, an agency that can render impartial judgments, and an enforcement power. "Those who are united into one Body, and have a common establish'd Law and Judicature to appeal to, with Authority to decide Controversies between them, and punish Offenders *are in Civil Society* one with another: but those who have no such common Appeal, I mean on Earth, are still in the state of Nature, each being, where there is no other, Judge for himself, and Executioner; which is, as I have before shew'd it, the perfect *state of Nature.*"[10] State power and the rule of law make possible the pursuit of interest in conditions of individual liberty and mutual security. Locke was sure that he could base obligation on individual satisfaction and simultaneously answer any political regime's most important question:

> If Man in the State of Nature be so free, as has been said; If he be absolute Lord of his own Person and Possessions, equal to the greatest, and subject to no Body, why will he part with his Freedom? Why will he give up this Empire, and subject himself to the Dominion and Controul of any other Power? To which 'tis obvious to Answer, that though in the state of Nature he hath such a right, yet the Enjoyment of it is very uncertain, and constantly exposed to the Invasion of others. For all being Kings as much as he, every Man his Equal, and the greater part no strict Observers of Equity and Justice, the enjoyment of the property he has in this state is very unsafe, very unsecure.[11]

Older theories of civil society had organized themselves around some general notion of the common good. Locke's work tended to empty it of substantial public content because its purpose was protecting particular interests. Hobbes had laid the foundations of such a position, but Locke accorded interest considerable influence even as he reduced the state to the enforcement functions of a civil society organized around property. His proposition that humans are naturally sociable meant that the state did not have to be as powerful as Hobbes's Leviathan. But a benign view of the state of nature did not mean that civil society could be constituted by public concerns. Even if civil society was originally established by an act of cooperation, individual interest was always clear and compelling in Locke's thinking, while common matters were derivative, thin, and inconsequential at best. Much of this was shaped by the course of the English Revolution, in which he was intimately involved. Like many other educated men of his day, Locke had every reason to believe that aristocracies and absolute monarchs posed the most pressing threat to liberty. There seemed to be ample evidence that the common good was substantially the same as the protection of private rights.

The priority Locke accorded to private interests—and to the rights that protect them—initiates liberalism's disposition to say that what is really important about people is the way they create and accumulate wealth. The sharp distinction Hobbes had drawn between human beings' "natural condition" and the political order underlay *Leviathan*'s emphasis on state power. In focusing attention on the economic processes of civil society,

Locke took an important step away from the ancient claim that politics stood at the center of social organization. The limited liberal state and the rule of law would make it possible for rights-bearing individuals to pursue their competing interests without having to kill one another.

As striking as Locke's political economy was, he was very much a man of his age. The decline of the embedded economy eroded the limits on the pursuit of interest that had protected precapitalist civil societies for centuries. Ancient principles of solidarity, justice, and morality had organized distribution in natural economies, where production had been driven by the needs of immediate consumption and markets had played only a marginal role. The development of production for exchange drove toward the disappearance of the embedded economy, the primacy of individual judgment, the reduction of social life to economic considerations, and a conception of politics as protective of a network of individual rights whose sum total was the common good. Market relations were penetrating everywhere and interest was fast becoming the central category of economic and political thought.[12] Public welfare no longer came from action intended to advance it. Natural law was subordinated to the logic of property and the market.

But even as he took an important step toward an autonomous and self-regulating economy, Locke was unable to effect a clean break with the past. He sought to retain important elements of natural law and did not reduce all social connections to market relations. Considerable elements of his thought still described politics as a defining component of civil society. The state was only beginning to separate out from society during his lifetime, and it was not yet possible to clearly isolate political power from the distribution of economic wealth and social influence. A fully modern liberal theory of civil society would have to wait.

A century separated the *Second Treatise* from Adam Smith's epochal *Wealth of Nations*.[13] The Enlightenment was marked by the expansion of markets, a renewed emphasis on the benefits of civilization, and further steps toward a distinctly modern conception of civil society. Capitalism and liberalism began to take definite shape during this period, and when both received authoritative expression in Smith's political economy the conditions were set for a distinctly modern theory of civil society. Locke's demonstration that property is derived from nature rather than from custom or privilege appealed to Enlightenment thinkers anxious to use natural law to undermine the authority of revealed truth and established power. Almost all of them agreed that property is an indispensable condition for moral autonomy. Only insofar as he was a property owner could the free individual exercise his reason and resist superstition and servility.

Before civil society came to be dominated by markets, it had been widely agreed that some entity external to the sphere of necessity would guarantee social order and civic peace. Classical theories of obligation were predicated on the need to transcend the divisions, rivalries, and insecurities of the struggle for survival. But the rapid growth of markets in commodities, labor, and land drove the near-universal eighteenth-century interest in the processes by which economic relationships could organize society without state compulsion. Enlightenment theorists replaced the Forms, God, sin, and nature with processes that were intrinsic to the social world. If property was both a natural right and a condition of moral independence, it followed that economic freedom rested at the heart of any proper social organization and that the state should guarantee maximum liberty to all individuals defined as free, self-interested proprietors. By the end of this period, the ancient notion that the source of social order was external to civil society was in full retreat.

It appeared that scholasticism and theology had finally been expelled from political theory. Grand Enlightenment ideas of perfectibility, progress, freedom, liberty, and reason accelerated the dissolution of ancient unities and gave rise to theories of civil society that rested on observed fact. The period's "recovery of nerve" and certainty that moral humans could use their reason to shape the social world and control nature was expressed in the *philosophes'* fierce commitment to secularism, humanism, and internationalism.[14] Increased economic activity required and stimulated more knowledge about the world than could be contained within the old limits of medieval dogmatism and a natural economy dominated by production for immediate use. Battered by the Reformation and eroded by markets, the theologically centered unity of medieval Christendom was in an advanced state of decomposition and distinct spheres of intellectual activity were beginning to appear.

The rebellion against Cartesian metaphysics and system-building encouraged the demarcation of definite fields for unfettered investigation.[15] The foundation of modern natural and social science was laid with the claim that discrete activities had their own laws and logic even if their findings conflicted with Scripture. The growing professionalization of the intellect was marked by the appearance of physics, chemistry, and psychology as identifiable disciplines; the separation of astronomy from astrology; and the liberation of literature, philosophy, and the social sciences from theology. The age of Universal Knowledge came to a close as the division of intellectual labor mimicked what was happening in society as a whole.

Dogma and ignorance were the great enemies of freedom. Directed against the claims of the Church, Enlightenment rationalism denied that any single set of convictions could claim *a priori* validity and fiercely defended an open spirit of scientific investigation. Drawing strength from Isaac Newton rather than René Descartes, the new approach began with the particular and proceeded to the general by way of analysis and experimentation. Toleration, the political counterpart to Enlightenment universalism, was the only policy that could stimulate further progress in an increasingly varied and differentiated world. The first victim of this view was the old medieval account of a hierarchically ordered society with an external source of motion. The Enlightenment's pervasive individualism was rooted in the claim that each individual is responsible to himself because only he can know his interests. An open society would finally eliminate the arbitrariness fostered by superstition and respect the pluralism inherent in nature and society alike.

But individualism does not easily yield a durable theory of political obligation, and early Enlightenment thinkers were vulnerable to the charge that the autonomy of the rational person threatened solidarity and community. Adam Smith would attempt his famous reconciliation of private desire with public virtue toward the end of the period, but for the moment the needs of commerce prefigured the theoretical separation of public from private. The growing independence of the state was expressed as French absolutism and English parliamentarianism. In both countries a formal apparatus of law and coercion began to stand apart from the personality of the monarch. Enlightenment thinkers frequently spoke of the "rule of law," and many of them pressed for the regularization and codification of often brutal and arbitrary legal systems.[16] They tended to rely on a secularized version of natural law that was external to and independent of the private individuals whose self-interested drives constituted civil society. Hobbes had argued that if the sovereign is the source of law, he cannot be limited in advance. But the alliance between the centralizing, leveling monarchs and the nascent bourgeoisie had begun to break down, and Enlightenment thinkers were deeply hostile to absolutism. Most eighteenth-century advocates of natural law sought to erect a barrier to unrestrained power by arguing that a law of reason antedates and limits it. The Scots would try to demonstrate that an innate moral sense animated reason, informed nature, and constituted civil society at the same time.

The Moral Foundations of Civil Society

One of the intellectual leaders of the eighteenth-century Scottish Enlightenment, Adam Ferguson wanted to limit arbitrary political power and attenuate the impact of private interest by basing civil society on a set of innate moral sentiments.[17] His work was part of a broader tendency to theorize civil society as a natural condition for moral development and intellectual progress instead of an artificial device for survival. Some Scottish Enlightenment thinkers thought they could find evidence of its naturalness in protective adult reactions to the helplessness of infants and a universal human inclination to live in social groups. For his part, Ferguson located the roots of human sociability in a general capacity to put oneself in another's place and see the world through another's eyes. This "fellow-feeling" permits individuals to participate in the lives of others and makes moral judgment possible by reconciling individuality with a civil society constituted by shared ethical relations.

Hobbes and Locke thought of civil society as a contractually produced and politically guaranteed instrument of individuals who come together to attain some conscious purpose. But their emphasis on private strivings failed to provide a satisfactory explanation of social ties, for it was no secret that people are often driven by altruism, solidarity, and generosity. Ferguson articulated a moralist rebellion against the logic of individual interest. He rooted civil society in "love of mankind," a quality that was dramatically different from the commercial interests some thinkers were placing at the center of human organization. "Affection, and force of mind, which are the band and strength of communities, were the inspiration of God, and original attributes in the nature of man," he asserted, warning that self-interest alone could account for the full range of social connections.[18] He agreed with many of his contemporaries that the "care of subsistence is the principal spring of human action," but it was clear to him that people form societies for reasons broader than mere survival.[19] Humans are moral creatures above all, and instrumental reason and individual advancement cannot provide a civilized life. "His fellow-creatures would be considered merely as they affected his interest. Profit or loss would serve to mark the event of every transaction, and the epithets *useful* or *detrimental* would serve to distinguish his mates in society, as they do the tree which bears plenty of fruit, from that which serves only to cumber the ground, or interrupt his view."[20]

"This," Ferguson insisted, "is not the history of our species." Addressing the "real" life of humans in society, he observed that kindness, mutual aid, and benevolence are as characteristic of human interactions as greed, cruelty, and callousness. Selfishness will drive people to live alone and in competition with their fellows, but natural sociability enables us to live with others, help them, and benefit from their disposition to do the same. Selfishness divides us from our fellows, but solidarity enables us to indulge "that habit of the soul by which we consider ourselves as but a part of some beloved community, and as but individual members of some society, whose general welfare is to us the supreme object of zeal, and the great rule of our conduct."[21]

> In what situation, or by what instruction, is this wonderful character to be formed? Is it found in the nurseries of affectation, pertness, and vanity, from which fashion is propagated, and the genteel is announced? in great and opulent cities, where men vie with one another in equipage, dress, and the reputation of fortune? Is it within the admired precincts of a court, where we may learn to smile without being pleased, to caress without affection, to wound with the secret weapons of envy and jealousy, and to rest our personal importance on circumstances which we cannot always with honor command? No: but in a situation where the great sentiments of the heart are awakened; where the characters of men, not their situations and fortunes, are the principal distinction; where the anxieties of interest, or vanity, perish in the blaze of more vigorous emotions; and where the human soul, having felt and recognized its objects, like an animal who has tasted the blood of its prey, cannot descend to pursuits that leave its talents and its force unemployed.[22]

Ferguson was unwilling to base civil society on contract and refused to speculate about a presocial or prepolitical state of nature. It is senseless to look back to a time when humans were without social bonds, for without these we were not human. The "great sentiments" which form the basis of human sociability are innate. Civil society is the mode of human existence; we were born in and for it and cannot be conceived outside it. Our moral development and material welfare are realized in intimate connection with others, and there is no contradiction between individual self-interest and the moral welfare of the community.[23] "It would seem, therefore, to be the happiness of man, to make his social dispositions the ruling spring of his occupations, to state himself as the member of a community, for whose general good his heart may glow with an ardent zeal, to the suppression of those personal cares which are the foundation of painful anxieties, fear, jealousy, and envy."[24] The state of nature is not some far-off vanished Eden but here and now, taking shape wherever people live together. It is not necessary to explain human beings' transition to civil society; we have always employed the moral power that nature gave us to forge associations with others. Civil society is, and always has been, our habitat.

> That condition is surely favorable to the nature of any being, in which his force is increased; and if courage be the gift of society to man, we have reason to consider his union with his species as the noblest part of his fortune. From this source are derived, not only the force, but the very existence of his happiest emotions; not only the better part, but almost the whole of his rational character. Send him to the desert alone, he is a plant torn from its roots; the form indeed may remain, but every faculty droops and withers; the human personage and the human character cease to exist.[25]

But humankind's moral and social history is a paradoxical one. Ferguson never tried to describe a presocial stage of human life, but his typology of human association progressed from an original "rudeness" to various degrees of "polish." The classical distinction between barbarism and civilization was still important. Rude people are naturally sociable but cannot develop ties beyond those of kinship because they live in conditions of poverty and subordination. A fully developed moral life cannot be established in such an environment, and the transition from rudeness to civil society was marked by the desire for security and individuals' consequent reluctance to "commit every subject to public use."[26] The moral possibilities of civil society have come with a heavy price. The accumulation of property has given rise to increasingly complex political institutions and "the individual having now found a separate interest, the bands of society must become less firm, and domestic disorders more frequent. The members of any community, being distinguished among themselves by unequal shares in the distribution of property, the ground of a permanent and palpable subordination is laid."[27]

Moral advance occurs in conditions of increasing inequality and is marked by intensifying dependence. The consequences were full of danger, and Ferguson worried that civil society might not be up to the challenge. Anticipating Jean-Jacques Rousseau's famous words, he framed the contours of the problem: "He who first said, 'I will appropriate this field; I will leave it to my heirs,' did not perceive, that he was laying the foundation of civil laws and political establishments. He who first ranged himself under a leader, did not perceive, that he was setting the example of a permanent subordination, under the pretense of which, the rapacious were to seize his possessions, and the arrogant to lay claim to his service."[28] Inequality and individualism signified that civil society was not an unadulterated moral advance over rudeness after all.

Locke knew that the unlimited appropriation of private property would produce economic and political inequality, but the vastly increased measure of prosperity and liberty in civil society seemed worth the price. Since Ferguson refused to locate civil society or the state in a contract, he believed that they were not the result of conscious decision but rather the unintended consequences of human action. "Every step and every movement of the multitude, even in what are termed enlightened ages, are made with equal blindness to the future; and nations stumble upon establishments, which are indeed the results of human action, but not the execution of any human design."[29] As powerfully attached to reason as any Enlightenment thinker, Ferguson also based civil society on the unintended results of human action. "No constitution is formed by concert, no government is copied from a plan."[30]

Indeed, the law of unanticipated consequences was one of Ferguson's important contributions to theories of civil society. It is important not to expect too much from deliberation and rationality, for a country's moral progress may come from the self-serving actions of people in securing their property, increasing commerce, or protecting their rights. Civil society is shaped by casual practices and habits as often as by explicit rules. The assumption of innate morality and sociability enabled Ferguson to use the theory of unintended consequences as an instrument of moral progress. Adam Smith, far more focused in matters of ideology, would deploy it with great effectiveness in his political economy. Ferguson did take a step toward extending it to economic affairs as he anticipated his friend's later outline of a self-sufficient market mechanism:

> Property, in the common course of human affairs, is unequally divided; we are therefore obliged to suffer the wealthy to squander, that the poor may subsist; we are obliged to tolerate certain orders of men, who are above the necessity of labor, in order that, in their condition, there may be an object of ambition, and a rank to which the busy aspire. We are not only obliged to admit numbers, who, in strict economy, may be reckoned superfluous, on the civil, the military, and the political list; but because we are men, and prefer the occupation, improvement, and felicity of our nature, to its mere existence, we must even wish, that as many members as possible, of every community, may be admitted to a share of its defence and its government.

Men, in fact, while they pursue in society different objects, or separate views, procure a wide distribution of power, and by a species of chance, arrive at a posture for civil engagements, more favorable to human nature than what human wisdom could ever calmly devise.[31]

If Ferguson used the law of unintended consequences to explain how self-serving action and economic inequality could serve moral progress, he was not entirely convinced that economic improvement was an unmixed blessing. Too much civilization might be disastrous to civil society itself because of the fragmentation unleashed by individual interest and the division of labor. Unrestrained economic growth meant that "society is made to consist of parts, of which none is animated with the spirit of society itself."[32] Echoing ancient warnings about how destructive economic affairs could be to the common moral life of civil society, Ferguson worried about the same individualism that was the wellspring of progress. "The members of a community may, in this manner, like the inhabitants of a conquered province, be made to lose the sense of every connection, but that of kindred or neighborhood; and have no common affairs to transact, but those of trade: Connections, indeed, or transactions, in which probity and friendship may still take place; but in which the national spirit, whose ebbs and flows we are now considering, cannot be exerted."[33] As more people came to regard civil society as a setting for the accumulation of wealth, Ferguson worried that public life would be marked by intolerable levels of corruption, despotism, and apathy. His warnings were similar to those voiced by many of his predecessors and contemporaries. "The effects of such a constitution may be to immerse all orders of men in their separate pursuits of pleasure, which they may now enjoy with little disturbance; or of gain, which they may preserve without any attention to the commonwealth."[34]

Ferguson's fears led him to political institutions and the law of unanticipated consequences. He could not pretend that the people of his age were motivated by the same noble commitment to the public good that drove the Greeks. Too much time had passed. Venality and corruption rested at the heart of the commercial order he saw developing, and he had to lower his expectations. Perhaps innate sociability was not a sufficiently strong organizing principle for a modern civil society after all.

We must be contented to derive our freedom from a different source; to expect justice from the limits which are set to the powers of the magistrate, and to rely for protection on the laws which are made to secure the estate, and the person of the subject. We live in societies, where men must be rich, in order to be great; where pleasure itself is often pursued from vanity; where the desire of a supposed happiness serves to inflame the worst of passions, and is itself the foundation of misery; where public justice, like fetters applied to the body, may, without inspiring the sentiments of candor and equity, prevent the actual commission of crimes.[35]

Maybe Hobbes was right. Perhaps coercion could serve decency in a civil society whose commercial activity threatened to submerge moral life beneath its requirements of individual profit and loss. Ferguson still believed that "bands of affection" constitute the only basis of a durable social life, but he feared that moral ties could not withstand the pressure of markets. Civil society was becoming a mechanism for the creation of wealth rather than the grounding for moral and civic life. Separation and privacy had replaced community and publicity. Ferguson contented himself by saying that happiness "depends more on the degree in which our minds are properly employed, than it does on the circumstances in which are destined to act, on the materials which are placed in our hands, or the tools with which we are furnished."[36] But he was suspicious of the market whose arrival he accepted, and his acute discomfort reflected his reliance on vague moral categories to gauge a future that was only dimly visible.

Ferguson stood at the beginning of the full development of market society and anticipated what the arrival of capitalism might entail for the embedded moral community that served as his model of civil society. But he could not see the future with great clarity. Considerably more advanced in 1767 than it had been in Locke's day, the commodification of human relations was undermining the old civil society as it established the conditions for the new.[37] Ferguson was able to articulate some of the themes that would drive classical British political economy's understanding even as he sought to moralize Locke and revitalize ancient traditions of ethical life. But the penetration of capitalist social relations was still fairly restricted by modern standards, and it would take a man with far greater vision than he to produce the first fully modern theory of civil society.

The Emergence of Bourgeois Civil Society

It was Adam Smith who first articulated a specifically bourgeois conception of civil society. His effort to integrate economic activity and market processes into a more general understanding of the anatomy of civilized life is a milestone in the development of modern thought. Taking note of the breakdown of mercantilism, the spread of markets, and the early appearance of large-scale industrial production, his work was a quantum leap over that of his predecessors and contemporaries. One of the classic texts of English political economy and political philosophy, *The Wealth of Nations* was published in 1776 and lies at the heart of all modern theories of civil society.

The profusion of themes Smith covered reveals how incomplete the division of intellectual labor still was. But the eighteenth century was the century of the political economists, and the ascendancy of economics over the other disciplines also reveals how far the division of labor had advanced. The inexorable spread of markets and their penetration of social relations required intellectuals to address questions of taxes, labor, price, value, and the like systematically. Population growth, tariffs, exports, and imports were central to debates about how to achieve a favorable balance of trade, establish the material conditions for modern civilization, and ensure the security and prosperity of the realm.[38]

Smith's attack on mercantilism crystalized his arguments against political regulation of economic affairs and anticipated the modern conception of civil society as a market-organized sphere of private advantage that stands apart from the state. He disputed the orthodox view that the wealth of a nation can be reduced to the amount of gold or silver in its coffers, the bedrock position that underlay mercantilism's preference for the international market and trade surpluses. Since the supply of precious metals was limited, mercantilist economists assumed that the pursuit of national political power was a zero sum game in which one nation's loss was another's gain. But Smith argued that the internal market was the foundation of national prosperity, advocated measures to stimulate consumption, and contended that mercantilism's interference with free trade worked against everyone's interests in the long run. He opposed the Corn Laws' stiff duties on imported grain, held that colonies should not be used as a source of gold and silver, and combated monopolies of all kinds. Taking note of the period's economic expansion, he pointed to the possibilities of a dynamic international economy in which the prosperity of each was the condition for the prosperity of all. The task of political economy and governmental policy was to provide sustenance for the population and revenue for the state so people could pursue their interests in conditions of peace and stability. Hobbes and Locke had said much the same, of course, but Smith was able to build upon a developed body of economic thought which had not been available a century earlier.

The French Physiocrats, preoccupied as they were with defending agriculture, helped drive the final nails into mercantilism's coffin. François Quesnay viewed the economy as a system that functioned according to its own laws and was thus open to scientific investigation. Each individual works for others, said the Physiocrats, even if he imagines that he works for himself alone. The economic system is smooth, harmonious, and self-correcting; it follows that the closer a nation comes to organizing itself according to the laws of nature, the more stable and prosperous it will be. The economist's job is to demonstrate how to increase production and national wealth. The ideology of improvement was developing as rapidly as the markets it served, and the Physiocrats' celebrated slogan—*laissez faire, laissez passer*—demanded that statesmen liberate their economies from the mercantilist protections that crippled individual initiative and social progress. Prices would find their natural levels, the division of labor would conform to the real distribution of talents, and free individuals would be able to pursue their interests in conditions of freedom. Where earlier projections had regarded politics as the source of stability, political economy was beginning to privilege economic processes.

Smith distanced himself from some important Physiocratic positions, but he shared many of its criticisms of orthodox economic doctrine. Mercantilism was tied to the powerful royal bureaucracies of the period and was unable to conceive of, much less adapt to, the requirements of a self-regulating market. It provided a credible explanation for the restrictive customs and rules of feudal guilds and towns but could not take into account the commercialization and commodification of land, labor, money, and objects of use. Smith was able to do what his predecessors could not. Indeed, the leading conception of *The Wealth of Nations*—the existence of a natural order and the benevolent effects of economic freedom—was neatly expressed in Book I's title claim that "produce is naturally distributed among the different ranks of the people."[39] Smith's celebrated analysis of the division of labor was a logical consequence of this initial assertion, and it culminated in a theory of civil society founded on self-interested economic activity supported by a sympathetic and active state.

Discussions of the division of labor go all the way back to Plato, and we have seen that Ferguson devoted considerable attention to the distribution of skills, resources, and wealth in the population. But Smith was special because he located the division of labor at the heart of civil society and connected it to the moral improvement that would accompany the unprecedented augmentation of human productivity.[40] The book's very first sentence asserted that "the greatest improvement in the productive powers of labor, and the greater part of the skill, dexterity, and judgement with which it is any where directed, or applied, seem to have been the effects of the division of labor."[41] Innate sociability and sympathy could not explain the fundamental relationships of civil society.

> It is the great multiplication of the productions of all the different arts, in consequence of the division of labor, which occasions, in a well-governed society, that universal opulence which extends itself to the lowest ranks of the people. Every workman has a great quantity of his own work to dispose of beyond what he himself has occasion for, and every other workman being exactly in the same situation, he is enabled to exchange a great quantity of his own goods for a great quantity or, what comes to the same thing, for the price of a great quantity of theirs. He supplies them abundantly with what they have occasion for, and a general plenty diffuses itself through all the different ranks of society.[42]

Smith was not discovering something new, of course; his great achievement was to link the division of labor to markets and place it at the center of civil society. The material and moral progress that resulted meant that "a workman, even of the lowest and poorest order, if he is frugal and industrious, may enjoy a greater share of the necessaries and conveniences of life than it is possible for any savage to acquire."[43] Resting as they do on the division of labor, markets allow individuals to multiply their particular skills and regularize their mutual dependence. Markets organized the reciprocal interactions that Ferguson had tried to explain in moral terms. The exchange of quantities of labor replaced Ferguson's "fellow-feeling" as the glue of civil society. "Every man is rich or poor according to the degree in which he can afford to enjoy the necessaries, conveniences, and amusements of human life," Smith explained. "But after the division of labor has once thoroughly taken place, it is but a very small part of these with which a man's own labor can supply him. The far greater part of them he must derive from the labor of other people, and he must be rich or poor according to the quantity of that labor which he can command, or which he can afford to purchase."[44]

Smith's civil society is a market-organized network of mutual dependence. Its transfers of labor require a specifically modern sense of individual freedom. No arbitrary restrictions should prevent anyone from working as he chooses, and Smith understood that markets require that labor stand on its own without being connected to or conditioned by anything else. His classic expression of the labor theory of value was part of an extensive argument against long apprenticeships, corporations, guilds, and other restrictions on the development of a free market in labor:

> The property which every man has in his own labor, as it is the original foundation of all other property, so it is the most sacred and inviolable. The patrimony of a poor man lies in the strength and dexterity of his hands; and to hinder him from employing this strength and dexterity in what manner he thinks proper without injury to his neighbor, is a plain violation of this most sacred property. It is a manifest encroachment upon the just liberty both of the workman, and of those who might be disposed to employ him. As it hinders the one from working at what he thinks proper, so it hinders the other from employing whom they think proper. To judge whether he is fit to be employed, may surely be trusted to the discretion of the employers whose interest it so much concerns.[45]

Now constituted by the division of labor and organized by markets, civil society transforms the voluntary exchanges of free individuals into the substance of a fully civilized life. The interactions of interest-pursuing individuals are translated by market mechanisms into a new social order consisting of landlords, wage-earners, and capitalists. The old social estates are gone from Smith's presentation, replaced by the three characteristically modern social classes organized around agriculture, manufacture, and trade. Three components of production constitute civil society—land, labor, and capital—and they yield three forms of reward: rent, wages, and profits. Smith's complex tripartite analysis revealed the anatomy of "the wealth of nations." Hobbes had identified human appetite as the motor of civil society's economic activity and social motion, but it was Smith who supplied a precise explanation. Civil society does not originate in consciousness, decisions, ingenuity, or reason; like Ferguson, Smith had no need of contract theory. The law of unintended consequences is incorporated in his famous description of the origin of civil society:

> This division of labor, from which so many advantages are derived, is not originally the effect of any human wisdom, which foresees and intends that general opulence to which it gives occasion. It is the necessary, though very slow and gradual consequence of a certain propensity in human nature which has in view no such extensive utility: the propensity to truck, barter, and exchange one thing for another.[46]

It didn't matter to Smith whether this "propensity" was innate to human nature or resulted from our capacity for reason and speech. Whatever its source, he proclaimed it common to all. Smith did not need to base a theory of obligation on contracts, but he agreed with Hobbes and Locke on one essential claim: people get assistance from others only on the basis of mutual self-interest. Unlike Ferguson, he did not expect to form a durable social order by relying on some innate sense of fellowship or morality. "It is not from the benevolence of the butcher, the brewer, or the baker, that we expect our dinner, but from their regard to their own interest. We address ourselves, not to their humanity but to their self-love, and never talk to them of our own necessities but of their advantages."[47]

Hobbes had appealed to an external coercive force to overcome the chaotic drives of isolated and insecure individuals. Locke had substituted natural rights and the rule of law. Ferguson had argued from a theory of moral sentiments. It fell to Smith to fully articulate the claim that a self-regulating market is the permanent engine of economic progress and prosperity. He accomplished the task by grounding civil society on a basic human "propensity to truck, barter, and exchange." Such a formulation obscured the fact that large-scale markets and their domination of society were fairly recent developments, but it fully expressed the growing tendency to regard both individual and social life from the standpoint of economics. If a natural "propensity to truck, barter, and exchange" drives the development of markets, a no less natural "desire" explains the necessity to save and accumulate:

> With respect to profusion, the principle, which prompts to expense, is the passion for present enjoyment; which, though sometimes violent and very difficult to be restrained, is in general only momentary and occasional. But the principle which prompts to save, is the desire of bettering our condition, a desire which, though generally calm and dispassionate, comes with us from the womb, and never leaves us till we go into the grave. In the whole interval which separates these two moments, there is scarce perhaps a single instant in which any man is so perfectly and completely satisfied with his situation, as to be without any wish of alteration or improvement, of any kind. An augmentation of fortune is the means by which the greater part of men propose and wish to better their condition. It is the means the most vulgar and the most obvious; and the most likely way of augmenting their fortune, is to save and accumulate some part of what they acquire, either regularly, or upon some extraordinary occasions. Though the principle of expense, therefore, prevails in almost all men upon some occasions, yet in the greater part of men, taking the whole course of their life at an average, the principle of frugality seems not only to predominate, but to predominate very greatly.[48]

Dissatisfaction with the present stands behind the "desire of bettering our condition," and this dissatisfaction is a permanent feature of human life.[49] It is natural to human beings, present in us "from the womb," and stands as a crucial factor in moral and economic progress. Smith's initial position that people exchange because of necessity had evolved into a natural drive to acquire as much as possible. Ferguson's innate moral sentiments had been replaced by accumulation and abstinence.

The Wealth of Nations helped create a powerful economic and moral argument for the untrammeled pursuit of individual self-interest and announced the appearance of civil society organized around "economic man." It is difficult to overstate the importance of this development. We have seen the classic republican suspicion of such activity and the desire to balance it with some sort of conscious orientation toward common affairs. Smith's great achievement was to articulate a market-driven theory of civil society whose automatic operation made the pursuit of self-interest a condition of the public good. The law of unintended consequences had served Ferguson's effort to limit the impact of individual interest. Smith used it to opposite effect. No longer did selfishness coexist with sympathy, or greed with charity. The drive for wealth and economic advantage was now the force behind all human activity in civil society. "The consideration of his own private profit, is the sole motive which determines the owner of any capital to employ it either in agriculture, in manufactures, or in some particular branch of the wholesale or retail trade. The different quantities of productive labor which it may put into motion, and the different values which it may add to the annual produce of the land and labor of the society, according as it is employed in one or other of those different ways, never enter into his thoughts."[50]

The theory of unintended consequences enabled Smith to bridge the gap between individual motivation and systemic consequences. Reason played no role in regulating social life or balancing the relationship between individual interest and general good, private appetite and public welfare. Mutual dependence rooted in self-interest and manifested in a natural "propensity" to exchange gave rise to consequences that no one could foresee. "Each individual," Smith wrote, "is continually exerting himself to find out the most advantageous employment for whatever capital he can command. It is his own advantage, indeed, and not that of the society, which he has in view. But the study of his own advantage naturally, or rather necessarily leads him to prefer that employment which is most advantageous to the society."[51] Self-aggrandizing individuals are driven toward the home market because it is a more lucrative arena for accumulation than colonies or international trade. Prefigured by Ferguson, Smith's famous "invisible hand" links private advantage to public welfare. Individual pursuit of self-interest provides "the wealth of nations." Markets summarize private vices as public virtues. Modern civil society is born.

> As every individual, therefore, endeavors as much as he can both to employ his capital in the support of domestic industry, and so to direct that industry that its produce may be of the greatest value, every individual necessarily labors to render the annual revenue of the society as great as he can. He generally, indeed, neither intends to promote the public interest, nor knows how much he is promoting it. By preferring the support of domestic to that of foreign industry, he intends only his own security; and by directing that industry in such a manner as its produce may be of the greatest value, he intends only his own gain, and he is in this, as in many other cases, led by an invisible hand to promote an end which was no part of his intention. Nor is it always the worse for the society that it was no part of it. By pursuing his own interest he frequently promotes that of the society more effectually than when he really intends to promote it. I have never known much good done by those who affected to trade for the public good.[52]

Common concerns have been replaced by the invisible logic of the marketplace. Civil society is now a determinate sphere for the pursuit of wealth, separate from the state and powered by its own laws of motion. Smith was not entirely sure that one could erase the gap between public and private by simply invoking the law of unanticipated consequences, but his work did provide a purely "economic" alternative to earlier theories of obligation that attempted to link the part to the whole through politics, natural law, theology, or ethics.

Smith is widely known as the theorist of the invisible hand and the self-correcting market. He certainly had every reason to believe that market societies were more efficient and fairer than mercantilist bureaucracies. The freer individuals are to make their own choices, the more smoothly the self-regulating character of markets will assert itself through the apparent chaos of individual choice. A system of "natural liberty establishes itself of its own accord. Every man, as long as he does not violate the laws of justice, is left perfectly free to pursue his own interest his own way, and to bring both his industry and capital into competition with those of any other man, or order of men."[53] Civil society, the self-interested realm of freedom, production, and exchange, can correct itself automatically provided that political authorities do not interfere. Smith's state had finally separated out from civil society, a theoretical reflection of the collapse of feudalism and the arrival of capitalism.

Popular belief to the contrary, though, Smith was not the theorist of the nineteenth century's "night-watchman state." Even as he expressed liberalism's characteristic disposition to favor private desires over the public good and society over the state, the system of natural liberty still reserved three important tasks to politics. On the most basic level, the state must protect civil society from external danger. This requires an army that stands apart from the armed citizens of premarket social orders. Its second task—"protecting, as far as possible, every member of the society from the injustice or oppression of every other member of it, or the duty of establishing an exact administration of justice"—requires a judicial apparatus to enforce contracts, protect property, and safeguard liberty. Smith feared that inequality might threaten social stability. Echoing Machiavelli, but significantly less interested in republican solutions, Smith fell back on state-organized coercion and the rule of law:

> But avarice and ambition in the rich, in the poor the hatred of labor and the love of present ease and enjoyment, are the passions which prompt to invade property, passions much more steady in their operation, and much more universal in their influence. Wherever there is great property, there is great inequality. For one very rich man, there must be at least five hundred poor, and the affluence of the few supposes the indigence of the many. The affluence of the rich excites the indignation of the poor, who are often both driven by want, and prompted by envy, to invade his possessions. It is only under the shelter of the civil magistrate that the owner of that valuable property, which is acquired by the labor of many years, or perhaps of many successive generations, can sleep a single night in security. He is at all times surrounded by unknown enemies, whom, though he never provoked, he can never appease, and from whose injustice he can be protected only by the powerful arm of the civil magistrate continually held up to chastise it. The acquisition of valuable and extensive property, therefore, necessarily requires the establishment of civil government. Where there is no property, or at least none that exceeds the value of two or three days labor, civil government is not so necessary.[54]

In the end, state power exists to protect property and inequality. The foundations of civil society have to be defended. "Civil government, so far as it is instituted for the security of property, is in reality instituted for the defense of the rich against the poor, or of those who have some property against those who have none at all."[55] But political authority is more than coercion. It has more "positive" tasks to undertake than raising an army and developing a legal and coercive apparatus. "The third and last duty of the sovereign or commonwealth is that of erecting and maintaining those public institutions and those public works, which, though they may be in the highest degree advantageous to a great society, are, however, of such a nature, that the profit could never repay the expense to an individual or small number of individuals, and which it, therefore, cannot be expected that any individual or small number of individuals should erect or maintain."[56] Even as he recognized the enormous creative power of markets, Smith reserved to the state the responsibility to provide "social goods" like roads, bridges, canals, mail, ambassadors, and consuls. In some respects, civil society was more extensive than the core institutions of the market. But Smith's recognition of public goods did not dilute his notion that a self-regulating market rested at the heart of civil society. Its needs and capacities defined the range of permissible state action.

Smith wanted a free market to organize society for many reasons, one of which was its impersonality. Ancient criteria of wealth, status, family background, honor, and the like were irrelevant in the new market economy of production, consumption, profits, sales, and performance. Quite understandably, he regarded the market as the most objective, impartial, and fair mechanism for organizing social life. It did not make the irrational distinctions that had characterized earlier periods. The economic foundation of a promising future, it can organize the mutual exchange of equivalent quantities of labor only in conditions of freedom and the rule of law. "In general, if any branch of trade, or any division of labor, be advantageous to the public, the freer and more general the competition, it will always be the more so."[57] Like Locke, Smith believed that "commerce and manufactures gradually introduce order and good government, and with them, the liberty and scrutiny of individuals, among the inhabitants of the country, who had before lived almost in a continual state of war with their neighbors, and of servile dependency upon their superiors."[58] Under certain circumstances, commerce could tame the state. A political apparatus is indispensable to civil society, but it is a dangerous instrument. The market rewards individuals on the basis of their contribution to prosperity, but the state is arbitrary, erratic, and partial by its very nature. Fundamentally parasitical on the productive body of civil society, its tendency to grow without limit would be devastating were it not for the market's ability to correct its inherent disposition to excess. Conditioned by bourgeois criticisms of residual aristocratic power and unproductive bureaucracies, Smith contrasted the decay of the old to the health of the new:

Great nations are never impoverished by private, though they sometimes are by public prodigality and misconduct. The whole, or almost the whole public revenue, is in most countries employed in maintaining unproductive hands. Such are the people who compose a numerous and splendid court, a great ecclesiastical establishment, great fleets and armies, who in time of peace produce nothing, and in time of war acquire nothing which can compensate the expense of maintaining them, even while the war lasts. Such people, as they themselves produce nothing, are all maintained by the produce of other men's labor. When multiplied, therefore, to an unnecessary number, they may in a particular year consume so great a share of this produce, as not to leave a sufficiency for maintaining the productive laborers, who should reproduce it next year. The next year's produce, therefore, will be less than that of the foregoing, and if the same disorder should continue, that of the third year will be still less than that of the second. . . .

The uniform, constant, and uninterrupted effort of every man to better his condition, the principle from which public and national, as well as private opulence is originally derived, is frequently powerful enough to maintain the natural progress of things toward improvement, in spite both of the extravagance of government, and of the greatest errors of administration. Like the unknown principle of animal life, it frequently restores health and vigor to the constitution, in spite, not only of the disease, but of the absurd prescriptions of the doctor.[59]

Despite his fears that a "profusion of government" could retard England's natural progress, Smith reserved important regulatory and productive functions to a state that was bound to grow as markets became more powerful. If its natural proclivities could be kept in check, the rule of law could assist the growth of markets. "Commerce and manufactures can seldom flourish long in any state which does not enjoy a regular administration of justice, in which the people do not feel themselves secure in the possession of their property, in which the faith of contracts is not supported by law, and in which the authority of the state is not supposed to be regularly employed in enforcing the payment of debts from all those who are able to pay. Commerce and manufactures, in short, can seldom flourish in any state in which there is not a certain degree of confidence in the justice of government."[60] A vigorous state and the universal rule of law is central to a bourgeois civil society organized around individual advantage and private interest. It makes possible the stable set of expectations that sustain economic progress.

Smith is generally known as an enthusiastic supporter of market society, and indeed he was. But he was also a moralist and shared Ferguson's reservations about the ideology of progress. He did not believe that the market could cure all social ills. The state was important, even if Smith limited it to protecting the market's outer boundaries, codifying its internal rules, and providing the necessary public goods that lay beyond its reach. He worried that commerce could make the rich soft, narrow, and corrupt. For all his interest in the possibilities of factory production, he viewed merchants with deep suspicion and insisted that a properly functioning market would maximize the material condition of those at the bottom of the economic ladder. But he also knew that the contradictory logic of civil society brutalized the direct producer and tended to undermine the conditions of social progress.[61] The paradoxical effects of economic progress and the division of labor meant that sharpened skills and enhanced productivity came with intellectual sclerosis and civic incapacity. "His dexterity at his own particular trade," Smith said of the new worker, "seems to be acquired at the expense of his intellectual, social, and martial virtues. But in every improved and civilized society this is the state into which the laboring poor, that is, the great body of the people, must necessarily fall, unless government takes some pains to prevent it."[62] His civic moralism always coexisted in an uneasy tension with his dedication to economic progress. For all his faith in natural freedom and markets, Smith knew that "every improved and civilized society" was built on the debasement of the direct producers. It was imperative that "government take some pains to prevent it."

Even if Smith reserved an important role to the state, his work dramatically shifted the understanding of civil society away from its ancient moorings. A political economy of the division of labor, a network of self-interested actions, and a regime of economic liberty lay at the heart of his thinking. Like Locke, he helped establish the liberal argument that the activities of people in markets, rather than in politics, is the real glue of civil society. Public virtue now emerged from the unintended results of self-interested economic action rather than from politics. Its source was the private desires and appetites of self-regarding individuals rather than the traditional orientation toward the common good. Detaching public virtue from its earlier political framework had relocated it to a framework of social relationships determined by the market processes of a distinctly capitalist economy. The market that lies at the heart of Smith's civil society is a self-correcting automatic network of independent individuals whose connections to each other are their private choices. The old unities were finally collapsing, replaced by the different spheres and isolated individuals of modernity.

The state's formal separation from the economy could not conceal that it was an instrumentality of market society. Smith had no desire to pretend that either sphere stood on its own. The state's task was to provide external security and a domestic environment in which market forces could organize social life. At the same time, the state's basic structure and range of action were set by the requirements of the market. Smith's break with mercantilism signaled that close public control was no longer necessary to ensure the extensive production of commodities at reasonable prices. The guilds, families, and estates that had dominated production for so long were vanishing, supplanted by more modern forms of economic organization. It would not be necessary to organize economic life through politics; the productive processes of capitalism are rooted in the market, and public activity could not conceal liberalism's preference for a "strong society" and a "weak state." As optimistic as he was, Smith had some reservations about the price that markets would extract, but he was not particularly worried about how it could be mitigated. It would take the shattering effects of the French Revolution and the new world of industrial production for the nineteenth century to generate a theory of civil society fully appropriate to modernity's economics and politics.

5

Civil Society and the State

Classical notions of civil society recognized that social life was carried on in separate spheres, but theorists did not organize their thinking around individual interests. For the most part, the Greeks and Romans situated private strivings in broader notions of citizenship. As the ancient world collapsed and Christianity directed itself toward faith and good works, medieval theorists sought to explain human actions in light of God's plan for the universe. All such efforts were suited to hierarchically organized natural economies in which economic life was constrained by other institutions and norms, production was undertaken primarily for reasons of subsistence, and personal gain was not a morally reputable guide to action.

The development of powerful markets in land, labor, and commodities undermined embedded economies and located individual interest at the heart of theory and practice. Thomas Hobbes's view that a competitive civil society had to be constituted by sovereign power anticipated the disintegration of the traditional commonwealth. John Locke identified interests with property and placed them at the center of civil society, but he knew little about markets and retained important elements of earlier traditions. The Scottish Enlightenment tried to regulate individual strivings with an innate moral sense, but Adam Smith's qualms about the market did not prevent him from expressing the period's general confidence that a social order populated by individual interest-maximizers could be organized by the "invisible hand." The coming of modernity saw liberalism detach markets from states and recognize interest as the constitutive force of civil society.

But ancient concerns about the disintegrating impact of particularism would not go away. Neither markets nor states were as developed in the rest of Europe as in France and England, and it fell to German thinkers to reconceptualize the moral content of universality in light of the French Revolution. Immanuel Kant tried to inform ethical action with reason and locate a public sphere at the heart of civil society. G. W. F. Hegel theorized the bureaucratic state as the highest moment of freedom in an effort to supersede the economically driven chaos of bourgeois civil society. Karl Marx's critique of Hegel's theory of the state would culminate in the modern era's most powerful understanding of civil society as a problematic and undemocratic arena of egoistic competition.

Civil Society and the Ethical Commonwealth

We have seen that moral sentiments and universal benevolence rested at the heart of much Scottish Enlightenment theorizing about civil society and even played a role in explaining "the wealth of nations." But they came to grief in David Hume's devastating attack on natural law attempts to unify mental processes. Hume's assertion that reason and morality occupy different spheres and yield different sorts of understandings found expression in the famous distinction he drew between the "is" and the "ought." A strict boundary separates moral precepts rooted in "the sentiments and affections of mankind" from the truths revealed by reason.

How can the common good be conceptualized in such an environment? Hume answered that it cannot be revealed by moral reasoning and does not exist apart from the sum of individual goods. The rules by which civil society functions are not derived from the moral law of nature; they are "artifices," and civil society is nothing more than a conventional arrangement for the pursuit of private goals. Instrumental reason helps individuals identify their interests and indicates the most efficient path to satisfying them. Experience and habit replaced *a priori* morality and virtue as the criteria of truth. People can be expected to follow ethical rules only if their immediate purposes are so served. No general good links individuals in any shared enterprise broader than the mutual pursuit of interest. Civil society is constituted by the external interactions of rational seekers after individual self-interest.

Immanuel Kant was the foremost philosopher of the Enlightenment, and his response to Hume began with the ancient contention that self-interest cannot supply an acceptable grounding for human life. Kant sought to base civil society on an intrinsic sense of moral duty that unites all human beings, but he also wanted to move past the weakness and naiveté of the Scots' theory of innate moral sentiments. His central claim—that a moral life can be lived only in a civil society founded on universal categories of right that are accessible to all—hinged on his profoundly important effort to derive a universal ethic appropriate to people who are fully self-governing in moral matters.

To say that Kant was an Enlightenment thinker is to say that he dispensed with an external authority that constituted morality or instructed people about the requirements of action. The Middle Ages were over and the role of religion was increasingly confined to private matters of faith; Kant announced that humans are morally free because they can know what is right without being told. People are able to derive valid moral rules as requirements that they impose on themselves. The Scots had said much the same but failed to recognize the extent to which moral obligations clash with powerful passions, prejudices, appetites, and desires. They had made things too easy; the deep meaning of ethical action, Kant knew, is to be found in how hard it is, how fiercely we resist controlling our behavior. But all is not lost. Even as individual interest drives toward anarchy, we have powerful motives to act as we know we should. The entire thrust of Kantian ethics was to derive a stable ethical foundation for civil society by basing it on the things we know we have to do just because they are right.

But how can people who are pulled by their particular interests make moral law? If morality dictates necessary acts that are independent of what the agent wants, what is to prevent a particular individual from exempting himself from a moral rule he finds inconvenient? Kant was convinced that a "moral metaphysic" could be derived from reason and used to generate a set of principles that stand on their own because they are independent of the vagaries of experience. But he knew that he had to answer *Leviathan* if he was to replace Hobbes's attempt to derive a "purely" political and instrumental theory of civil society with something more morally defensible.[1]

Kant's "critical philosophy" argued that there is a radical difference between the natural world of what is and the moral world of what ought to be. In this it echoed Hume's contention that morality cannot be derived from the chaos and mutability of experience. But people are able to make some systematic sense of the world all the same, and they do so because they can understand and use transcendent ideas that are not derived from experience, whose objects are entirely hypothetical, and which have no empirical reality. People use reason as a speculative tool all the time, and Kant understood equality as a universal ability to share in a transcendent quality of lawfulness. Seeking to rescue reason from Hume, Kant located it in the will.[2]

Kant's great achievement resulted from his investigation of how the mind organizes the perceptions presented to it by the senses. The forms of order we use are not externally imposed; they are an aspect of the human mind as such, a fundamental capacity we all have to structure our experience rationally, understand patterns, discover first principles, and arrive at laws. Moral laws are like laws of nature and also originate outside the realm of experience; we can understand their *a priori* quality because our "practical reason" is governed by the same patterns that allow our "pure reason" to grasp the patterns of nature. Moral freedom is a fundamental possibility of the human condition because the rational will is determined by its own inner lawfulness. Even with the powerful pull of individual interest, moral lawmaking is an intrinsic capacity of the human mind.

The advance from dependence to autonomy described humanity's maturation toward moral freedom. "*Enlightenment is man's emergence from his self-incurred immaturity,*" Kant announced. "Immaturity is the inability to use one's own understanding without the guidance of another. This immaturity is *self-incurred* if its cause is not lack of understanding, but lack of resolution and courage to use it without the guidance of another. The motto of enlightenment is therefore: *Sapere aude!* Have courage to use your *own* understanding!"[3] Universal moral categories can rescue human life from the calculus of self-interest, and every person can derive them.

Freedom is a potential for independence from the necessity of the sensible world. If the will is completely determined by its own lawfulness, it is still limited because we are not God and cannot always know what is right with complete clarity. Kant knew that we have our own desires and goals that insistently demand our attention. Private interest cannot be ignored or erased, for the human condition is marked by a continual tension between what we want to do and what we ought to do. But we have a powerful ally. Reason allows an insight into what the hypothetical perfectly rational agent would decide to do in any particular situation, and this constitutes the "ought" that must govern moral deliberations. Such deliberation is well within the capacity of all people. Moral freedom is obedience to the moral laws of practical reason that the will gives itself. These considerations led Kant to the "categorical imperative."

The guide to moral action appropriate to imperfectly rational agents, the categorical imperative supplies the only standard of judgment that a perfectly rational agent would choose: "So act that the maxim of your will could always hold at the same time as the principle giving universal law."[4] We use this standard all the time. When we ask what would happen if everyone undertook a particular course of action, we express our membership in and responsibility to the human race as a whole. Recognizing that we live in a civil society full of people whose legitimate ends are worthy of respect *in their own right* makes one a "legislative member of a possible realm of ends." There are moral limits to the ends we may pursue, and those limits are the morally defensible ends of the people with whom we share the world.

Kant was sure that organizing civil society around a community of ends was ethically better than constituting it according to the requirements of the market. He was equally convinced that treating people as ends in themselves is how we reconcile our particular goals with universal moral requirements. None of this should be a surprise, he said. People express their ethical concerns in real life as a set of self-imposed duties toward others that require determinate actions for no other reason than because they are right. Understanding duties in this way enables us to overcome the barbarism of using others as instruments for satisfying our private interests. Kant's civil society was a moral community that required autonomous people to subject their action to the universal ethical standards of the categorical imperative.[5]

Civil society for Kant represented a set of possibilities appropriate to civilized people, and many commentators have noted that the categorical imperative is really a set of procedures. Indeed, Kant was a formalist and an intentionalist. He insisted that moral law cannot contain any "matter" or content, originating as it does in a determinate quality of mind. Moral law can only provide a way of dealing with what our senses present to the mind.

If Kant refused to derive ethics from politics, he certainly based his politics on ethics. An ethics of duty led to a politics of rights. The law must maximize people's opportunities to make their own decisions in conditions of freedom and must enable them to live by the choices they make. Kant insisted that moral autonomy and the demands of the categorical imperative require a protected space within which people can freely determine their own action. Freedom cannot be restricted to any particular element of the population but must be generally available to all. Protected by the rule of law, rights, and civil liberties, civil society reflects the common and equal moral capacity of all its members. But one's ability to live according to the choices one has made is deeply affected by economic and social factors, and later theorists justly took Kant to task for limiting equality to the formal criteria of classical liberalism.

The Scots were too naive, Kant thought. Enlightenment demands more than universal moral precepts, and we cannot be dependent on the benevolence of others. Beneficent action is important and people engage in it all the time, but it cannot serve as the wellspring of justice or as the organizing principle of civil society. Concerned with maximizing peoples' opportunities to follow their interests, Kant looked to politics and history for signs of moral enlightenment and found them in the French Revolution. Formerly passive observers were participating in the events of the day, he thought; the people of France gave themselves the constitution they wanted, and it was no accident that they used it to organize a republic. So long as there were no predetermined political outcomes and civil liberties remained in place, Kant regarded the Revolution as the first home of a genuine public sphere organized around the universal and public use of reason. Once he became convinced that civil liberties had been compromised, he withdrew his support.

Kant's central political concern was with the principles of legitimacy, and his procedural approach dictated an emphasis on how people develop the rules by which they choose to live. As we have seen, the content of those rules was not at issue, nor were any substantive factors that might shape peoples' ability to live according to duties they had elaborated for themselves. Only the fullest measure of public deliberation, discussion, and decision can yield moral rules that approach universal validity. People have a basic right to be subjected only to laws that are capable of receiving universal assent, and this requires publicness. Maturity requires the "freedom to make *public* use of one's reason in all matters" and can come to life only in the presence of others.[6] Kant regarded critical, independent thought as the most important weapon against dogma and authoritarianism. Publicity and rights would rescue reason from experience and allow it to serve moral development:

> The *public use of man's reason must always* be free, and it alone can bring about enlightenment among men; the *private* use of reason may quite often be very narrowly restricted, however, without undue hindrance to the progress of enlightenment. By the public use of one's own reason I mean that use which anyone may make of it *as a man of learning* addressing the entire *reading public.* What I term the private use of reason is that which a person may make of it in a particular *civil* post or office with which he is entrusted.[7]

As a characteristic of the soul, inner freedom means self-government understood as independence from opinion and dogma. As a quality of public life, it requires a free sphere of thought and action that is immunized from outside interference. Always aware of the "radical evil" that lurks in the human heart, Kant knew that nature, feeling, and experience can serve morality only if integrated into a broader perspective than immediate desire. He looked to "critical reason" to bring universal moral standards to bear on particular arguments and individual experiences. It is only in public that "the court of reason" can overcome the limitations of immediate experience and free institutions can serve enlightenment by making thought available to others. Kant's public sphere describes the processes and institutions of civil society through which thought is made public so it can be critically considered from a universal point of view.[8] It would be clear before long, however, that liberal civil society was constituted by considerably more than thought; Kant was unable to adequately theorize the influence of power because the internal operations of civil society were not sufficiently clear.

The free use of critical reason does not guarantee agreement, however—it simply provides a set of rules for debate. A public sphere protected by laws and institutions can make disagreement serve enlightenment because debate can blunt the antisocial edge of individual interest. "The means which nature employs to bring about the development of innate capacities is that of antagonism within society, in so far as this antagonism becomes in the long run the cause of a law-governed social order."[9] This "antagonism within society," largely generated in dogma and commerce, is what Kant called man's "unsocial sociability"—the contradiction between the human tendency to form civil societies and an accompanying resistance to do so. Driven by a desire to live with others and a no less powerful drive to live alone, humanity's problem is how to build a morally defensible public sphere that can serve freedom and respect autonomy.

Only the *Rechtsstaat*, the law-governed state, can reconcile individual moral autonomy with the requirements of public order. Reason requires that human relations be governed and public conflicts be settled according to the universal standards of the categorical imperative. Any rule of conduct that allows one to live in freedom and simultaneously respects the freedom of all others has the standing of "right." An ethically legitimate state will take the form of a republic based on civil liberties and the rule of law—the best form within which each individual can seek happiness and not impair others' ability to do the same. Indeed, "the highest formal condition of all other external duties is the *right* of men *under coercive public laws* by which each can be given what is due to him and secured against attack from any others." When applied in more general terms to the moral life of people in civil society, the categorical imperative requires a state. "*Right* is the restriction of each individual's freedom so that it harmonizes with the freedom of everyone else (in so far as this is possible within the terms of a general law). And *public right* is the distinctive quality of the *external laws* which makes this harmony possible." A measure of coercion is necessary for freedom.

Civil society is constituted by "a relationship among *free* men who are subject to coercive laws, while they retain their freedom within the general union with their fellows."[10] Autonomy requires obedience.

A republic respects the equality and independence of all citizens, but Kant agreed with Hobbes that it must also subject them to the coercive command of law. Civil society is founded on participation and guarantees freedom from the will of others, but egocentric man is disposed to abuse his liberty and "requires a master to break his self-will and force him to obey a universally valid will under which everyone can be free."[11] Kant expressed the equality of people as political subjects in terms that Hobbes would have understood: "no-one can coerce anyone else other than through the public law and its executor, the head of state."[12]

> All right consists solely in the restriction of the freedom of others, with the qualification that their freedom can co-exist with my freedom within the terms of a general law; and public right in a commonwealth is simply a state of affairs regulated by a real legislation which conforms to this principle and is backed up by power, and under which a whole people can live as subjects in a lawful state. This is what we call a civil state, and it is characterized by equality in the effects and counter-effects of freely-willed actions which limit one another in accordance with the general law of freedom. Thus the *birthright* of each individual in such a state (i.e. before he has performed any acts which can be judged in relation to right) is absolutely *equal* as regards his authority to coerce others to use their freedom in a way which harmonizes with his freedom.[13]

Freedom and authority describe humankind's ability to rule itself, and they take shape as a single sovereign will to which people voluntarily submit. A union of free persons under law can serve justice if individuals are treated as ethical ends, citizens are their own lawgivers, and the moral rules under which people live are public and universal. This requires equality of opportunity, the right to vote, the rule of law, the separation of powers, and a constitutional government. As a sphere of moral life,

> the civil state, regarded purely as a lawful state, is based on the following *a priori* principles:
> 1. The *freedom* of every member of society as a *human being*
> 2. The *equality* of each with all the others as a *subject*
> 3. The *independence* of each member of a commonwealth as a *citizen*.[14]

The three *a priori* principles of freedom, equality, and autonomy do not originate in experience or history; they are the political equivalents of the moral requirements that Kant derived from the categorical imperative. Treating other people as moral ends in their own right, understanding that they cannot be means to our ends, and becoming a "legislative member of a possible realm of ends" can constitute civil society as a republic organized around respect for freedom, equality, and independence.[15] Kant's civil society requires a liberal public sphere that can reconcile individuality with universality and antagonism with membership through the institutions of a law-governed republic.

> The greatest problem for the human species, the solution of which nature compels him to seek, is that of attaining a civil society which can administer justice universally. The highest purpose of man—i.e. the development of all natural capacities—can be fulfilled for mankind only in society, and nature intends that man should accomplish this, and indeed all his appointed ends, by his own efforts. This purpose can be fulfilled only in a society which has not only the greatest freedom, and therefore a continual antagonism among its members, but also the most precise specification and preservation of the limits of this freedom in order that it can co-exist with the freedom of others.[16]

There can be no freedom without law, no civil society without the state, and no peace without coercion. The antagonisms between people—based on their natural differences, manifested in their different interests, and exacerbated by economic competition—can assist humankind's moral growth if constrained by a state that forces free people to act in accordance with the moral duties they legislate for themselves. Kant's strong commitment to individual moral autonomy was paired with an equally strong commitment to the state, law, and obedience. A constitutional monarchy would protect civil society from democracy and despotism alike. Civil liberties could be reconciled with a political authority that administers the law impartially and universally. Despite his support for the French, Kant was adamantly opposed to revolutions. He held that the traditional right of revolution would make the people the judges in their own case and implied a return to humankind's original condition. Morality could not be served by the dissolution of civil society; only political reform and the gradual spread of republican institutions could facilitate moral progress and inaugurate an international regime of "perpetual peace." The constitutional state is a better guarantor of the moral law than any other institution because its organization recognizes the contradictory relationship between freedom and necessity.

> All right consists solely in the restriction of the freedom of others, with the qualification that their freedom can co-exist with my freedom within the terms of a general law; and public right in a commonwealth is simply a state of affairs regulated by a real legislation which conforms to this principle and is backed up by power, and under which a whole people live as subjects in a lawful state. This is what we call a civil state, and it is characterized by equality in the effects and counter-effects of freely willed actions which limit one another in accordance with the general law of freedom.[17]

Authority may be necessary for moral freedom, but Kant's notion that everyone is capable of moral judgment represented a radical break with prevailing ideas about the moral capacity of ordinary people. Even if they agreed that all people were capable of moral reasoning, earlier thinkers tended to see God as the author of all good and pictured human beings as undependable and willful subjects. Such a view had supported theories of civil society and the state from Augustine to Hobbes. Kant's contribution to modern theories of civil society consisted in his conception of a public life infused with moral purpose that is accessible to all. Civil society represents the organization of humanity into a moral realm of ends and makes it possible for people to realize ethical ends through the duties they impose on themselves. Kant's "republic of letters" might have been based on an overly optimistic view about the potential of individual action, the capacity of formal liberties, and the power of procedures, but his effort to ground a moral theory of civil society on a stronger foundation than competition and self-interest would deeply inform the work of Hegel and Marx. A powerful ethical critique of the market was present in embryonic form, and it would not be particularly difficult for subsequent thinkers to demonstrate that formal equality, republican institutions, and civil liberties were not sufficient to protect moral autonomy. Kant's formalism prevented him from probing deeply into the network of material relations that constituted civil society, and it fell to Hegel to move past Kant's separation of the subjective and objective conditions of freedom and craft a theory of civil society that was simultaneously a theory of the state.

The "Giant Broom"

An entire generation of theorists were transformed by the French Revolution's promise that civil society and the state could finally be organized on a rational basis. If social and political institutions could reflect the freedom and interest of the individual, the Revolution also marked the definitive appearance of the modern state, whose formal separation from economic processes would encourage the rapid development of civil society. As in all revolutions, construction proceeded in tandem with demolition. The emancipation of the individual required the destruction of the hierarchical and corporate structures that had shaped French life for centuries. Not all intermediate institutions disappeared, but those that were founded on birth and privilege did not survive the Revolution's "giant broom."[18]

The division of the French people into three estates was abolished on the famous night of August 4, 1789, and formally ended by decree three months later. This struck directly at the fusion of state and society that had characterized medievalism. All citizens were declared equal without distinctions of birth. All special privileges of towns, cantons, provinces, regions, and principalities were abolished. The state was no longer the personal property of the monarch, and his will was no longer the expression of sovereignty. From now on, declared the Constituent Assembly, the state would be at the service of its citizens. It would also act directly on them, since it was now the representative of the entire community and the agent of universal values. Many of the intermediate bodies that had stood between it and the individual were abolished or transformed.

The abolition of feudal privilege directly affected the fortunes of the Church. With its property, courts, assemblies, autonomous financial institutions, tithes, and the like, it had been a "state within the state" for centuries. All these privileges disappeared and the Church began its long transformation into a spiritual institution. Religious orders, teaching and charitable congregations, the Order of Malta, ancient *collèges*, hospitals, and the like disappeared. Much Church property passed to the nation, and members of the clergy were even state employees for a time.

The nobility did not have an articulated corporate expression like the Church, but it had been represented in the Estates General and provincial assemblies. It lost all its hereditary titles, coats of arms, privileges, and authority. Serfdom and personal manorial rights were ended without compensation and aristocratic courts disappeared. All formal distinctions between noble land and that of commoners were eliminated. Fiefs, customary rights, primogeniture, and other feudal privileges vanished. The Constituent Assembly's elimination of the formal distinctions between nobles and commoners paved the way for the modern state of universal citizenship and uniform laws. At the same time, it stimulated the development of a modern civil society whose roots lay in property rather than in birth and which could be sustained by economic processes rather than by political power.

The political structure that emerged from the Revolution's early events was a weakened and decentralized one, but the logic of France's protracted emergency pushed toward centralization. The revolutionary state acted directly on its citizens at the expense of intermediate feudal institutions and ancient provincial dreams of autonomy and local control. It subjected the economy to political supervision throughout the long revolutionary crisis, but after Thermidor the centralized Jacobin structure collapsed and was replaced for a time by a liberal structure that released the economy from political guidance. But before long the Napoleonic Wars required further centralization. Bonaparte consolidated the rationalized state by organizing the relationship between the central government and local administrations, codifying a network of uniform national laws, establishing a system of primary education, promoting a single national language, and initiating a uniform system of weights and measures. Waterloo brought his dream of European empire to an end, but many of the Revolution's most far-reaching political advances remained in place. Indeed, the continuing popularity of a universal public educational system financed by a national tax, administered from Paris, and organized around a uniform curriculum testifies to the Revolution's continuing appeal. The same could be said of such institutions as a national health system and public provision of childcare. The struggle over the future of these universal and democratic legacies of the Revolution lies at the heart of contemporary European politics.

The French Revolution was a revolution for national unity as much as anything else, and abolishing the customary privileges of towns, provinces, clergy, and nobility facilitated the growth of powerful central institutions and equality before the law. The intermediate bodies that had curbed state power were swept away, and national unity was achieved through centralized administrative uniformity, a national army, hostility to local particularism, and a single market with a uniform set of customs and tariffs. The chaotic diversity of feudalism and the prerogatives of personal power were gone. Traditional local autonomy and medieval associations had long meant privilege and inequality. Democracy came with centralization, and the result was a specifically modern bifurcation of spheres. Political liberties could now be extended to an entire continent because citizenship was formally abstracted from the distribution of economic power and made a function of residence. The French Revolution was so powerful precisely because the state was no longer dependent on the wealth, status, and other "private" attributes of feudalism. The formal separation of politics from economics announced the appearance of modernity's universal state and particularistic civil society.

But the explicit separation of spheres could not hide their real interconnections. Since the French Revolution, many central concerns of modern political theory have been driven by the "real" relationship between the state and civil society. The formal separation between them has accelerated the substantive economic and social inequality of civil society, now seen as the sphere of private pleasure. But the foundations of economic exploitation appeared to lie outside the arena of politics and did not seem amenable to political solution. Civil society could freely develop as the realm of property and interest precisely because of legal and institutional barriers to political supervision. The market converted political equality into a condition of economic inequality and thus expressed the twin horns of the dilemma that gave rise to Hegel's theory of the state. The social content of the French Revolution, expressed in the sans-culottes' call for a regulated economy and the equality of conditions, would survive Thermidor and Waterloo. It would mark European politics throughout the nineteenth century and continues to shape much of the contemporary political environment.

The Revolution's immediate results, however, were legal equality and economic freedom. The destruction of old hierarchies and corporations made possible the development of the modern state and civil society. As profoundly important as they were, the Revolution's political accomplishments only established the terrain on which future democratic struggles would be conducted. Equality before the law brought a series of distinctly modern social problems into the open that could not emerge as long as they were hidden behind feudal social and political relations. Few modern thinkers understood this as clearly as Georg Wilhelm Friedrich Hegel.

The "System of Needs"

The French Revolution seemed to have completed the Reformation by making the individual the self-reliant master of his life in the profane world as well as in spirit. It signaled that free rational activity could give concrete expression to the inner freedom announced by Luther. To a whole generation of German thinkers—one of whom was Kant—the Revolution marked the appearance of human beings as the autonomous subjects of their own moral development. For the first time, it seemed, people could become free as they organized the world according to the requirements of reason.

Like Kant, Ludwig van Beethoven, Johann Gottlieb Fichte, Friedrich Schelling, and many others in his generation, Hegel recognized the Revolution as the dawn of a new era. But he was equally convinced that Kant had gone too far in his attempt to rescue reason from Hume—and this meant, paradoxically, that he had not been able to go far enough. His critique of Kant was founded on the claim that separating essence from appearance made ultimate reality opaque to human understanding and weakened reason's ability to contribute to freedom. Hegel began with Aristotle's conviction that reality is intelligible, that reason can discover the real nature of things, and that freedom is summarized in our ability to order the world in accordance with our intentions.

Completed just before the Battle of Jena forced Hegel to flee the university town with the manuscript in 1806, *The Phenomenology of Mind* attempted to do away with Kantian dualism and asserted that ultimate reality—*Geist*—is manifested in all its phenomenological appearances and can be understood by human reason in its progress through each of them. Aristotle's teleology had treated *logos* as a fixed given, but Hegel viewed *Geist* as unfolding in all its manifestations and hence as discoverable in history. No universal can exist as an abstraction on its own, independent of the particularities that make it up. Spirit, another way of understanding *Geist*, is conscious activity. Kant was wrong, Hegel announced. The essence of things can become manifest in the world. Reason does not exist *a priori*; it can only be realized in practice, as the summation of the real, sensual interactions of which human history is made.

This critique of Kant's "introversion" led Hegel to deny that the categorical imperative can furnish universal moral rules. All it can do is provide a standard for choosing between alternatives whose origins are external to the choosing will. Relegating ethics to the inner legislation of moral duty had left it without any concrete referent in the real world of social relations. The Kantian claim that nothing can be known "in its essence" limited reason's power and ended with the suggestion that the heart can know things that the mind cannot grasp; "this self-styled 'philosophy' has expressly stated that 'truth itself cannot be known,' that that only is true which each individual allows to rise out of his heart, emotion, and inspiration, about ethical institutions, especially about the state, the government, and its constitution." The discovery of universal principles is the ultimate human achievement, and reason is what gives us knowledge of them. But Kant had denied the emancipatory possibilities of the mind and settled for less than he should have. The "quintessence of shallow thinking," Hegel insisted, "is to base philosophic science not on the development of thought and the concept but on immediate sense-perception and the play of fancy."[19]

Kant's abstract "formalism" led him to separate the moral absolute from concrete reality through his claim that morality cannot be translated into empirical reality. He had preserved the individual and an ethic, but he had no way of bringing the subjective and objective conditions of freedom together. Hegel was not willing to leave truth to chance by accepting Kant's implication that all authentic convictions have equal moral weight. He proposed to develop a metaphysics of absolute knowledge that fused essence and appearance. Freedom is not given by a "natural" structure of the self as Kant had claimed, but is created only in interaction with other individuals. The will can be independent of internal desire and external circumstance only in relation to other wills. We are not born free, Hegel suggested. We become free, and we do so as we become conscious of our history as social beings.

Knowledge lies in Spirit, and reason enables us to discover it as we decipher the meaning of a history we have made. Humanity's progress through the Enlightenment and the French Revolution to "the moral life of the Spirit" is *Geist*'s passage from consciousness through self-consciousness, reason, spirit, and religion to Absolute Knowledge. *Geist* comes to self-consciousness through the culmination of humankind's self-expression in history—through art, religion, and philosophy. Freedom has always existed. It is a matter of how we come to know it, and this is the purpose of reason. It can free us from the contingent and the false, for "it is only as thinking intelligence that the will is genuinely a will and free."[20] Freedom enables man to "be himself" as he becomes the conscious subject of his own history.

The world-historic importance of the French Revolution was that it raised freedom to the principal and conscious aim of society and state for the first time.[21] This breakthrough in thought was paralleled by a breakthrough in action. It is now possible for us to organize our lives on the basis of our reason in conditions of freedom. "The right of individuals to be subjectively destined to freedom is fulfilled when they belong to an actual ethical order, because their conviction of their freedom finds its truth in such an objective order, and it is in an ethical order that they are actually in possession of their own essence or their own inner universality. When a father inquired about the best method of educating his son in ethical conduct, a Pythagorean replied: 'Make him a citizen of a state with good laws.'"[22]

Freedom demands that human beings be able to act in accordance with the requirements of reason. For the first time in history, our ability to shape civil society now lies in our ability to apply the results of free thought to the conditions of our lives. Hegel announced the birth of the human being as the conscious subject of his own history, and in so doing he transcended Kant's categorical imperative. Freedom is a structure of interactions in the world in which the self-determination of each is a condition of the self-determination of others. Human history is the domain in which freedom comes into being as the summation of all practical relations. Its emancipatory content is to be found in the structures of human history.

Hegel's conception of freedom stands at the beginning of all modern theories that consider civil society apart from the state. It was he who first elaborated modernity as distinct spheres and put an end to earlier theoretical trends in the process. The three spheres of social life—the family, civil society, and the state—are different structures of ethical development, separate and related moments of freedom in which individual self-determination is realized in larger ethical communities within which free persons make moral choices. If *Geist* is revealed in history, freedom passes through the different historical moments of social life.

The family constitutes ethical life in its "natural" phase but must conceal it behind the screen of immediate personal relations and express it as a set of domestic duties. Its ethical limitations cannot be separated from its private purpose. It tends to suppress differences between its members because it is structured by love, altruism, and a concern for the whole. In case of conflict, the needs of others and of the whole must trump those of the individual. Each member must be ready to sacrifice for every other member; no family can exist for long if its members are driven by self-interest. If the basis of its ethical life is mutual self-sacrifice, family morality "consists in a feeling, a consciousness, and a will, not limited to individual personality and interest, but embracing the common interests of the members generally."[23] The minimal condition of ethical life is family unity, but it is impermanent and dissolves as children reach maturity, differentiate themselves from their parents, and go out into the world to acquire property and form new families. Their subjectivity is soon expressed as the ownership of external things. Property becomes a condition of identity and freedom even as it dissolves the family by transforming its children into competing self-interested proprietors.[24]

Civil society is the "negation" of the essential but limited ethical moment of the family.[25] If the family is constituted by renunciation and unity, civil society is ethical life in competition and particularity. Its inhabitants act with their own interests in mind, are concerned with the satisfaction of their individual needs, and are continually driven to treat others as means to their own end. But if it violates the conditions of ethical life, civil society's mutual selfishness can still form the basis of an ethical association. "In civil society each member is his own end, everything else is nothing to him. But except in contact with others he cannot attain the whole compass of his ends, and therefore these others are means to the end of the particular member."[26] Where the family unites its members on the basis of their commonalities, civil society divides its members on the basis of their differences. Individuals are compelled to behave selfishly and instrumentally toward each other, but they cannot help satisfying each other's needs, advancing their mutual interests, and constructing a set of durable social relations. "In the course of the actual attainment of selfish ends . . . there is formed a system of complete interdependence, wherein the livelihood, happiness, and legal status of one man is interwoven with the livelihood, happiness, and rights of all. On this system, individual happiness, etc., depend, and only in this connected system are they actualized and secured."[27] Hegel knew his Adam Smith. The invisible hand can turn selfishness into enlightenment and transform egoists into self-conscious and respected members of civil society; "by a dialectical advance, subjective self-seeking turns into the mediation of the particular through the universal, with the result that each man in earning, producing, and enjoying on his own account is *eo ipso* producing and earning for the enjoyment of everyone else."[28]

Hegel's civil society preserves the ethical moment of the family as it transcends it. It is a higher sphere of ethical life because it can accommodate the differences that proved fatal to family life and is the unique creation of a modernity shaped by individuality and competition. "Civil society," he observed, "is the [stage of] difference which intervenes between the family and the state."[29] His was the first systematic effort to theorize a competitive sphere of self-interest in radical distinction from the state.

His standpoint was that of the isolated individual of the early nineteenth century who, emancipated from the "political" entanglements of feudalism, became "civil" in the modern—that is, economic—sense of the term. "The concrete person, who is himself the object of his particular aims, is, as a totality of wants and a mixture of caprice and physical necessity, *one* principle of civil society. But the particular person is essentially so *related* to other particular persons, that each establishes himself and finds satisfaction by means of the others and at the same time purely and simply by means of the form of universality, the second principle here."[30] Inhabited by economic man, constituted by private concerns, and organized by the market, civil society thrives because modernity is free from the particularisms, privileges, and inequalities of medievalism. For the first time, a person can pursue his own interests and act for his own sake. A network of social relations standing apart from the state and rooted in individual interests, civil society links self-serving individuals to one another in an autonomous chain of social connections.[31] It is a sphere of moral freedom and individual interests. The progress of Spirit has become manifest in civil society as surely as it had in the family.

Civil society is a moment in freedom, but it is a limited and dangerous moment because it drives toward making itself the only determination for human beings. Acutely aware of the enormous power of market relations, Hegel knew that the appearance of bourgeois civil society was changing the world. "Civil society is . . . the tremendous power which draws men into itself and claims from them that they work for it, owe everything to it, and do everything by its means."[32] The political revolution in France and the economic transformation unleashed in England were altering the social fabric of the human condition as such. Civil society is "the system of needs," and Hegel had no doubt that it was organized by the market. The end of the embedded economy marked the appearance of the totalizing commodity form:

> Originally the family is the subjective unit whose function it is to provide for the individual on his particular side by giving him either the means and the skill necessary to enable him to earn his living out of the resources of society, or else subsistence and maintenance in the event of his suffering a disability. But civil society tears the individual from his family ties, estranges the members of the family from one another, and recognizes them as self-subsistent persons. Further, for the paternal soil and the external inorganic resources of nature from which the individual formerly derived his livelihood, it substitutes its own soil and subjects the permanent existence of even the entire family to dependence on itself and to contingency. Thus the individual becomes a son of civil society which has as many claims upon him as he has rights against it.[33]

But civil society's totalizing power is also its fatal flaw. Any particular demand can be satisfied in the short run, but civil society constantly generates new ones. Its infinite multiplication of needs gives rise to the poverty that paralyzes it. Civil society constantly breeds inequality, and Hegel's discovery that poverty is the great problem it poses but cannot solve precipitated his turn toward the state. Civil society's paradoxical motion leads it from choice, self-interest, and autonomy to isolation, dependence, and subservience. Civil society creates "want and destitution" as part of its normal operation.[34] There is nothing natural about it, Adam Smith notwithstanding: "the need for greater comfort does not exactly arise within you directly; it is suggested to you by those who hope to make a profit from its creation."[35] Hegel was familiar with English and Scottish political economy, and his famous words about the inevitability of pauperism were rooted in the discovery that civil society produces fatal extremes of wealth and poverty:

> When the standard of living of a large mass of people falls below a certain subsistence level—a level regulated automatically as the one necessary for a member of the society—and when there is a consequent loss of the sense of right and wrong, of honesty and the self-respect which makes a man insist on maintaining himself by his own work and effort, the result is the creation of a rabble of paupers. At the same time this brings with it, at the other end of the social scale, conditions which greatly facilitate the concentration of disproportionate wealth in a few hands.[36]

The "system of needs" is a state of mutual dependence. The individual's work can no longer guarantee him that his needs will be met. In the end, civil society is an alienated, unfree, and unjust sphere, for a power alien to the individual and over which he has no control determines whether his needs will be fulfilled. Transformed into the negation of freedom by its own dynamic, civil society generates a uniquely dangerous mass of politicized and alienated poor people; "a rabble is created only when there is joined to poverty a disposition of mind, an inner indignation against the rich, against society, against the government, etc." Earlier social orders had been able to defend themselves with arguments drawn from God or nature, but the French Revolution had closed that path. "Against nature man can claim no right, but once society is established, poverty immediately takes the form of a wrong done to one class by another. The important question of how poverty is to be abolished is one of the most disturbing problems which agitate modern society."[37] Poverty in Hegel's civil society moved social theory past the political accomplishments of the French Revolution:

> When the masses begin to decline into poverty, (a) the burden of maintaining them at their ordinary standard of living might be directly laid on the wealthier classes, or they might receive the means of livelihood directly from other public sources of wealth (e.g. from the endowments of rich

hospitals, monasteries, and other foundations). In either case, however, the needy would receive subsistence directly, not by means of their work, and this would violate the principle of civil society and the feeling of individual independence and self-respect in its individual members. (b) As an alternative, they might be given subsistence indirectly through being given work, i.e. the opportunity to work. In this event the volume of production would be increased, but the evil consists precisely in an excess of production and in the lack of a proportionate number of consumers who are themselves also producers, and thus it is simply intensified by both of the methods (*a*) and (*b*) by which it is sought to alleviate it. It hence becomes apparent that despite an excess of wealth civil society is not rich enough, i.e. its own resources are insufficient to check excessive poverty and the creation of a penurious rabble.[38]

Civil society's inability to fully overcome the natural inequality of savagery limits its ethical potential. Its basis in particularity and egoism undermines the formal possibilities of liberty. As long as a general anarchy of interests prevails, excessive wealth will go hand in hand with excessive poverty. They culminate in what Hegel called "barbarism," a condition that exacerbates all the defects of nature and is the living negation of freedom. "Men are made unequal by nature, where inequality is in its element, and in civil society the right of particularity is so far from annulling this natural inequality that it produces it out of mind and raises it to an inequality of skill and resources, and even to one of moral and intellectual attainment."[39] Civil society cannot overcome nature because freedom requires more than liberation from the constraints of feudalism. Civil society cannot provide people with a self-determined ethical whole because its economic relations negate the possibilities of freedom in history. The anarchy of a sphere of self-serving proprietors cannot produce integration, rationality, universality, and freedom. A higher ethical category must be found from outside the market-driven logic of civil society.

Hegel's "state" is the ethical sphere of universality and integration that completes civil society's necessity and particularity. It is the final realization of Spirit in history because it is founded on freedom instead of coercion.[40] Its strength rests not on force but on its ability to organize rights, freedom, and welfare into a coherent whole that serves freedom because it is not driven by interest, "nor is its fundamental essence the unconditional protection and guarantee of the life and property of members of the public as individuals. On the contrary, it is that higher unity which even lays claim to this very life and property and demands its sacrifice."[41] The state is an ethical category because it reconciles civil society's antagonisms and embraces humankind's universal concerns in the broadest sense of the term.[42]

Individuals can be fully self-actualized and concretely free only if they are devoted to ends that are broader than their own immediate interests—indeed, beyond *anyone's* immediate interests. But civil society's pauperism makes this impossible, and the rational unity of Hegel's state is the locus of humanity's highest collective ends. It provides meaning because it harmonizes particular interests and completes the march of Spirit in history. It acts on individuals not through coercion or law but because it fulfills our rational nature on the highest level of our social connections to others. As the completion of the ethical moments of the family and civil society, then, the state fulfills because it stands apart. Its logic is different from that of civil society and its generality carries with it the objective requirements of moral progress. "If the state is confused with civil society, and if its specific end is laid down as the security and protection of property and personal freedom, then the interest of the individuals as such becomes the ultimate end of their association, and it follows that membership of the state is something optional. But the state's relation to the individual is quite different from this. Since the state is mind objectified, it is only as one of its members that the individual himself has objectivity, genuine individuality, and an ethical life. Unification pure and simple is the true content and aim of the individual, and the individual's destiny is the living of a universal life."[43] The individual is fulfilled in the state because it makes possible "the rational life of self-conscious freedom, the system of the ethical world."[44]

The state is more than a mechanism for keeping the peace, promoting the prince's interests, or protecting natural rights. It is not an artifice or convention but arises out of the very logic of civil society. The infinite multiplication of needs and the variety of ways in which individuals seek their own satisfaction "give rise to factors which are a common interest, and when one man occupies himself with these his work is at the same time done for all. The situation is productive too of contrivances and organizations which may be of use to the community as a whole. These universal activities and organizations of general utility call for the oversight and care of the public authority."[45] The universality of the state is the culmination of humanity's ethical development precisely because it stands as the living negation of civil society's antagonistic chaos. The elements of modernity that make for free and rational association must be liberated from private interests and submitted to an organizing power that stands above civil society's competition and antagonism. The state is an "independent and autonomous power" in which "the individuals are mere moments" in "the march of God in the world."[46] Its task of transcendence is the realization of a higher order of justice than that made possible by individual exchange:

> The differing interests of producers and consumers may come into collision with each other; and although a fair balance between them on the whole may be brought about automatically, still their adjustment also requires a control which stands above both and is consciously undertaken. The right to the exercise of such control in a single case (e.g. in the fixing of the prices of the commonest necessaries of life) depends on the fact that, by being publicly exposed for sale, goods in absolutely universal daily demand are offered not so much to an individual as such but rather to a universal purchaser, the public; and thus both the defense of the public's right not to be defrauded, and also the management of goods inspection, may lie, as a common concern, with a public authority.[47]

The ethical moment of the state is prepared in the family and civil society, but a gulf separates the endless needs and private rights of individuals from the universal interests of the broader ethical community.[48] The state rescues humankind by transforming civil society's dependence into interdependence. Its preservation of universality fulfills the ethical potential of civil society's individualism, guarantees autonomy, and safeguards freedom. "In contrast with the spheres of private rights and private welfare (the family and civil society), the state is from one point of view an external necessity and their higher authority; its nature is such that their laws and interests are subordinate to it and dependent on it. On the other hand, however, it is the end immanent within them, and its strength lies in the unity of its own universal end and aim with the particular interest of individuals, in the fact that individuals have duties to the state in proportion as they have rights against it."[49] The state makes the egoistic individual of civil society fit for civilization.

> The state is the actuality of concrete freedom. But concrete freedom consists in this, that personal individuality and its particular interests not only achieve their complete development and gain explicit recognition for their right (as they do in the sphere of the family and civil society) but, for one thing, they also pass over of their own accord into the interest of the universal, and, for another thing, they know and will the universal; they even recognize it as their own substantive mind; they take it as their end and aim and are active in its pursuit. The result is that the universal does not prevail or achieve completion except along with particular interests and through the co-operation of particular knowing and willing; and individuals likewise do not

live as private persons for their own ends alone, but in the very act of willing these they will the universal in the light of the universal, and their activity is consciously aimed at none but the universal end.[50]

In the family, reason was hidden behind feeling and sentiment; in civil society, it appeared as an instrument of individual self-interest. Only in the state does reason become conscious of itself and serve human liberation by making it possible for us to structure our action in accordance with our understanding of the common good. Hegel was confident that he had made Kant's ethics real because he had made them social; now a person "has rights as he has duties, and duties insofar as he has rights."[51] The state is the morally indispensable environment in which the individual can find freedom in conscious association with others. It provided Hegel with the social context that could ground Kant's subjective sense of moral duty and make humanity's moral life a true end in itself. "What the service of the state really requires is that men shall forgo the selfish and capricious satisfaction of their subjective ends; by this very sacrifice they acquire the right to find their satisfaction in, but only in, the dutiful discharge of their public functions. In this fact, so far as public business is concerned, there lies the link between universal and particular interests which constitutes both the concept of the state and its inner stability."[52] Only conscious public duty makes it possible for individual interest and egoism to serve universality and freedom. The state is the objective and necessary ethical sphere that is independent of all subjective wants, the inclusive sphere of conscious choice that transcends the family's biologic accident and civil society's arbitrary self-interest. Its universality allows it to guarantee freedom of personhood, moral subjectivity, family life, and social action. It preserves the family and civil society as it transcends them in commonality and universality. Civil society is made whole in the state.

Hegel's important contributions to theories of civil society allowed him to conceive it in radically different terms than his predecessors because of the presence of a market-constituted economic order composed of independent persons and their interests understood as distinct from the state. People are "bourgeois" in this civil society because they are oriented toward their private interests; but even if its logic is different, the state cannot exist apart from civil society. Hegel's World Spirit came to rest in the reactionary Prussian bureaucracy, but *The Philosophy of Right* was remarkably far-sighted for having been written in 1821. The nineteenth-century economic explosion lay in the future, and Hegel was not able to mount a comprehensive critique of existing social relations. It was enough for him to understand how the market distorts the moral potential of individual needs. The reconciliation of these interests lay in a universal structure that could attenuate the destructiveness of civil society's market processes. The full force of Hegel's insight that egoism and particularity cannot constitute freedom could not yet rest on a solid analysis of industrial production. Providing such a grounding fell to Karl Marx, and he developed it as he came to terms with Hegel's theory of civil society and the state.

The Politics of Social Revolution

It was Marx's critique of Hegel's theory of civil society and the state that led him to the 1848 *Communist Manifesto*. He began with the standard notion of a civil society organized around individual interest but soon encountered the limits of Hegel's attempt to theorize the state apart from the "system of needs." Even if civil society was constituted by necessity, competition, the division of labor, property, class, pauperism, and the like, Hegel had never brought political economy to bear on the production of social life. Marx came to understand Hegel's weakness early in his career, and his criticism yielded a materialist orientation that owed much to its statist roots even as it became grounded in the material processes of civil society.

Marx was not alone. European social theorists were beginning to raise "the social question" in light of the French Revolution's evident failure to eliminate economic inequality, and the wide variety of approaches testified to the newness and importance of the problem. The assorted socialists, communists, democrats, republicans, and anarchists who comprised the pre-Marxian left disagreed about much, but they were all trying to understand a new set of social problems and economic forces that seemed impervious to political solution.[53] Marx himself came to theoretical maturity during the 1840s, a period of rapid industrialization and political conflict that saw him reject Hegel's state as a false universal and move toward a materialist critique of social conditions.[54] Where the *Philosophy of Right* terminated in the Prussian state, Marx's criticism of Hegel would take him to the negation of civil society.

His early activity as a radical-democratic journalist quickly got him in trouble with the Prussian censors, and his first encounters with the state led him to question Hegel's hope that a selfless bureaucracy could articulate the public good. Arbitrary censorship and economic regulations favoring the already powerful made it impossible to conceptualize state power independently of civil society. Social "position" was supplanting "character" and "science" in a divided and backward Germany, and the bureaucracy was becoming the weapon of "one party against another" instead of serving as "a law of the state promulgated for all its citizens."[55] Much of Marx's early development was driven by his growing suspicion that the state could not do the job that Hegel had assigned it.

He decided that Hegel failed to understand the "real" relation between the state and civil society. "Family and civil society are the premises of the state; they are the genuinely active elements, but in speculative philosophy things are inverted."[56] Hegel's idealism had led him toward the integrative principle of the state, but Marx had learned an important lesson from his confrontation with the Prussian censors. "In the bureaucracy," he concluded, "the identity of state interest and particular private aim is established in such a way that *the state interest* becomes a *particular* private aim over against other private aims."[57] Civil society's network of particular material interests structured the state and seriously compromised its ability to serve as mankind's "ethical whole." The bureaucratic state could not be the agent of the universal ethical community. Marx's move to a materialist analysis would change theories of the state and civil society forever.

The occasion for his reconsideration was a dispute that had broken out within the German Left. The French Revolution had extended legal emancipation to the German areas administered by French law. The gains made by German Jews had been repealed after Waterloo, but by the early 1840s demands for equality were being raised in all the large towns of the Rhineland. In the course of the ensuing debate Bruno Bauer, a prominent Young Hegelian, staked out what seemed to be the most radical position on the matter: religious belief itself was the most important obstacle to progress. The problems faced by German Jews could not be resolved with political equality. Only emancipation from *all* religion could protect German democracy from feudal reaction.

Marx suggested that Bauer was missing the forest for the trees and hence could not penetrate deeply enough to solve "the Jewish question." Driving religion out of politics would not eliminate economic and political inequality. It was clear to Marx that the criticism of the German state had to be broadened because the problem with the state was deeper than its arbitrariness and authoritarianism. There was something fundamentally wrong with all statist approaches to civil society. Freedom of religion was important but insufficient. "The division of the human being into a *public man* and a *private man*, the *displacement* of religion from the state into civil society, this is not a stage of political emancipation but its completion; this emancipation therefore neither abolishes the *real* religiousness of man, nor strives to do so."[58] Underneath its apparent radicalism, Bauer's critique did not go far enough.

Marx's crucial discovery that civil society itself had to be democratized deepened Hegel's revelation of its totalizing power. Separating private affairs from politics freed the state from civil society, but it simultaneously liberated civil society from the state. If public life now functions independently of property, class, religion, and the like, it is no less true that property, class, and religion can develop independently of political influences. Their hold over human beings has not been weakened by their formal separation from politics; on the contrary, emptying civil society of direct political content has strengthened both spheres' motive forces. "The consummation of the Christian state is the state which acknowledges itself as a state and disregards the religion of its members. The emancipation of the state from religion is not the emancipation of the real man from religion."[59] Indeed, the separation of Church and state in America was the indispensable condition for its citizens' unprecedented political freedom and their equally unprecedented subordination to religion.

As powerful as it was, then, the French Revolution had not touched the foundations of bourgeois civil society. The "rights of man" encouraged people to pursue their private interest in isolation from, and in opposition to, all other competing members of civil society. "The right of man to liberty is based not on the association of man with man, but on the separation of man from man. It is the *right* of this separation, the right of the *restricted* individual, withdrawn into himself."[60] Given the power of newly liberated civil society's pull toward private interest, the political revolution meant that "the *state* can free itself from a restriction without man being *really* free of this restriction, that the state can be a free *state* without man being a *free man*."[61] Equality before the law, a secular political order, the right of divorce, and other political liberties were enormous accomplishments. But the limits of a formally democratic state only highlighted the importance of democratizing the civil society on which it rested.

Where Hegel theorized the state as freedom from the antagonisms of civil society, Marx's materialism led him to criticize the state as part of a more general criticism of civil society. As important an advance as political emancipation had been, a regime based on the protection of individual rights was not a sufficient condition for emancipation. "The sole bond holding them together," Marx said of civil society's individuals, "is natural necessity, need and private interest, the preservation of their property and their egoistic selves."[62] After all was said and done, the Revolution had established civil society as the basis of an entire social order and self-serving individuals as the basis of civil society. "Political emancipation was at the same time the emancipation of civil society from politics, from having even the *semblance* of a universal content. Feudal society was resolved into its basic element—*man*, but man as he really formed its basis—*egoistic* man. This *man*, the member of civil society, is thus the basis, the precondition, of the *political* state. He is recognized as such by this state in the rights of man."[63]

A liberated civil society killed Hegel's hope that the state could provide a universal ethical category. Limiting emancipation to political freedom and legal equality did not go far enough. "Hence man was not freed from religion, he received freedom of religion. He was not freed from property, he received freedom of property. He was not freed from the egoism of business, he received freedom to engage in business."[64] Hegel had correctly grasped the problem but, paradoxically, his statism was too weak for the task at hand. The rule of law and the moral state could not eliminate pauperism because the market processes of civil society that give rise to inequality are beyond direct political remedy. Marx concluded that Hegel's state was a false universal. "None of the so-called rights of man, therefore, go beyond egoistic man, beyond man as a member of civil society, that is, an individual drawn into himself, into the confines of his private interests and private caprice, and separated from the community."[65]

Marx's whole approach would be built on the important difference that separates "the radical revolution" which aims at "*general human* emancipation" from "the partial, the merely *political* revolution, the revolution which leaves the pillars of the house standing."[66] His crucial contribution was to make civil society itself the object of democratic activity. Liberation demands a comprehensive criticism and transformation of *all* existing relationships. Equality before the law and political revolution were yielding to social democracy and the transformation of civil society.

What is the agent of this "real, human emancipation"? Earlier democratic transformations had been led by a section of the population whose advanced position made it the embodiment of civil society's social relations. "No class of civil society can play this role," Marx observed, "without arousing a moment of enthusiasm in itself and in the masses, a moment in which it fraternizes and merges with society in general, becomes confused with it and is perceived and acknowledged as its *general representative*, a moment in which its demands and rights are truly the rights and demands of society itself; a moment in which it is truly the social head and the social heart. Only in the name of the general rights of society can a particular class lay claim to domination."[67] The bourgeoisie had been able to lead the struggle against feudalism because its demands for liberty and protection had acquired a general force across the entire social order. It had defended a young and still-vulnerable bourgeois civil society against the *ancien régime*, but Marx was beginning to call the very foundations of that civil society into question. The struggle for "human emancipation" could be led only by that section of the population whose conditions placed it in opposition to the entire existing order. Where should one look to find an agent of German emancipation?

> In the formation of a class with *radical* chains, a class of civil society which is not a class of civil society, an estate which is the dissolution of all estates, a sphere which has a universal character by its universal suffering and claims no *particular right* because no *particular wrong* but *wrong generally* is perpetrated against it; which can no longer invoke a *historical* but only a *human* title; which does not stand in any one-sided antithesis to the consequences but in an all-round antithesis to the premises of the German state; a sphere, finally, which cannot emancipate itself without emancipating itself from all other spheres of society and thereby emancipating all other spheres of society, which, in a word, is the *complete loss* of man and hence can win itself only through the *complete rewinning of man*. This entire dissolution of society as a particular estate is the *proletariat*.[68]

Hegel had looked to the state to integrate civil society from the outside. Marx looked at the constitutive processes of civil society itself and found the universal class there. History's emancipatory class is the propertyless proletariat, the living negation of civil society even though its labor is the foundation upon which the entire social order rests. Its appearance as the agent of emancipation signifies that democratizing bourgeois civil society is the same as abolishing it. "By proclaiming the *dissolution of the hitherto existing world order* the proletariat merely states the *secret of its own existence*, for it is in fact the dissolution of that world order. By demanding the *negation of private property*, the proletariat merely raises to the rank of a *principle of society* what society has made the principle of the *proletariat*, what, without its own cooperation, is already incorporated in it as the negative result of society."[69] The proletarian revolution is the negation of civil society and the consequent liberation of humanity, even if it was not yet clear what this might mean.

Marx's understanding of agency was dramatically different from that of his contemporaries on the European Left. The proletariat was no longer the largest, poorest, or most hard-working section of the population. It was lack of property that made the proletariat the subversive agent without whom civil society cannot exist. Marx would later define it more precisely as the class that sells its labor power, but for the moment its universality lay in its negation of civil society: "the emancipation of the workers contains universal human emancipation—and it contains this, because the whole of human servitude is involved in the relation of the worker to production, and all relations of servitude are but modifications and consequences of this relation."[70] Every social relation can be understood in relation to the proletariat's situation in civil society, the "real" grounding of history.[71]

By the time Marx and Engels wrote *The Communist Manifesto* in 1848, Marx had gone well beyond earlier theories. The criticism of Hegel's state had become the criticism of bourgeois civil society. "Merely political" emancipation had yielded to social revolution. This is what Marx meant in the "Tenth Thesis on Feuerbach" when he observed that "the standpoint of the old materialism is *civil* society; the standpoint of the new is *human* society, or ·associated humanity."[72] As powerful and comprehensive as the French Revolution had been, its demolition of feudalism was a precursor to a far more radical social revolution that would transform civil society *and* the state. "The condition for the emancipation of the working class is the abolition of all classes, just as the condition for the emancipation of the third estate, of the bourgeois order, was the abolition of all estates and all orders. The working class, in the course of its development, will substitute for the old civil society an association which will exclude classes and their antagonism, and there will be no more political power properly so-called, since political power is precisely the official recognition of antagonism in civil society."[73]

Marx's orientation toward concrete social conditions had been pulling him toward political economy since his earliest criticisms of Hegel. The more convinced he became that the state could not be comprehended apart from the material organization of civil society, the more important it was to understand the mediations between them. In one of his few instances of self-investigation, Marx connected his misgivings about Hegel to the appearance of *Capital*. "The first work which I undertook to dispel the doubts assailing me was a critical re-examination of the Hegelian philosophy of law. . . . My inquiries led me to the conclusion that neither legal relations nor political forms could be comprehended whether by themselves or on the basis of a so-called general development of the human mind, but that on the contrary they originate in the material conditions of life, the totality of which Hegel, following the example of English and French thinkers of the eighteenth century, embraces within the term 'civil society'; that the anatomy of this civil society, however, has to be sought in political economy."[74] His earlier theoretical critique of Hegel had to be supplemented by concrete investigation.

Capital is Marx's definitive analysis of the social relations of bourgeois civil society. It begins by identifying the point of departure and "dominant moment" of capitalism as resting in production. Classical political economy had treated production, consumption, distribution, and exchange as separate processes, but Marx was convinced that any social order could be understood as a "mode of production." The chaos of the market made it appear that civil society was shaped by a variety of unrelated economic processes. Marx's insight meant that all social relations were moments of production, no matter how independent they seemed.[75] "But in bourgeois society the commodity form of the product of labor—or the value form of the commodity—is the economic cell form."[76] The commodity form stands at the center of capitalism as a productive system, and *Capital* began at the beginning. "The wealth of those societies in which the capitalist mode of production prevails, presents itself as 'an immense accumulation of commodities,' its unit being a single commodity. Our investigation must therefore begin with the analysis of a commodity."[77]

If they are the "cell form" of civil society, commodities are more than simple articles of commerce. They are produced by people in historically defined circumstances, and they embody a specific set of social relations. To analyze a commodity is to uncover the social relations congealed in it, and Marx's celebrated discussion of the "fetishism of commodities" unmasked their social character. *Capital* revealed that a specific set of social relations are changing hands when commodities are being exchanged. The market mystifies these relations, and Marx set out to reveal what was hidden by the separation of the state from civil society.

> Since the producers do not come into social contact with each other until they exchange their products, the specific social character of each producer's labor does not show itself except in the act of exchange. In other words, the

labor of the individual asserts itself as a part of the labor of society, only by means of the relations which the act of exchange establishes directly between the products, and indirectly, through them, between the producers. To the latter, therefore, the relations connecting the labor of one individual with the rest appear, not as direct social relations between individuals at work, but as what they really are, material relations between persons and social relations between things.[78]

If commodities embody social relations and the market creates and organizes class relations, it does so according to the logic of wage labor, commodity production and exchange, profit maximization, and capital accumulation. Ferguson, Smith, and Hegel had sensed how powerful the market could be, but Marx demonstrated how it continually drives toward the endless multiplication of human needs that Hegel had identified as civil society's Achilles' heel. Its apparent simplicity masks its unprecedented totalizing power. The commodity form penetrates into every nook and cranny of civil society:

> This sphere that we are deserting, within whose boundaries the sale and purchase of labor-power goes on, is in fact a very Eden of the innate rights of man. There alone rule Freedom, Equality, Property and Bentham. Freedom, because both buyer and seller of a commodity, say of labor-power, are constrained only by their own free will. They contract as free agents, and the agreement they come to is, but the form in which they give legal expression to their common will. Equality, because each enters into relation with the others, as with a simple owner of commodities, and they exchange equivalent for equivalent. Property, because each disposes only of what is his own. And Bentham, because each looks only to himself. The only force that brings them together and puts them in relation with each other, is the selfishness, the gain and the private interests of each. Each looks to himself only, and no one troubles himself about the rest, and just because they do so, do they all, in accordance with the preestablished harmony of all things, or under the auspices of an all-shrewd providence, work together to their mutual advantage, for the common weal and in the interest of all.[79]

Marx's early criticism of Hegel had demonstrated that the state is shaped by civil society rather than the other way around. Social transformation and the abolition of civil society marked the path to "human emancipation," but it was not clear how the proletariat could accomplish its task. If the material processes of civil society are dominant and the state is little more than an epiphenomenon, was there any role for politics in "real, practical" emancipation?

The formal separation between state and civil society had permitted the rapid development of markets and the accompanying democratizing of the political order. But Marx knew that, as important as the distinction was, it was more apparent than real. Capital ruled politically as well as economically, and *Capital*'s account of enclosures, the factory laws, colonization, and the like left little doubt that state activity had been an indispensable condition for the expansion of civil society. The state may be an illusory community, but Marx appreciated the importance of politics very early in his career: "every class which is aiming at domination, even when its domination, as is the case with the proletariat, leads to the abolition of the old form of society in its entirety and of domination in general, must first conquer political power in order to represent its interest as the general interest, which in the first moment it is forced to do."[80] Nor was such a focus limited to a theory of revolution. Every effort to democratize civil society, from imposing democratic supervision on its market processes to abolishing or severely curtailing them, would require the application of state power. But the state itself had to be democratized, for the structure of political power expresses the way civil society is organized.

The formal separation of state and civil society and Marx's materialist criticism of Hegel notwithstanding, the struggle to abolish civil society would necessarily assume a political form. "Since the state is the form in which the individuals of a ruling class assert their common interests, and in which the whole civil society of an epoch is epitomized, it follows that all common institutions are set up with the help of the state and are given a political form."[81] Marxism has always privileged political action in the effort to democratize civil society, an orientation it has shared with most of the Left for a long time. Their different historic trajectories explain why liberalism and socialism conceive of the relationship between the state and civil society in such different ways, a dispute that lies behind much contemporary theory and practice.

The political revolutions that accompanied the transition to capitalism generally broke out after more or less finished forms of bourgeois civil society had slowly developed within the structures of feudalism. Wage labor, production for exchange, and the accumulation of capital had largely supplanted medieval property and production for use prior to feudalism's final political crises. This is why the fundamental task of bourgeois revolutions was breaking the political supremacy of the aristocracy. Since the basic structures of market relations were largely in place before political power passed to the bourgeoisie itself, its "open" and political revolution did little more than adjust a political structure to a largely transformed civil society.

The transition to socialism differs markedly from that of its predecessors because the foundations of the socialist order are absent from bourgeois society and cannot be generated within the boundaries of private property. Marx always held that the social relations of a classless society do not and cannot grow up spontaneously within capitalist social relations but develop only as part of the democratization of civil society itself. The use of state power was central to his theory of revolution because he saw it as the indispensable condition for a transformation of civil society that begins before the social and material conditions for its completion are in place. Hegel had located the active motor, the "real home," the positive moment of historical development in the state. Marx located the active motor, the "real home," the positive moment of bourgeois development in civil society. This is why he ended with the seizure and use of state power as the precondition to social revolution. Its apparent "victory" was the proletarian revolution's beginning:

> The first step in the revolution by the working class, is to raise the proletariat to the position of ruling class, to win the battle of democracy.
>
> The working class will use its political supremacy to wrest, by degrees, all capital from the bourgeoisie, to centralize all instruments of production in the hands of the State, i.e., of the proletariat organized as the ruling class; and to increase the total of productive forces as rapidly as possible.
>
> Of course, in the beginning, this cannot be effected except by means of despotic inroads on the rights of property, and on the conditions of bourgeois production; by means of measures, therefore, which appear economically insufficient and untenable, but which, in the course of the movement, outstrip themselves, necessitate further inroads upon the old social order, and are unavoidable as a means of entirely revolutionizing the mode of production.[82]

Bourgeois theories of revolution and democracy had developed as rights-based theories of weak government, suspicion of politics, and the conviction that the operations of the market were the surest guarantees of democracy, freedom, and equality in civil society. But Marx revealed civil society as a sphere of compulsion and reserved a central role to a powerful political apparatus to lead the attack on its social relations. Reducing the thrust of the commodity form would require state action in such areas as banking, labor, agriculture, communications, transportation, and education. A series of state interventions in civil society expressed the immediate political goals of the workers' movement and established the minimal conditions for its further development.[83] So would the more dramatic "abolition of the bourgeois relations of production, an abolition that can be effected only by a revolution."[84] The "ultimate results" of the workers' revolution may be social transformation, but its "immediate goal" is the seizure and use of state power. "Revolution in general—the *overthrow* of the existing power and *dissolution* of the old relationships—is a *political* act. But *socialism* cannot be realized without *revolution*. It needs this *political* act insofar as it needs *destruction* and *dissolution*. But where its *organizing activity* begins, where its *proper object*, its *soul*, comes to the fore—there socialism throws off the *political* cloak."[85] The connection between the politics of social revolution and the transformation of civil society revealed the contradictory imperatives of Marx's project:

> When, in the course of development, class distinctions have disappeared, and all production has been concentrated in the hands of a vast association of the whole nation, the public power will lose its political character. Political power, properly so called, is merely the organized power of one class for oppressing another. If the proletariat during its contest with the bourgeoisie is compelled, by the force of circumstances, to organize itself as a class, if, by means of a revolution, it makes itself the ruling class, and, as such, sweeps away by force the old conditions of production, then it will, along with these conditions, have swept away the conditions for the existence of class antagonisms and of classes generally, and will thereby have abolished its own supremacy as a class.
>
> In place of the old bourgeois society, with its classes and class antagonisms, we shall have an association, in which the free development of each is the condition for the free development of all.[86]

The "when" of this summary statement has proved enormously difficult. Marx knew that his project was a difficult one. Using the state as a tool to mitigate the damage inflicted by the market might hold matters in abeyance for the short run, but a deep contradiction lies at the heart of his view that civil society could be democratized by using state power against the market. It has always been unclear just how this could be accomplished, and the history of twentieth-century communism furnishes precious little positive guidance. If the state would eventually "wither away" with the transformation of civil society, as Engels famously claimed, how would this happen in the absence of individual interests and the rights that protect them? It was one thing to use the category of civil society as an analytic instrument for the study of capitalism. But Marxism is a theory of communism as much as a critique of capitalism, and it has been difficult to conceptualize the relation between state and society because it is never easy to discern a future that one imagines to be dramatically different from the present. Marx's vision of communism was limited because he never specified just what "human emancipation" meant. It is clear that the communist free association of producers is incompatible with civil society's alienation, powerlessness, and necessity. But "merely political" emancipation had allowed for the expression of civil society's multitudinous interests, and social revolution seemed to imply that such interests would no longer drive individual action or social structure. This has not been a crushing problem for Marxism understood as a critique of capitalism, but it remains central to a more ambitious project that has yet to adequately theorize a proletarian state or a post-bourgeois society, much less organize them.

Fratricidal children of the Enlightenment, Marxism and liberalism share modernity's theoretical differentiation between the state and civil society while retaining a sense of their connections. Marx accepted Hegel's desire to overcome the distinction and took his distance from liberal claims that a sharp distinction between the two spheres is a condition of freedom. He also brought one strand of modern theory to a temporary close. If civil society was constituted by economic processes and markets, it would not survive a socialist revolution. It was one thing to conceptualize a state that would moderate the effects of capitalism while preserving its basic structure and respecting civil society as a system of needs. But if abolishing inequality, poverty, and necessity required social revolution, then a powerful proletarian state had to act directly on a civil society by which it was no longer effectively constrained. In the end, abolishing civil society would imply much more than abolishing the market that lay at its core. The implications of this dilemma are at the heart of all contemporary politics—and not just those of the Left. But if "human emancipation" was not the issue, then civil society could be theorized as a mediating sphere of organization and association whose goal was to temper state power even as it left the market untouched and inequality unaddressed. It is to this second strand of modern thought that we now turn.

6

Civil Society and Intermediate Organizations

When premodern theorists of civil society considered economic affairs, they almost always treated them as threats to civil society. Considered by themselves, commerce and trade were thought to be destructive of the bonds that held social life together. Only when markets began to organize civil society was it possible to differentiate social or economic categories from political or religious ones. As we have seen, the first strand of modern thought concerning civil society conceptualized it as a market-organized sphere of necessity. This view came to a head with Karl Marx and continues to drive the Left's critique of capitalism. Marx drew his understanding of civil society from G. W. F. Hegel's analysis of "the system of needs," and Hegel had infused the public sphere with a much stronger notion of power than Immanuel Kant's "introversion" had made possible. Although they understood civil society in broad terms, Hegel and Marx agreed that class, production, interest, and competition lay at its core, and both men paid close attention to the processes by which it creates and distributes wealth.

But economics does not play a particularly important role in the second strand of modern thought. Rooted in aristocratic criticisms of royal absolutism, it describes civil society as an intermediate sphere of voluntary association and activity standing between the individual and the state. This view, which rests at the heart of much contemporary theory, is closely identified with the work of Alexis de Tocqueville, but its roots can be found in the Baron de Montesquieu's fear of modernity's centralizing monarchies, Jean-Jacques Rousseau's preference for an intimate small-scale republic, and Edmund Burke's attack on the French Revolution. All three came together in Tocqueville's remarkably influential body of thought, whose antistatist thrust and disregard of the material processes of civil society helps explain its contemporary popularity.

The Aristocratic Republic

Born in 1689, Montesquieu belongs to the first generation of Enlightenment thinkers. The writings of Thomas Hobbes, Isaac Newton, and John Locke were fresh and controversial, and the Glorious Revolution had provided a moderate alternative to Stuart absolutism. Like many of his contemporaries, Montesquieu was attracted to England because its tolerant and flexible social order seemed to have brought a century of upheaval to a close without falling into the extremes of despotism or anarchy. England had apparently accomplished everything that proponents of balanced government since Aristotle's time had hoped for. The division of society into the three estates of king, nobility, and people was mirrored in the institutions of Crown, Lords, and Commons. It appeared that the ancient dream of balancing monarchy, aristocracy, and democracy had been made concrete by combining the principles of the one, the few, and the many in a happy and judicious constitution. State and society were one; economic activity and political power mutually defined one another in an informal arrangement that worked to the benefit of all. The aristocracy had lost its dominant role but had not been destroyed, and its inherited property could still act as a buffer between the centralizing Crown and the unruly population.

Montesquieu's thinking took shape in a period dominated by the long struggle between aggressive French monarchies and aristocracies trying to retain their ancient privileges. Much more powerful than its English counterpart, the leveling Crown often enlisted the bourgeoisie and the people on its side by curbing the lords and subjecting aristocratic institutions to intense pressure. The French Crown tended to regard local privileges with hostility. Since the aristocracy's power rested on custom, the kings often forged temporary alliances with a nascent bourgeoisie that stood to gain from uniform market relations. Montesquieu saw this developing, and his desire to protect the nobility's *parlements*, courts, estates, and other organizations stands behind his important contribution to the second branch of modern thought.

The aristocracy had always justified its monopoly of the land by arguing that since its power and property were independent of both the will of the monarch and the passions of the crowd, it was the only estate that could mediate between them. It tended to appeal to the king by warning about the dangers of mob rule, and to the people by invoking the threat of royal despotism. Montesquieu was not interested in natural law or the social contract and based his argument on a notion of political virtue that could balance existing estates of the realm. England fascinated him throughout his life, and *The Spirit of the Laws* spoke for a whole generation of aristocratic thinkers who sought to apply British lessons to Continental conditions without relying on *a priori* assertions of natural rights whose existence could not be proven. Montesquieu's important contribution to modern theories of civil society is rooted in his defense of intermediate associations and his theory of a balanced constitution.

His political taxonomy followed ancient patterns. It distinguished between three forms of government: a republic, in which the people as a whole (democracy) or certain families (aristocracy) hold sovereign power; a monarchy, in which a prince holds power but exercises it according to established laws; and despotism, a lawless corruption of monarchy in which a prince governs alone according to his own whims or caprices. The distinction between monarchies and despotisms was the important one. Both forms are governed by a single prince, but stable monarchies are marked by a complicated gradation of intermediate institutions that makes possible the rule of law and reflects the "spirit" of honor. A prudent monarchy depends on the presence of intermediate organizations.

Despotisms are marked by an empty space between the sovereign and the people because the intermediate institutions that could deflect central power have been destroyed or tamed. Everyone becomes a slave of the royal will and is ruled by fear and lawless coercion. Despotism can best be described as monarchy without the aristocracy's intermediate bodies; "if you abolish the prerogatives of the lords, clergy, nobility, and towns in a monarchy, you will soon have a popular state or a despotic state."[1] Liberty requires that power be broken up and distributed by the institutions of an aristocratic republic:

> Intermediate, subordinate, and dependent powers constitute the nature of a monarchical government, that is, of the government in which one alone governs by fundamental laws. I have said intermediate, subordinate, and dependent powers; indeed, in a monarchy, the prince is the source of all political and civil power. These fundamental laws necessarily assume mediate channels through which power flows; for, if in the state there is only the momentary and capricious will of one alone, nothing can be fixed and consequently there is no fundamental law.
>
> The most natural, intermediate, subordinate power is that of the nobility. In a way, the nobility is the essence of monarchy, whose fundamental maxim is: *no monarch, no nobility; no nobility, no monarch*; rather, one has a despot.[2]

Montesquieu considered monarchies more stable than despotisms because their intermediate bodies enable them to forge mutually beneficial relationships between the king and the nobles.[3] This requires that political power be distributed according to status and wealth. At a time when civil society could not yet be theoretically distinguished from the economy or the state, "differences in rank, origin, and condition that are established in monarchical government often carry with them distinctions in the nature of men's goods, and the laws regarding the constitution of this state can increase the number of these distinctions."[4] A despot will always be unhappy with such a situation, but a wise monarch understands that preserving local privilege and social differences is essential to the health of the entire polity. "There must be privileges in governments where there are necessarily distinctions between persons. This further diminishes simplicity and produces a thousand exceptions."[5]

A monarch accepts the restrictions on his power imposed by a complex civil society, but a despot's realm is uniform and flat. "Despotism is self-sufficient; everything around it is empty. Thus when travelers describe countries to us where despotism reigns, they rarely speak of civil laws."[6] The despot is the private man elevated to public leadership; he cannot rule a stable kingdom because he knows only his own desires and cannot tolerate different centers of power. "The monarch, who knows each of his provinces, can set up various laws or permit different customs. But the despot knows nothing and can attend to nothing; he must approach everything in a general way; he governs with a rigid will that is the same in all circumstances; all is flattened beneath his feet."[7] Despotic power cannot be constrained by the "intermediate, subordinate, and dependent" associations whose roots lie outside the sphere of state action. "Just as the sea, which seems to want to cover the whole earth, is checked by the grasses and the smallest bits of gravel on the shore, so monarchs, whose power seems boundless, are checked by the slightest obstacles and submit their natural pride to supplication and prayer."[8] Despotic leveling is the great enemy of liberty and stability because it attacks the hierarchies that undergird moderate and responsible rule.

> Thus, when a man makes himself more absolute, his first thought is to simplify the laws. In these states he begins by being struck more by particular drawbacks than by the liberty of the subjects with which he is not concerned.
> One can see that there must be at least as many formalities in republics as in monarchies. In both governments, formalities increase in proportion to the importance given to the honor, fortune, life, and liberty of the citizens.

Men are all equal in republican government; they are equal in despotic governments; in the former, it is because they are everything; in the latter, it is because they are nothing.[9]

When Montesquieu defended liberty, he was talking about the nobility's hereditary property and established privileges. Like his contemporaries, he was no democrat. Indeed, their hostility to the aristocracy makes despotism and democracy twin threats to his understanding of freedom. The only solution is to organize "a society of societies," a federation of intermediate bodies that can serve liberty by constraining both executive power and mob violence. The mixed state thus formed would combine the civic virtue of a republic with the external power of a monarchy and protect against internal decay and foreign conquest. It would be as difficult for an aspiring despot to consolidate power across a wide expanse of existing organizations as it would be to organize sedition. Thus, the bodies at the base of the "federal republic" do more than control the king; they also structure the state by providing an alternative to the shapelessness of despotism and democracy. "This form of government," said Montesquieu, "is an agreement by which many political bodies consent to become citizens of the larger state that they want to form."[10] James Madison and Tocqueville would agree.

It was Montesquieu who first placed intermediate organizations at the center of civil society. Since the monarch's will can never be a dependable standard taken by itself, liberty requires "moderate governments" to curb ambition and power with the institutions of aristocratic privilege.[11] In an argument that Madison, Alexander Hamilton, and John Jay would use to defend bicameral legislatures, he observed that

> in a state there are always some people who are distinguished by birth, wealth, or honors; but if they were mixed among the people and if they had only one voice like the others, the common liberty would be their enslavement and they would have no interest in defending it, because most of the resolutions would be against them. Therefore, the part they have in legislation should be in proportion to the other advantages they have in the state, which will happen if they form a body that has the right to check the enterprises of the people, as the people have the right to check theirs.
>
> Thus, legislative power will be entrusted both to the body of the nobles and to the body that will be chosen to represent the people, each of which will have assemblies and deliberations apart and have separate views and interests.[12]

Liberty depends on the structure of the state in the last instance, and Montesquieu admired the English because he thought they had developed a system that preserved the material interests of the commons, the lords, and the king by balancing them against one another. Each order of the old regime could play a role in the new executive and legislative branches.[13] As essential as they are, secondary associations cannot safeguard liberty if they are unsupported by culture or unprotected by law. A substratum of "mores, manners, and received examples" work with a body of law to protect the integrity of civil society's "intermediate, subordinate, and dependent" bodies from the will of the sovereign and the appetites of the mob. Intermediate organizations embedded in what later analysts would call a "civic culture" constitute Montesquieu's civil society.[14]

It is no accident that England produced Adam Smith's political economy, and it is equally understandable that modernity's earliest theories of the state were developed in France. Alarmed by monarchy's tendency to go over to despotism, Montesquieu tried to protect local privilege with a ramified structure of intermediate organizations and a mixed constitution. He admired the English combination of free political institutions and commercial activity. Commerce encourages frugality, peace, regularity, planning—qualities that are essential to life in civil society. It creates centers of private privilege that work with political associations to moderate the arbitrariness of royal power. Taken together, aristocratic associations and commerce tend to create strong centers of interest that can resist central power and encourage peace and moderation.[15]

Montesquieu was not the first theorist of civil society to identify the interests of a particular class with those of the whole. He could not have imagined that both the nobility and the monarchy would be swept away by a democratic revolution that drew sustenance from ancient notions of the unitary moral community. For the moment, other thinkers would not be so sure that the baron had correctly identified the conditions of social health. After all, his penchant for intermediate associations was caught up with the interests of the aristocracy. Perhaps another tradition could be brought to bear.

Civil Society and Community

The Scottish Enlightenment's claim that civil society rested on an innate moral sensibility implied that social and political institutions were to be evaluated in light of their effect on the human capacity for ethical judgment and action. It was from the vantage-point of a moralized civil society that the Scots had assessed the impact of markets on social life, the responsibilities of the state, and the obligations of citizens. Suitably impressed with English liberty and Scottish moral economy, Montesquieu had tried to combine stability and virtue in a balanced constitution organized around intermediate associations. But his attempt came with a price.

Unwilling to protect the nobility, Jean-Jacques Rousseau built a moral theory of civil society whose root in community tried to adapt Roman virtue and Machiavellian republicanism to the spread of markets and the entrenched power of aristocrats and kings. His enormous impact on the French Revolution came from this fusion of the Scottish Enlightenment's individualistic moralism with the ancient commitment to disinterested public action and the common good. His entire worldview was animated by a simple but explosive claim: "man is naturally good, and it is entirely by his institutions that he is made wicked." But if civil society makes human beings evil, it alone can rescue them. Operating well within the boundaries of social contract theory, Rousseau's analysis of civil society began with a description of a hypothetical state of nature. It was not important to him whether the state of nature ever "really" existed; like others, Rousseau used the category as a way of talking about civil society.

Rousseau populated the state of nature with isolated and amoral individuals whose mutual indifference meant that they could do each other neither harm nor good. People in the state of nature lived for themselves and sought what was necessary for their individual self-preservation. In a peculiar way, their lack of social connections saved them. The pervasive insecurity that drove Hobbesian man to the violent subjugation of others was absent because people were not yet able to take account of others:

> Wandering in the forests, without industry, without speech, without domicile, without war and without liaisons, with no need of his fellow-man, likewise with no desire to harm them, perhaps never even recognizing anyone individually, savage man, subject to few passions and self-sufficient, had only the sentiments and intellect suited to that state; he felt only his true needs, saw only what he believed he had an interest to see; and his intelligence made no more progress than his vanity. If by chance he made some discovery, he was all the less able to communicate it because he did not recognize even his own children. Art perished with the inventor. There was neither education nor progress; the generations multiplied uselessly; and everyone always start-

ing from the same point, centuries passed in all the crudeness of the first ages; the species was already old, and man remained ever a child.[16]

Rousseau wanted to establish a basis for social life that did not depend on something as immutable as social instinct or as arbitrary as self-interest. He did not want to fall back on reason because its individualism seemed too insecure. Instead, he sought its source in human nature. There are two natural principles "anterior to reason," he declared: "one interests us ardently in our well-being and our self-preservation, and the other inspires in us a natural repugnance to see any sensitive being perish or suffer, principally our fellow-men."[17] His debt to the Scots shaped his view that a natural sense of sympathy is our only innate social disposition. It represents the social and moral potential of life in civil society, fulfills a state of nature composed of asocial and amoral people, tempers the potentially destructive effect of self-interest, and makes it possible for civil society to harmonize individual self-concern and the general interest. Natural man is prepared for civilization not by reason but because

> pity is a natural sentiment which, moderating in each individual the activity of love of oneself, contributes to the mutual preservation of the entire species. It carries us without reflection to the aid of those whom we see suffer; in the state of nature, it takes the place of laws, morals, and virtue, with the advantage that no one is tempted to disobey its gentle voice; it will dissuade every robust savage from robbing a weak child or an infirm old man of his hard-won subsistence if he himself hopes to be able to find his own somewhere. Instead of that sublime maxim of reasoned justice, *Do unto others as you would have them do unto you*, it inspires all men with this other maxim of natural goodness, much less perfect but perhaps more useful than the preceding one: *Do what is good for you with the least possible harm to others*. In a word, it is in this natural sentiment, rather than in subtle arguments, that we must seek the cause of the repugnance every man would feel in doing evil, even independently of the maxims of education. Although it may behoove Socrates and minds of his stamp to acquire virtue through reason, the human race would have perished long ago if its preservation had depended only on the reasonings of its members.[18]

"Man is born free, and everywhere he is in chains," Rousseau famously proclaimed. His disagreement with Hobbes and Locke on the nature of the social bond was an important one. It is not enough to unite individuals with coercion and the threat of overwhelming force, nor can self-interest and instrumental reason provide a sufficiently durable motivation for human association. Civil society is formed by individuals who are naturally free and potentially moral. It enables them to transcend their natural isolation by drawing on their desire for security and their disposition to sympathy. Anticipating Kant, who repeatedly acknowledged his debt to Rousseau, the Genevan asserted that civil society makes civilization possible because it rests on our capacity for autonomous moral judgment. "The social order is a sacred right that serves as a basis for all the others" because at bottom civil society is a moral association:

> There will always be a great difference between subjugating a multitude and governing a society. If scattered men, however many there may be, are successively enslaved by one individual, I see only a master and slaves; I do not see a people and its leader. It is an aggregation, if you wish, but not an association. It has neither public good nor body politic. That man, even if he had enslaved half the world, is nothing but a private individual. His interest, separate from that of the others, is still nothing but a private interest. If this same man dies, thereafter his empire is left scattered and without bonds, just as an oak tree disintegrates and falls into a heap of ashes after a fire has consumed it.[19]

Hobbes's "scattered agglomeration" can become a fully human association only if personal dependence is overcome in a higher order of social and moral life.[20] Drawing on Plato and the Scots, Rousseau replaced Hobbes's sovereign, Locke's natural rights, and Montesquieu's nobility with a moralized civil society that preserves autonomy by rooting it in a dense network of social interactions. If "the total alienation of each associate, with all his rights, to the whole community" is Rousseau's famous formulation of the social bond, it is also the description of a civil society that alone can remedy the defects of the natural state. Authority has moral worth only when individuals do not experience it as an alien, external, coercive power but voluntarily subject themselves to it. If Locke's "man" was fully formed before the transition to civil society, Rousseau's "savage" became a moral being *in* civil society. This required the renunciation of "natural independence" for something more enriching and secure, for the free personality can come into existence only in close proximity to others. Civil society substitutes internalized moral duty for blind nature and arbitrary coercion as the basis for human association. It makes possible a new, and properly human, moral order:

> The passage from the state of nature to the civil state produces a remarkable change in man, by substituting justice for instinct in his behavior and

giving his actions the morality they previously lacked. Only then, when the voice of duty replaces physical impulse and right replaces appetite, does man, who until that time only considered himself, find himself forced to act upon other principles and to consult his reason before heeding his inclinations. Although in this state he deprives himself of several advantages given him by nature, he gains such great ones, his faculties are exercised and developed, his ideas broadened, his feeling ennobled, and his whole soul elevated to such a point that if the abuses of this new condition did not often degrade him beneath the condition he left, he ought ceaselessly to bless the happy moment that tore him away from it forever, and that changed him from a stupid, limited animal into an intelligent being and a man.[21]

If civil society is the source of both our chains and our freedom, Rousseau found its paradoxical outline in each individual's acknowledgment of total dependence on a community of moral equals. This makes personal dependence a thing of the past and ushers in a reign of freedom; "as each gives himself to all, he gives himself to no one; and since there is no associate over whom one does not acquire the same right one grants him over oneself, one gains the equivalent of everything one loses, and more force to preserve what one has."[22] The moral bond between individual and community found expression in Rousseau's "general will" and expressed the old republican notion that the common good constitutes civil society by providing each individual with a socialized inner sense of moral duty. Neither majority rule nor royal power, the general will is the political expression of the common good and provides the moral link between individual and community.

Rousseau believed that classical liberalism could not explain the moral process by which human beings become human beings in civil society. The Hobbesian and Lockean contracts created states but not civil societies because they could do no more than facilitate the mutual pursuit of self-interest. But civil society has to be constituted by something more durable than a mechanism to enforce contracts and defend property. Rousseau was not particularly demanding about its form, thinking of it as any community guided by the general will and ruled by law. Every legitimate government is a republic in which "the public interest governs and the commonwealth really exists."[23] Most important is his conviction that moral freedom cannot be exercised against others but can be realized only in and through a social life organized according to the objective requirements of the general will. "For if some rights were left to private individuals, there would be no common superior who could judge between them and the public."[24] In the absence of a compelling sense of shared moral duty, competition will always drive each individual to regard every other individual as his instrument, and the strong will always reduce the weak to the personal dependence and poverty that make human life, civil society, and moral community impossible. Human beings gained nothing by moving to civil society if the common interest is nothing more than a "social contract" by which all agree to follow their interests and stand out of the way so others can do the same. Grafting Hobbes's state or Smith's market onto the state of nature could not make for a moral life worthy of human beings.

Rousseau's social contract, then, was not designed to preserve natural man. It was designed to wrench him out of the state of nature and make him fully human. It established civil society as a moral association of individuals who participate fully in the political life of the community. "Instantly, in place of the private person of each contracting party, this act of association produces a moral and collective body, composed of as many members as there are voices in the assembly, which receives from this very same act its unity, its common *self,* its life, and its will."[25] Everyone has the capacity to be an independent moral agent, and Rousseau knew that every life is endowed with a special kind of value and dignity. In its present corrupt state, civil society makes it impossible for people to realize their full potential. *The Social Contract* called for a community organized around the general will because the good of the whole makes it possible for each individual to realize his deepest and truest aims. Only an orientation toward universality can enable individuals to organize their unstable private interests. The general will protects individuals and the community from the narrow destructiveness of particularism, mistrust, intolerance, prejudice, and exclusion. It provides the mediations between individual and community that enable personal goals and common interests to serve one another.

Rousseau's politicized and moralized theory of civil society summarized his attack on enlightened self-interest and the rational calculation of advantage. Civil society is more than an association whose value is the range of opportunities for advantage it offers its individual members. Its general will makes it possible for citizens to translate their private interests into general rules that become binding. Like other social contract theorists, Rousseau knew that people have individual desires. The problem was keeping civil society from tearing itself to pieces, and this is why he sought to connect its individuals with the binding moral connections that forge an identity between part and whole. This is accomplished with a general will that achieves moral force when it transcends the pull of temporary advantage and is expressed politically. "It is not good for him who makes the laws to execute them, nor for the body of people to turn its attention away from general considerations to particular objects," Rousseau said. "Nothing is more dangerous than the influence of private interests on public affairs; and the abuse of laws by the government is a lesser evil than the corruption of the legislator, which is the inevitable result of private considerations."[26] Rousseau's attempt to marry Plato to Machiavelli enabled him to identify a fatal weakness in liberal theories of civil society: without a commitment to publicness and a political understanding of morality, market society was little better than Hobbes's war of all against all. The human capacity for moral choice requires the constant presence and public activity of others. It is no wonder that Kant found inspiration in Rousseau.

> The better constituted the State, the more public affairs dominate private ones in the minds of the citizens. There is even less private business, because since the sum of common happiness furnishes a larger portion of each individual's happiness, the individual has less to seek through private efforts. In a well-run City, everyone rushes to assemblies. Under a bad government, no one likes to take even a step to go to them, because no one takes an interest in what it is done there, because it is predictable that the general will won't predominate, and finally because domestic concerns absorb everything. Good laws lead to the making of better ones; bad laws bring about worse ones. As soon as someone says what do I care? about the affairs of the State, the State should be considered lost.[27]

If civil society can betray moral freedom by connecting people through ties of personal dependence, it also contains the solution to that betrayal. Rousseau's paradoxical attempt to guarantee personal independence by fusing it with objective social welfare precipitated his often misunderstood claim that "the general will is always right and always tends toward the public utility."[28] Only the frank recognition of complete and compelling mutual dependence can create a moral community supported by the best traditions of civil republicanism. Rousseau's well-known fear that private concerns, factions, and partial associations would destroy civil society was rooted in his conviction that only a relatively small, unitary, and intimate community could provide the appropriate grounding for the politics of moral duty. The larger the state and the more interests comprised by civil society, the more likely will its individual members orient themselves to their private concerns. Such a situation was profoundly troubling to Rousseau, who clearly and unambiguously articulated the classic republican view that private interests tend to drive against the general will and the common good. Public welfare cannot arise from any network of partial associations:

> If, when an adequately informed people deliberates, the citizens were to have no communication among themselves, the general will would always result from the large number of small differences, and the deliberation would always be good. But when factions, partial associations at the expense of the whole, are formed, the will of each of these associations becomes general with reference to its members and particular with reference to the State. One can say, then, that there are no longer as many voters as there are men, but merely as many as there are associations. The differences become less numerous and produce a result that is less general. Finally, when one of these associations is so big that it prevails over all the others, the result is no longer a sum of small differences, but a single difference. Then there is no longer a general will, and the opinion that prevails is merely a private opinion.[29]

Rousseau's hostility to factions and intermediate associations marked his decisive break with Montesquieu. The general will was the vehicle of independence and civilization precisely because it is general, extensive, and abstract. Neither the general will nor the law can address individual, particular cases. Uniformity makes morality possible, and Rousseau took his distance from Montesquieu's desire to protect local differences and aristocratic privilege. "Given this idea, one sees immediately that it is no longer necessary to ask who should make the laws, since they are acts of the general will; nor whether the prince is above the laws, since he is a member of the State; nor whether the law can be unjust, since no one is unjust toward himself; nor how one is free yet subject to the laws, since they merely record our wills."[30] Rousseau's search for a general and compelling moralizing agency led him to the general will and the political community as the highest expression of civil society. "The more the social bond stretches, the looser it becomes, and in general a small state is proportionately stronger than a large one."[31] A civil society of free public citizens is a small and intimate community whose moralizing power is uncompromised by factions or intermediate associations. Sovereignty is a direct attribute of the entire community and can be neither divided nor represented.

Rousseau articulated one of the most powerful challenges to the private concerns and partial associations of liberal theory and pre-Revolutionary French society. An Enlightenment enemy of the *ancien régime*'s hierarchy, customs, and obscurantism, he was also a critic of his colleagues' single-minded reliance on reason and individual interest. "What will become of virtue when one must get rich at any price?" he asked. "Ancient thinkers incessantly talked about morals and virtue. Those of our time talk only of business and money."[32] Civil society could not survive the application of reason to the unlimited pursuit of self-interest. It civilizes human beings because it removes them from personal dependence on others, and it does so by making them entirely dependent on the abstract community. It is their home precisely because "the general will, to be truly such, should be general in its object as well as in its essence; that it should come from all to apply to all; and that it loses its natural rectitude when it is directed toward any individual, determinate object."[33] Civil society's mutualism, solidarity, reciprocity, and impersonal dependence provided the antidote to modernity's instrumental reason and calculating efficiency. Such a view drove against partial associations, factions, and mediation. Rousseau echoed Montesquieu's view that freedom was defined locally and knew that people had private interests, but he left an empty space between political authority and the citizen which he hoped to fill with the liberating chains of a moral community. Such a conception raised just as many questions as it addressed. Perhaps such a community was not enough. Perhaps the general will needed further determination.

The Customs of Civil Society

Edmund Burke's conservative attack on Rousseau and the French Revolution came from his fear that leveling, centralization, and equality could not help but destroy civil society.[34] Experience demonstrated to him that arbitrary schemes hatched in the brains of would-be Saviors of Humanity could not substitute for the active, living social forces that make up civil society. Disaster awaits any attempt to impose arbitrary ideological categories on a recalcitrant social structure. History and customs will win out in the end.

Attacking the theory and practice of democratic leveling and popular sovereignty, Burke attributed the Revolution's violence to its assault on the creative and regenerative capacity of civil society. The best intentions in the world cannot create a new order. As soon as their recklessness took them outside the historical and customary limits of moderate reform, the French had no choice but to drift into an assault on civilization itself. The British, by contrast, had understood the power of custom and history, and the Glorious Revolution had respected the traditional customs, practices, and institutions from which all liberty comes.

If Montesquieu relied on the aristocracy to defend freedom and Rousseau located civil society in a community, Burke looked to the past. History and usage establish a delicate balance among the elements of any constitution, and it is wise not to meddle with them. "The engagement and pact of society, which generally goes by the name of the constitution, forbids such invasion and such surrender. The constituent parts of a state are obliged to hold their public faith with each other and with all those who derive any serious interest under their engagements, as much as the whole state is bound to keep its faith with separate communities. Otherwise competence and power would soon be confounded and no law be left but the will of a prevailing force."[35] Montesquieu had identified a deep wellspring of liberty. Customs endure because they preserve a balance among the historically grounded elements of civil society. Prudence demands that history's lessons be heeded.

Burke's emphasis on the integrating power of custom explains why he was not particularly worried about faction or conflict. Social peace demands preserving existing centers of power. Having studied Montesquieu, he rebuked the French for abandoning the aristocratic institutions that had contained the masses and held the monarchy in check. They should have taken English events to heart and built on the foundations left them by their ancestors. With some modest modifications, the *ancien régime*'s political and social institutions were perfectly adequate instruments for the country. "Through that diversity of members and interests, general liberty had as many securities as there were separate views in the several orders, whilst, by pressing down the whole by the weight of a real monarchy, the separate parts would have been prevented from warping, and starting from their allotted places."[36] Civil society is constituted by complementary relationships among social groups whose mutual compatibility has deep historical roots. No good can come from misplaced ambition. History cannot be trampled underfoot or reshaped in the name of any ideology. Stability, order, tradition, custom, property, and religion constitute the foundations of any stable civil society. They are constituted and defended by the same intermediate institutions that Montesquieu had identified, Rousseau had ignored, and the Revolution had destroyed.

> From Magna Charta to the Declaration of Right it has been the uniform policy of our constitution to claim and assert our liberties as an *entailed inheritance* derived to us from our forefathers, and to be transmitted to our posterity—as an estate specially belonging to the people of this kingdom, without any reference whatever to any more general or prior right. By this means our

constitution preserves a unity in so great a diversity of its parts. We have an inheritable crown, an inheritable peerage, and a House of Commons and a people inheriting privileges, franchises, and liberties from a long line of ancestors.[37]

None of this was a monopoly of the English. "You had all these advantages in your ancient states," Burke told the French, "but you chose to act as if you had never been molded into civil society and had everything to begin anew. You began ill, because you began by despising everything that belonged to you."[38] The root of the error lay in the Revolution's contempt for history and custom. Its leaders substituted abstract categories for the possibilities that existing institutions made available, and the results could only be disastrous. If they had taken the time to look around, the French would have seen that social leveling runs counter to nature and can only pervert the natural order of things; the "true moral equality of mankind" lies in a "protected, satisfied, laborious, and obedient people" understanding that hierarchy makes virtue possible. But the French allowed themselves to be driven by "that monstrous fiction which, by inspiring false ideas and vain expectations into men destined to travel in the obscure walk of laborious life, serves only to aggravate and embitter that real inequality which it can never remove, and which the order of civil life establishes as much for the benefit of those whom it must leave in a humble state as those whom it is able to exalt to a condition more splendid, but not more happy."[39] Civil society is constituted by inequality.

> But now all is to be changed. All the pleasing illusions which made power gentle and obedience liberal, which harmonized the different shades of life, and which, by a bland assimilation, incorporated into politics the sentiments which beautify private society, are to be dissolved by this new conquering empire of light and reason. All the decent trapery of life is to be rudely torn off. All the superadded ideas, furnished from the wardrobe of a moral imagination, which the heart owns and the understanding ratifies as necessary to cover the defects of our naked, shivering nature, and to raise into dignity in our own estimation, are to be exploded as a ridiculous, absurd, and antiquated fashion.[40]

The Enlightenment was the issue. Its universalism and aggressiveness pitted it against the private privileges and public inequalities that sustain civil society. If this continued, warned Burke, "the commonwealth itself would, in a few generations, crumble away, be disconnected into the dust and powder of individuality, and at length dispersed to all the winds of heaven."[41]

Inequalities between different classes of men have received institutional expression for many years and must be respected by prudent leaders. Legislation must "furnish to each description such force as might protect it in the conflict caused by the diversity of interests that must exist and must contend in all complex society" because any attempt to impose a politically derived uniformity on a differentiated civil society is a prescription for disaster.[42] Only a frank recognition that inequality stabilizes social relations could enable France's intermediate institutions to protect civil society from the Crown and the mob. No matter how much they needed reform, Burke said of the *ancien régime's parlements* and courts, they embodied longevity and independence. Appointed by the monarch, they were largely outside his control because they sat for life and rested on aristocratic laws of inheritance. This independence meant that they could resist "arbitrary innovation" by protecting property, tradition, and stability against king and people.[43] If they had not been destroyed in the recklessness of revolution, they could have been "one of the balances and correctives to the evils of a light and unjust democracy."[44] Montesquieu was right; differences in quality were more important than considerations of "substance and quantity." Intermediate organizations could preserve civil society by defending its diverse roots.

Montesquieu crafted his defense of intermediate organizations to limit the power of the king. Burke adapted it to attack the French Revolution in the name of custom, tradition, and local power. Rousseau's civil society politicized the Scottish concern with moral community by adding important elements from the ancient tradition of civic republicanism. It fell to Alexis de Tocqueville to adapt all three to modern conditions of democracy and equality. His theory of civil society as the nonstate sphere of intermediate associations arose from his assessment of French history and American democracy. Founded on localism and the politics of interest, it stands with Marxism at the heart of all contemporary theories of civil society.

American Lessons

"Among the novel objects that attracted my attention during my stay in the United States," wrote Tocqueville in 1835, "nothing struck me more forcibly than the general equality of condition among the people." Addressing himself to his fellow Frenchmen, the young aristocrat resolved to explain "the prodigious influence that this primary fact exercises on the whole course of society" because he was convinced that Europe was destined to be shaped by the same forces that he discerned in America.[45] He was equally convinced that it was time to put the past to rest and understand the opportunities and dangers that economic equality presented in politics and civil society alike. "I soon perceived that the influence of this fact extends far beyond the political character and the laws of the country, and that it has no less effect on civil society than on the government," he continued.[46] Explicitly locating civil society "beyond the political character and the laws of the country" and outside "the government," Tocqueville would craft his very influential understanding of it as a sphere of mediating organizations between the individual and the state. In so doing, he adapted Montesquieu to post-Revolutionary conditions of economic equality and political democracy.

The first thing that struck Tocqueville about America was the weakness of the state. His explanation made one of the first distinctions between a "strong society, weak state" America and "strong state, weak society" Europe that has had such a powerful influence on contemporary theorizing. The lack of an entrenched feudal tradition and concomitant absence of an *ancien régime*, the scarcity of great cities and consequent importance of local municipalities, the relative absence of a bureaucracy and accompanying tradition of decentralization, geographical isolation and the absence of a large standing army—all these factors, especially when combined with broad social equality, a culture of self-reliance, and a low level of class conflict, explained why America had not developed the powerful state tradition that marked Continental history. "Nothing is more striking to a European traveler in the United States than the absence of what we call the government, or the administration. Written laws exist in America, and one sees the daily execution of them; but although everything moves regularly, the mover can nowhere be discovered. The hand that directs the social machine is invisible."[47] Like Adam Smith, Tocqueville wanted to identify this "hand." Unlike Smith, he directed his attention away from the economy and toward culture. The consequences of his choice are still with us.

This orientation led him to his famous description of municipal life and its culmination in the town meeting. The "life and mainspring" of American liberty was "the intervention of the people in public affairs, the free voting of taxes, the responsibility of the agents of power, personal liberty, and trial by jury"—practices that exist only imperfectly in Europe but are "recognized and established by the laws of New England."[48] The Americans had combined Athenian democracy and traditional republicanism in the towns, the first organized forms of political life in the New World. Tocqueville's reading of Montesquieu informed his homage to local municipal institutions:

> In New England, townships were completely and definitely constituted as early as 1650. The independence of the township was the nucleus around which the local interests, passions, rights, and duties collected and clung. It gave scope to the activity of a real political life, thoroughly democratic and republican. The colonies still recognized the supremacy of the mother country; monarchy was still the law of the state; but the republic was already established in every township.
>
> The towns named their own magistrates of every kind, assessed themselves, and levied their own taxes. In the New England town the law of representation was not adopted; but the affairs of the community were discussed, as at Athens, in the marketplace, by a general assembly of the citizens.[49]

New England's municipalities mediated between the people and broader political institutions by representing local interests.[50] Their strong links to the population provided institutionalized patterns of self-government, and their provincialism domesticated the democratic state. They were perfectly structured to channel and tame popular participation, for "the township, at the center of the ordinary relations of life, serves as a field for the desire of public esteem, the want of exciting interest, and the taste for authority and popularity; and the passions that commonly embroil society change their character when they find a vent so near the domestic hearth and the family circle."[51] Local municipalities could defend liberty without going over to democratic excess precisely because of their narrow horizons:

> The native of New England is attached to his township because it is independent and free; his co-operation in its affairs ensures his attachment to its interests; the well-being it affords him secures his affection; and its welfare is the aim of his ambition and of his future exertions. He takes a part in every occurrence in the place; he practices the art of government in the small sphere within his reach; he accustoms himself to those forms without which liberty can only advance by revolutions; he imbibes their spirit; he acquires a taste for order, comprehends the balance of powers, and collects clear practical notions on the nature of his duties and the extent of his rights.[52]

The French Revolution's centralized state would never be appropriate in America because such a state's love of regularity, predictability, and routine makes it impotent when compared to a vibrant culture of local activity. "However enlightened and skillful a central power may be," Tocqueville declared, "it cannot of itself embrace all the details of the life of a great nation.

Such vigilance exceeds the powers of man. Its force deserts it when society is to be profoundly moved, or accelerated in its course; and if once the cooperation of private citizens is necessary to the furtherance of its measures, the secret of its impotence is disclosed."[53] The counterpoints to French centralism were strong local institutions supported by an individualistic and parochial culture that safeguarded liberty by constraining state power and keeping people close to home.

Local self-rule was perfectly suited to an American culture of self-reliance; "everyone is the best judge of what concerns himself alone, and the most proper person to supply his own wants. The township and the county are therefore bound to take care of their special interests; the state governs, but does not execute the law."[54] Americans look to themselves and their neighbors and ask for public assistance only when private initiatives fail. Their tradition of localism, the habits that come with political freedom, and a culture of self-reliance made it easy for the intermediate organizations of American civil society to represent the population's concerns to the state. This made it unique. "In no country in the world has the principle of association been more successfully used or applied to a greater multitude of objects than in America. Besides the permanent associations which are established by law under the names of townships, cities, and counties, a vast number of others are formed and maintained by the agency of private individuals."[55]

Tocqueville's culturally driven notion of American civil society attached a profoundly individualistic people to the general welfare in conditions of widespread social equality. His approach was radically different from Rousseau's. Free institutions, the rule of law, and freedom of association were essential if equality, democracy, and solidarity were to be reconciled. "Feelings and opinions are recruited, the heart is enlarged, and the human mind is developed only by the reciprocal influence of men upon one another. I have shown that these influences are almost null in democratic countries; they must therefore be artificially created, and this can only be accomplished by associations."[56] The American disposition to form voluntary organizations distinguished her from Europe and allowed her to avoid both state leveling and aristocratic privilege.

> Americans of all ages, all conditions, and all dispositions constantly form associations. They have not only commercial and manufacturing companies, in which all take part, but associations of a thousand other kinds, religious, moral, serious, futile, funereal or restricted, enormous or diminutive. The Americans make associations to give entertainments, to found seminaries, to

build inns, to construct churches, to diffuse books, to send missionaries to the antipodes; in this manner they found hospitals, prisons, and schools. If it is proposed to inculcate some truth or foster some feeling by the encouragement of a great example, they form a society. Wherever at the head of some new undertaking you see the government in France, or a man of rank in England, in the United States you will be sure to find an association.[57]

Voluntary associations fuse personal interest and the common good, and this explains why Tocqueville was so impressed by Americans' energy and intensity—especially when contrasted with Europeans' love of routine, uniformity, and moderation. "In no country in the world do the citizens make such exertions for the common weal. I know of no people who have established schools so numerous and efficacious, places of public worship better suited to the wants of the inhabitants, or roads kept in better repair. Uniformity or permanence of design, the minute arrangement of details, and the perfection of administrative system must not be sought for in the United States; what we find there is the presence of a power which, if it is somewhat wild, is at least robust, and an existence checkered with accidents, indeed, but full of animation and effort."[58] Echoing Montesquieu and Madison, Tocqueville hoped that civil society would serve liberty by diluting the influence of any single interest, weakening the majority, and guarding against the excesses of the very democracy that stimulated their appearance.[59] He drew on his observations to derive a general rule that could safeguard liberty in a democratic age:

> There are no countries in which associations are more needed to prevent the despotism of faction or the arbitrary power of a prince than those which are democratically constituted. In aristocratic nations the body of the nobles and the wealthy are in themselves natural associations which check the abuses of power. In countries where such associations do not exist, if private individuals cannot create an artificial and temporary substitute for them I can see no permanent protection against the most galling tyranny; and a great people may be oppressed with impunity by a small faction or by a single individual.[60]

Tocqueville never paid much attention to economic matters; his few references to the disintegrative influence of commerce were limited to cursory observations about its effects on association. His genius lay in his ability to contain equality, localism, and materialism in a greatly expanded notion of civil society. He attributed America's focus on material wealth to its democratic social structure, which was also the root of the people's unique propensity to associate. He also agreed with Locke, Montesquieu, and Madison that commerce could serve liberty by creating multiple centers of power in civil society. "I do not know if a single trading or manufacturing people can be cited, from the Tyrians down to the Florentines and the English, who were not a free people also. There is therefore a close bond and necessary relation between these two elements, freedom and productive industry."[61] But the pursuit of wealth in American conditions could also divide. "When social conditions are equal," he said, "every man is apt to live apart, centered in himself and forgetful of the public."[62] Tocqueville was acutely aware that the Americans were in uncharted waters. The prescribed legal and contractual codes, norms of social cohesion, hierarchical structures, and habits of deference that had structured medieval society were irrelevant in America and disappearing from Europe. Burke's complaints notwithstanding, the Enlightenment had won. The members of a democratic commercial republic have no essential ties to one another; each being the equal of all, no one is obligated to anyone else except when his own interests are at stake. Tocqueville was all the more impressed with Americans because he knew that civil society is difficult to create out of such raw materials. "It must be acknowledged that equality, which brings great benefits into the world, nevertheless suggests to men . . . some very dangerous propensities. It tends to isolate them from one another, to concentrate every man's attention upon himself; and it lays open the soul to an inordinate love of material gratification."[63] Left to itself, equality produces a society of strangers; "not only does democracy make every man forget his ancestors, but it hides his descendants and separates his contemporaries from him; it throws him back forever upon himself alone and threatens in the end to confine him entirely within the solitude of his own heart."[64]

This made it all the more important for civil society to provide the principles of association that are not spontaneously generated by politics or commerce. "The Americans have combatted by free institutions the tendency of equality to keep men asunder, and they have subdued it," Tocqueville announced.[65] Voluntary association can stimulate citizen activity and connect individual interest to the welfare of the community. Local control over public matters bring the lessons of Athenian democracy and classic republicanism to the egalitarian conditions of modern life. Tocqueville's voluntary activity replaced Rousseau's moral community.

> It is difficult to draw a man out of his own circle to interest him in the destiny of the state, because he does not clearly understand what influence the destiny of the state can have upon his own lot. But if it is proposed to

make a road cross the end of his estate, he will see at a glance that there is a connection between this small public affair and his greatest private affairs; and he will discover, without its being shown to him, the close tie that unites private to general interest. Thus far more may be done by entrusting to the citizens the administration of minor affairs than by surrendering to them in the control of important ones, towards interesting them in the public welfare and convincing them that they constantly stand in need of one another in order to provide for it. A brilliant achievement may win for you the favor of a people at one stroke; but to earn the love and respect of the population that surrounds you, a long succession of little services rendered and of obscure good deeds, a constant habit of kindness, and an established reputation for disinterestedness will be required. Local freedom, then, which leads a great number of citizens to value the affection of their neighbors and of their kindred, perpetually brings men together and forces them to help one another in spite of the propensities that sever them.[66]

The antistatist core of Tocqueville's preference for voluntary activity rests at the heart of much contemporary fascination with civil society, but for the moment his argument was a pragmatic one. "A government might perform the part of some of the largest American companies, and several states, members of the Union, have already attempted it; but what political power could ever carry on the vast multitude of lesser undertakings which the American citizens perform every day, with the assistance of the principle of association?" he asked. A more complicated and interdependent future would only intensify the problem. "It is easy to foresee that the time is drawing near when man will be less and less able to produce, by himself alone, the commonest necessaries of life. The task of the governing power will therefore extend it every day. The more it stands in the place of associations, the more will individuals, losing the notion of combining together, require its assistance; these are causes and effects that unceasingly create each other. Will the administration of the country ultimately assume the management of all the manufactures which no single citizen is able to carry on?"[67] The lessons taught by American social structure, culture, and history could be generalized. Montesquieu's critique of royal despotism was never far from Tocqueville, who drew on it to write a manifesto of civil society that lies at the center of almost all contemporary theorizing:

A government can no more be competent to keep alive and to renew the circulation of opinions and feelings among a great people than to manage all the speculations of productive industry. No sooner does a government attempt to go beyond its political sphere and enter upon this new track than it exercises, even unintentionally, an insupportable tyranny; for a government can only dictate strict rules, the opinions which it favors are rigidly enforced, and it is never easy to discriminate between its advice and its commands. Worse still will be the case if the government really believes itself interested in preventing all circulation of ideas; it will then stand motionless and oppressed by the heaviness of voluntary torpor. Governments, therefore, should not be the only active powers; associations ought, in democratic nations, to stand in lieu of those powerful private individuals whom the equality of conditions has swept away.[68]

We are at the heart of Tocqueville's theory of civil society. The responsibilities of government must be limited to "its political sphere." Civil society is populated by voluntary associations that are oriented to the pursuit of private matters and are generally unconcerned with broad political or economic affairs. Strengthened by the peculiar American disposition to associate in pursuit of local interests, civil society replaces aristocrats with groups of equals and blunts the thrust of the democratic state in the process. It is the essential condition of liberty and is America's answer to Europe's dilemma. "In democratic countries the science of association is the mother of science; the progress of all the rest depends on the progress it has made."[69]

Tocqueville was impressed by the New World's informality, energy, and creativity, but he worried about its capacity for statism and feared that the rich network of intermediate associations, traditions of localism, and political freedom might not be enough to turn a commercial society's isolated individuals toward the common good. Even with their powerful attachment to local voluntarism, Americans had to learn the importance of tempering the French Revolution's universalism with the recognition of local inequalities. "The Americans hold that in every state the supreme power ought to emanate from the people; but when once that power is constituted, they can conceive, as it were, no limits to it, and they are ready to admit that it has the right to do whatever it pleases. They have not the slightest notion of peculiar privileges granted to cities, families, or persons; their minds appear never to have foreseen that it might be possible not to apply with strict uniformity the same laws to every part of the state and to all its inhabitants."[70] Civil society could help a Europe that was finally sloughing off its ancient aristocratic structures. "Many of these local authorities have already disappeared," said Tocqueville; "all are speedily tending to disappear or fall into the most complete dependence. From one end of Europe to the other the privileges of the nobility, the liberties of cities, and the power of provincial bodies are either destroyed or are on the verge of destruction." But this was not an unambiguous blessing, for the French Revolution's tendency to destroy all the "secondary powers of government" is a real threat to liberty.[71] The contradictory logic of history meant that egalitarian America might help class-bound Europe preserve liberty by protecting local centers of privilege from the universalistic thrust of the democratic state. Perhaps civil society could put some of the secondary benefits of feudalism to use:

> I firmly believe that an aristocracy cannot again be founded in the world, but I think that private citizens, by combining together, may constitute bodies of great wealth, influence, and strength, corresponding to the persons of an aristocracy. By this means many of the greatest political advantages of an aristocracy would be obtained without its injustice or its dangers. An association for political, commercial, or manufacturing purposes, or even for those of science and literature, is a powerful and enlightened member of the community, which cannot be disposed of at pleasure or oppressed without remonstrance, and which, by saving its own rights against the encroachments of the government, saves the common liberties of the country.[72]

In an age when popular political power threatened liberty, civil society could protect freedom with inequality. "To lay down extensive but distinct and settled limits to the action of the government; to confer certain rights on private persons, and to secure to them the undisputed enjoyment of those rights; to enable individual man to maintain whatever independence, strength, and original power he still possesses; to raise him by the side of society at large, and uphold him in that position; these appear to me the main objects of legislators in the ages upon which we are now entering."[73] The free institutions that protect localism and association do so by limiting the power of majorities with a measure of inequality.

> The government of a democracy brings the notion of political rights to the level of the humblest citizens, just as the dissemination of wealth brings the notion of property within the reach of all men; to my mind, this is one of its greatest advantages. I do not say that it is easy to teach men how to exercise political rights, but I maintain that, when it is possible, the effects which result from it are highly important; and I add that, if there ever was a time when such an attempt ought to be made, that time is now. Do you not see that religious belief is shaken and the divine notion of right is declining; that morality is debased and the notion of moral right is therefore fading away? Argument is substituted for faith, and calculation for the impulses of sentiment. If, in the midst of this general disruption, you do not succeed in connecting the notion of right with that of private interest, which is the only im-

mutable point in the human heart, what means will you have of governing the world except by fear? When I am told that the laws are weak and the people are turbulent, that the passions are excited and the authority of virtue is paralyzed, and therefore no measures must be taken to increase the rights of the democracy, I reply that for these very reasons some measures of the kind ought to be taken; and I believe that governments are still more interested in taking them than society at large, for governments may perish, but society cannot die.[74]

America had managed the formidable task of "connecting the notion of right with that of private interest, which is the only immutable point in the human heart." Finding a place for liberty, excellence, and virtue in the new conditions of equality, commerce, and democracy depended on the sorts of institutions Americans had perfected: town meetings, freedom of the press, indirect elections, federalism, an independent judiciary, separation of church and state, and a multitude of independent associations. Tocqueville hoped that the Americans could show Europe how to limit the egalitarian and universal democratic state by reserving considerable power to a civil society that could mediate between the isolated individuals of a commercial society and an increasingly centralized and intrusive governmental apparatus.

Rousseau had given voice to ancient republican virtues of citizenship and community and articulated a revolutionary conception of civil society. Burke feared modernity's leveling and sought stability in custom and inequality. Tocqueville's ambivalence about the Revolution was reflected in his recognition that the *ancien régime* was irresistibly yielding to equality and democracy, but he shared Montesquieu's fear of central power and wanted to limit its scope with local institutions and voluntary associations. His civil society protected liberty because it was based on localism, particularism, and entrenched privilege. Relatively unconcerned about the internal dynamics of the economy, Tocqueville was able to leave the market out of his scheme because his assumption about American equality of conditions effectively removed the economy from democratic critique. Such an assertion was problematic enough in 1830, but is impossible to maintain a century and a half later.[75] None of this, however, would prevent some European intellectuals from turning once again to Tocqueville and his idealized America.

PART III

Civil Society in Contemporary Life

7

Civil Society and Communism

The roots of the contemporary interest in civil society lie in the 1980s contention of some Eastern European intellectuals that the accelerating crisis of communism was "the revolt of civil society against the state." Deeply hostile to the claims of self-described vanguard parties and to their bureaucratized version of politics, a dissident literature slowly took shape that identified "actual existing socialism" with a grasping and intrusive state apparatus, obsolete central planning of heavy industrial production, and pervasive repression of social initiatives originating outside the control of the party-state. Drawing from liberal constitutionalism, Tocqueville, and the Western literature on "totalitarianism," early analysts developed a sustained critique of what they said was Marxism's lack of limits, tendency to politicize everything, betrayal of democracy, and drive to direct or absorb any spontaneous activity arising from civil society. Rooted in broad popular desires for political democracy, the critique pointedly ignored economic matters and initially presented itself as a renovation of socialist thought. Its judgments certainly were not new, but they received considerable support from a deepening economic crisis and from the Right's political triumph in England and the United States. By the end of the decade, a pervasive distrust of politics and the state had turned these analysts toward private property and the market, and they soon became part of a broad consensus about why Soviet-style communism had collapsed. But the impact of their critique was considerably broader; its antistatist core resonated in the West and has become an important part of the sustained attack on living standards and the welfare state that dominates contemporary public life.

Since "actual existing socialism" developed as a state-led strategy of economic growth and social organization, the dissident critique gravitated toward liberal theories of civil society that centered on constraining state power. Constitutionalist arguments for political rights, civil liberties, and the rule of law sought to define a sphere of public life free of arbitrary bureaucratic intervention. Autonomous voluntary organizations came to be seen as democratic sites of self-organization and important obstacles to the relentless expansion of the party-state. Liberal constitutionalism could provide an important measure of protection from the state, but that turned out to be the only part of the solution to which the new theories of civil society were able to address themselves.

Modern socialism, the Enlightenment twin of liberalism, has always rested on the extension of democracy into the economy; indeed, this is why Marx called himself a "social democrat" in the first place. The understanding of civil society as self-organization pure and simple tended to view the state as the chief obstacle to democracy and to leave the economy out of consideration. But if civil society was theorized as a chaotic sphere of production, interest, and inequality, then the internal dynamics of the economy could be subject to scrutiny. This orientation has rested at the heart of all socialist theories of civil society. From the mild redistributive policies advocated by some to the full-blown abolition of the market preferred by others, equality and democracy seemed to require the use of state power to interfere with private property and the logic of commodification. Born in devastating war and economic catastrophe, this commitment to abolish the market, overcome the commodity form, and reunite civil society and the state accounts for much of communism's theoretical and practical appeal. It has also accounted for some of its deepest difficulties. Lenin's hope that the deep contradictions of the transition to socialism could be managed by the use of political power became a general principle for twentieth-century communism. But questions of democracy have forced themselves to the center of socialist political thought. Liberalism developed a theory of civil society because it wanted to democratize the state. Marxism developed a theory of the state because it wanted to democratize civil society. The twists and turns of contemporary history would bring them face to face in Eastern Europe.

Totalitarianism

Karl Marx's great project was his critical analysis of bourgeois civil society. He spent relatively little time describing how he thought communism would be organized. But he did present a fairly coherent outline of the transition to socialism, and we have seen that it was driven by his expectation that the central structures of capitalism would continue to exist for some time after the workers' political "victory." His projection that the seizure of power would precede and make possible the transformation of civil society implied that a powerful political apparatus would play an important guiding and directing function. Exactly how this state could be sufficiently strong to accomplish its difficult tasks and be accountable to the population at the same time was not very clear, but Marx certainly expected it to be actively supported by the overwhelming majority of the population. The unavoidable tension between this state and a still-bourgeois civil society need not be fatal to social or political democracy under such conditions.

Vladimir Ilich Lenin understood this, but the particular circumstances of the Russian Revolution would locate questions of political democracy at the heart of a society whose backwardness made it singularly unable to satisfactorily address them. "We must now set about building a proletarian socialist state in Russia," he soberly told the members of the Petrograd Soviet immediately after the successful insurrection of October 25, 1917.[1] Once its political and institutional foundations were in place, the social revolution could begin. But transforming civil society proved to be much more difficult than seizing state power. Things would have been difficult enough without the devastation of World War I, but the pressing need to defeat domestic counterrevolution and foreign intervention strengthened the forces of centralization and made it difficult to hold the party and state accountable to elements of the very civil society they were dedicated to transform. The initial hope that a revolutionary state could be organized on the decentralized basis of direct democracy, workers' supervision, and soviet power quickly yielded to the realization that a formidable political organ would be necessary for some time. The "withering away of the state" would have to wait at least until counterrevolution was defeated and economic modernization begun.[2]

Even victory in the civil war did little but redraw the parameters of a crisis that would prove permanent. Lenin knew that the New Economic Policy's turn toward the market would encourage dangerous economic forces to reassert themselves, but he was confident that capitalism could be turned to the advantage of socialism. He had often expressed the hope that the state-led transition to a stateless society would be comparatively rapid and easy, but as it became clear that revolutionary Russia stood alone he repeatedly turned to the vanguard party for help. The party's virtual fusion with the state permitted the Bolshevik regime to organize a Red Army, neutralize the political opposition, and mobilize an exhausted population for reconstruction and social revolution. Lenin knew that his reliance on a monolithic party and state was dangerous and he repeatedly warned his colleagues that only workers' supervision and control could turn the revolution's inescapable centralism to the advantage of socialism. Bureaucracy cannot be avoided, he often acknowledged, but its damaging effects can be limited with continuous working-class supervision. By the end of his life, he had become painfully aware that this would be considerably easier to proclaim in theory than to organize in practice.

Lenin's death in 1924 did little to resolve the deep contradictions inherent in using the state to transform civil society. Every one of the revolution's goals seemed to require strengthened state power and a party-led drive toward social mobilization and economic modernization. The important industrialization debates of the late 1920s occurred in the context of widespread agreement among the Soviet leadership that the capital for industry would have to come from the peasantry. The only question was the swiftness with which it would be extracted. Lenin had always recommended caution, patience, and the power of example in the effort to convince Russia's enormous and skeptical peasantry of the advantages of cooperation and collectivization. But socialist revolution had come to a devastated and besieged society whose leadership was now compelled to start at the very beginning: with the production of the means of production. In the end, Joseph Stalin won the complex political struggle with Nikolai Bukharin and Leon Trotsky by insisting that socialism could be built as an active alliance between the peasants and workers without hurting either class. Once a policy of land collectivization and rapid industrialization was agreed on, the state would take the lead.[3]

World War II and the subsequent confrontation with the United States only magnified the role of the state as heavy industry, a permanent state of emergency, and military necessity came to characterize Soviet socialism. The Soviet economy had rested on a war footing from the very beginning and relied upon centralized planning, strict political control, and a determination to hold market forces in check. However it was understood, civil society became increasingly problematic under such conditions. If it was Tocqueville's sphere of independent nonstate organizations, it seemed to have been entirely swallowed up by a party-state that was directing all its efforts toward social revolution. If it was the market-organized sphere of class, exploitation, and alienation, Soviet theorists proclaimed that it had largely disappeared by 1936. Either way, civil society did not figure prominently in socialist political theory for some time—and this would make it particularly difficult to comprehend what was to transpire in Eastern Europe during the 1980s.

The problems only intensified as a modern economy began to take shape. Claims that the USSR had developed a "mature" socialism that was setting in place the material conditions for communism were belied by increasing bureaucratization, social stratification, and political demobilization. Generous social services stood alongside an authoritarian political structure and a command economy built around the requirements of iron and steel. As the society matured, it became progressively more difficult to organize state affairs as if a planned economy could function on the basis of continuous mobilization and heroic examples from past industrialization, collectivization, and military campaigns.

The course of the Russian Revolution came to dominate progressive political thought for most of the century, but its appropriateness to advanced capitalism was always an open question. The vicissitudes of history transformed it into the preeminent model of state-driven industrialization of underdeveloped societies without deep traditions of political democracy. Marxist theory and its own experience had taught the Bolshevik leadership that a civil society which had not yet been fully transformed would spontaneously generate bourgeois impulses and counterrevolution, and independent social initiatives were always regarded with deep suspicion. Theory and practice came together to reinforce the view that the state was the most dependable weapon in the struggle to remold a recalcitrant social order. The Russian Revolution's critics had often described it as a Jacobin-inspired war against civil society and painted a dreary picture of a passive citizenry, a fractured and immobile civil society, and a powerful interventionist state. A full-scale theory of totalitarianism brought different strands of the analysis together.

As World War II's "grand alliance" with the Soviet Union yielded to hostility and cold war, a coherent anticommunist position solidified in the West. Basing much of their analysis on the traditional Anglo-American suspicion of the state, some intellectuals suggested that any effort to regulate civil society in the name of general interests was the first step toward despotism. Written toward the end of the war and ostensibly directed against Nazism and communism, Friedrich Hayek's *The Road to Serfdom* declared that both "are merely variants of the same totalitarianism which central control of all economic activity tends to produce."[4] Economic planning for broad social purposes will inevitably degenerate into an assault on civil society and the destruction of the rule of law, Hayek repeatedly asserted. He acknowledged that some state activity is necessary to protect contracts and guarantee legal equality, but Western societies ought to seek a minimal level of public intervention in the market's network of private calculations and actions. A competitive market economy can function without external coercion so long as the law does not explicitly favor any of civil society's private individuals. Plurality and limits can be guaranteed only by a capitalist economy and a structure of rights. Liberalism, Hayek said, "regards competition as superior not only because it is in most circumstances the most efficient method known but even more because it is the only method by which our activities can be adjusted to each other without coercive or arbitrary interventions of authority."[5] Exchange relations provide the only effective mechanism by which the activities of self-interested individuals can be coordinated dispassionately. The market's regulative capacity becomes even more important as society becomes more complex, and practical considerations of efficiency reinforced Hayek's suspicion of using coercive political power to supervise the market. A healthy civil society requires strong markets and weak states:

> There would be no difficulty about efficient control or planning were conditions so simple that a single person or board could effectively survey all the relevant facts. It is only as the factors which have to be taken into account become so numerous that it is impossible to gain a synoptic view of them that decentralization becomes imperative. But, once decentralization is necessary, the problem of co-ordination arises. . . . As decentralization has become necessary because nobody can consciously balance all the considerations bearing on the decisions of so many individuals, the coordination can clearly be effected not by "conscious control" but only by arrangements which convey to each agent the information he must possess in order effectively to adjust his decisions to those of others. And because all the details of the changes constantly affecting the conditions of demand and supply of the different commodities can never be fully known, or quickly enough be collected and disseminated, by any one center, what is required is some apparatus of registration which automatically records all the relevant effects of individual actions and whose indications are at the same time the resultant of, and the guide for, all the individual decisions.
>
> This is precisely what the price system does under competition, and which no other system even promises to accomplish.[6]

All collectivisms, said Hayek—and here fascism and communism are the same—seek to organize civil society in the name of some politically defined "public good." But there is no general good apart from the private purposes of individuals. Even the suggestion that some goods are more important than others denies that the individual knows his own interests and is the first step on the road to despotism. Individual interest provides the only solid grounding for freedom and autonomy. "It is this recognition of the individual as the ultimate judge of his ends, the belief that as far as possible his own views ought to govern his actions, that forms the essence of the individualist position."[7] Any suggestion that civil society can be organized in accordance with a purposeful end must assume more agreement about social goals than really exists and is deeply dangerous. An open and incomplete ethical code should guide a state that has no moral content and "should confine itself to establishing rules applying to general types of situations and should allow the individual freedom in everything which depends on the circumstances of time and place, because only the individuals concerned in each instance can fully know these circumstances and adapt their action to them."[8]

Hayek's obsession with the dangers of planning made it impossible for him to see the dangers of the market. He was not alone in this, of course; as he knew, liberalism has always been acutely aware of the threat of arbitrary political power and has paid less attention to the threat posed by concentrations of private wealth. His denunciation of planning conflated communism with social democracy and the liberal welfare state and made it sound as if Keynesianism was Stalinism's little brother. He knew that the combination of strong markets and weak states always produces substantial economic inequality, but he believed that arbitrariness was the chief threat to liberty and was convinced that it could be eliminated if public decisions were driven by market criteria.[9] "Inequality is undoubtedly more easily borne, and affects the dignity of the person much less, if it is determined by impersonal forces than when it is due to design," he assured his readers.[10] There is no credible public good apart from the summation of particular interests and "individual freedom cannot be reconciled with the supremacy of one single purpose to which the whole society must be entirely and permanently subordinated."[11] The privileged position of individual interest in liberal theories of civil society drove Hayek's denunciation of any attempt to organize conscious social supervision over economic processes. Economic regulation always risked political despotism.

Ever since Aristotle, political thinkers have described autocracy as a political formation marked by arbitrariness, unaccountability, and a lack of limits. Hayek linked it to planning, but Carl Friedrich and Zbigniew

Brzezinski adapted elements of classical theory and modern liberalism in an influential cold war portrayal of totalitarianism as a novel configuration of specific procedures, institutions, and processes.[12] Characterized by a relentless drive to enforce ideological unity, level social differences, and organize high levels of manipulated participation, totalitarianism is autocracy adapted to the conditions of twentieth-century mass industrial society. Like Hayek, they identified its root in the attempt to subject civil society's spontaneous drives to predetermined ends. Where Hayek was attacking all planning in the West, however, Friedrich and Brzezinski were crafting a specifically anticommunist position that left the door open to state involvement in the economy. Their approach differed from Hayek's because it paid more attention to a complicated and aggressive revolutionary ideology that claims jurisdiction over all aspects of human life and is organized by an all-powerful party-state. Constantly seeking unanimity, a permanent ideological campaign backed by state-sanctioned terror penetrates everywhere. A revolution of unprecedented ambition is extended "to every nook and cranny of society. Thus change becomes the order of the day."[13] No social sphere can protect its autonomy from the relentless intrusion of a hyperpoliticized revolutionary project to remold civil society and improve human nature. Highly refined instruments of rule make it possible to set goals that are more ambitious than earlier revolutionary projects—particularly when they are backed by a state monopoly of communications and the means of violence. For Brzesinski and Friedrich—and cold war liberalism generally—fascism and communism were cousins.

The totalitarian state's unprecedented ability to persuade and punish helps it organize "a central control and direction of the entire economy through the bureaucratic coordination of formerly independent corporate entities, typically including most other associations and group activities."[14] Whether expressed as communist industrialization or fascist war, totalitarianism's overweening ambition and ruthless aggressiveness crush civil society's autonomous spheres and intermediate organizations. Its logic drives it to extend its grasp, engulf ever-wider spheres, penetrate everywhere. Aristotle, Montesquieu, Burke, and Tocqueville had warned that the inclination to erase distinctions and impose universal standards tends to wipe out the mediating bodies that protect the individual. For Friedrich and Brzezinski, modern totalitarianism's *modus operandi* differs only in its agent. Fused with the state, the revolutionary party deploys a highly politicized bureaucracy and organizes a level of control that is without historic precedent. The all-powerful directing party-state that combines the power of ideology and the use of coercion is a defining feature of modern totalitarianism.

Friedrich and Brzezinski knew that economic planning had become a permanent feature of the twentieth century. Unlike Hayek, they had no problem with it in principle; what worried them was communism's project to transform civil society. The drive to politicize economic matters is inherent in modern autocracy as such and becomes a condition of its survival and growth. "Totalitarian planning is a necessary concomitant of the total revolution that these regimes set in motion—without it they would easily degenerate into anarchy—and it is this *political* quality that sets it apart from democratic economic planning." Hayek could not allow for the possibility of "democratic economic planning,"[15] but Friedrich and Brzezinski did not want to eviscerate the state as such because it could help maintain social cohesion, stimulate economic growth, and conduct the cold war. Unlike "democratic planning" carried on by dispassionate and apolitical experts, totalitarianism cannot respect the autonomous spheres that protect individual autonomy and private judgment. It can never leave well enough alone. When animated by a comprehensive ideology and organized by a militant party, the revolutionary state's access to advanced techniques of mobilization, organization, persuasion, and coercion make it a particularly dangerous enemy of liberal civil society's plurality and autonomy. Totalitarianism was always an ideal toward which modern autocracies aimed and, its unprecedented power notwithstanding, isolated "islands of resistance" did manage to hold out:

> In spite of the efforts of the totalitarians to destroy all separate existences, there remain in these dictatorships some groups that manage to offer some resistance to totalitarian rule. The family, the churches, the universities and other centers of technical knowledge, the writers and artists—each in response to the rationale of their being—must, if they are to survive, resist the total demands of the totalitarians. As we have seen, the totalitarian regimes seek to divide and rule in the most radical and extreme way; each human being should, for best effect, have to face the monolith of totalitarian rule as an isolated "atom." By being thus atomized, the people with its many natural subdivisions becomes the "mass," and the citizen is transformed into the mass man. This mass man, this isolated and anxiety-ridden shadow, is the complete antithesis to the "common man" of the working free society. It is, therefore, rather misleading to speak of the subjects of such regimes as "citizens." They are rather denizens or even serfs of the ruling party, and only the

members of that party as participants in governing the society can rightfully be said to be citizens, at least according to Aristotle's carefully developed notion of citizens.[16]

It was not particularly clear why some intermediate organs survived the totalitarian drive to convert them into instruments of the party-state. Surely their ability to preserve themselves must have rested on something more substantial than "the rationale of their being." If such important institutions as families, churches, universities, and the arts managed to retain a measure of autonomy, perhaps totalitarianism was not so total after all. The undeniable development of alternative centers of power would later cause many Sovietologists to abandon the concept of totalitarianism altogether, but it remained popular during the height of the cold war. Indeed, the classic model of a revolutionary party-state that penetrated, crushed, and reorganized a devastated civil society lay at the center of Hannah Arendt's influential and elitist claim that totalitarianism is a specific feature of an unstable civil society and of the masses who inhabit it.[17] A half century of war, revolution, depression, and crisis led her to worry about the breakdown of the social bonds with which nineteenth-century class identifications had organized European civil society. Enormous economic forces were transforming the world, and the political consequences of their relentless leveling, centralizing, and penetrating troubled her. Arendt's analysis of totalitarianism relocated the threat to autonomy from Montesquieu's despot to a particular form of modernity that negated the very possibility of civil society.

The disintegration of Europe heralded the appearance of those unique and pathological creations of modern life, mass man and mass society. Where civil society is marked by plurality and differentiation, mass society is empty because its inhabitants are unconnected and atomized. "The chief characteristic of mass man is not brutality and backwardness, but his isolation and lack of normal social relationships."[18] Totalitarianism, Arendt held, is the direct result of the entry of these rootless, classless masses into public life. Its basic unit is the lonely, marginalized, and angry individual whose search for stability and predictability makes him ready to overthrow civil society and participate in a frantic effort to create a new one. Alienated and isolated, deracinated mass man is as unable to articulate his own interests as he is to organize around them. He cannot act rationally because he has no ability to identify and act on any authentic interests. This is what accounts for the peculiar destructiveness of twentieth-century politics. Totalitarianism is so dangerous and unstable because it "functions independently of all calculable action in terms of men and material, and is completely indifferent to national interest and the well-being of its people."[19] Mass society makes impossible a classic bourgeois civil society constituted by rational individuals who pursue their interests because they are protected from others:

> Totalitarian movements are possible wherever there are masses who for one reason or another have acquired the appetite for political organization. Masses are not held together by a consciousness of common interest and they lack that specific class articulateness which is expressed in determined, limited, and obtainable goals. The term masses applies only where we deal with people who either because of sheer numbers, or indifference, or a combination of both, cannot be integrated into any organization based on common interest, into political parties or municipal governments or professional associations or trade unions. Potentially, they exist in every country and form the majority of those large numbers of neutral, politically indifferent people who never join a party and hardly ever go to the polls.[20]

Economic crisis is particularly dangerous because it throws these rootless individuals together. It is because mass man does not understand his interests and cannot organize to pursue them that he can be mobilized around a program of social destruction, Arendt's "new terrifying negative solidarity."[21] Liberal social theory had always sought to tame politics by anchoring it to a calculus of localism and self-interest. The rise of movements that attempted to redress social and economic inequities with political remedies unnerved Arendt, as it did Hayek. Political participation that is not connected to the immediate pursuit of self-interest is a dangerous and uniquely characteristic feature of mass society.

Arendt's analysis of totalitarianism's reckless disposition to shatter tradition and remake civil society was remarkably similar to Burke's attack on the French Revolution. She distinguished totalitarianism by its systematic suffocation of spontaneity. Its drive toward total domination, its claim that anything is possible, its tendency to erase all differences, and its propensity to treat "humanity" as if it were a single individual drives totalitarianism to eradicate independent contacts between people and the civil society that makes such contacts possible. Totalitarianism is marked by political isolation and private loneliness, and the destruction of civil society's intermediate structures is what makes the phenomenon so invasive. Erasing the distinction between civil society and the state is a prelude to an attack on the distinction between the public and private spheres of life. "While isolation concerns only the political realm of life, loneliness concerns human life as a whole. Totalitarian government, like all tyrannies, certainly could not exist without destroying the public realm of life, that is, without destroying, by isolating men, their political capacities. But totalitarian domination as a form of government is new in that it does not content itself within this isolation and destroys private life as well. It bases itself on loneliness, on the experience of not belonging to the world at all, which is among the most radical and desperate experiences of man."[22] Less worried by economic inequality than by the rise of mass politics, Arendt transformed a social analysis into the nostalgic politics of moderation and authority.

Crafted by Western social science in the early years of the cold war, the literature on "totalitarianism" was adapted to conditions in Eastern Europe and played an important role in the rediscovery of civil society. The failure of reform efforts in 1956 and 1968 led dissident intellectuals to conclude that "actual existing socialism" could not be reformed from within and that both Marxist theory and communist practice required the systematic application of state power to "coerce" civil society. Many retained the critique of mass society and concluded that a deep totalitarianism lurked at the heart of Marxism as such; "far from promising the fusion of civil with political society, the Marxian perspective of unified man is more likely to engender, if put into practice, a cancerous growth of omnipotent bureaucracy, trying to shatter and paralyze civil society and leading the (rightly blamed) anonymity of public life to its extreme consequences."[23] Others reassessed the Soviet industrialization and collectivization drives and contended that Stalinism was an inevitable outgrowth of Leninism. Still others used constitutionalist and pluralist categories to analyze social orders they continued to call "totalitarian," even though the development of more articulated socialist societies were already encouraging some Western analysts to discard the notion altogether. In some cases the notion of power was simply redefined to save the category; instead of terror, midnight raids, and concentration camps, totalitarianism meant "the ongoing capacity to limit all scope for independent action in every possible sphere of activity. In other words, it has nothing to do with the degree of violence or terror applied. Power remains 'totalitarian' even when the forms of repression are less visible (albeit still virtually present)."[24] Totalitarianism now described the unequal relation between an ideologically driven party-state and a fragmented civil society, even if overt terror had largely disappeared, the beginnings of autonomous spheres could be discerned, and a degree of pluralism was apparent in "mature" socialist societies. The more indiscriminate the use of "totalitarianism," the weaker was its explanatory power.

The gradual abandonment of the identity between totalitarianism and terror did not necessarily signal the abandonment of the concept. Totalitarianism may have been bureaucratized, but some observers thought it no less despotic. What passed for "socialism," on this analysis, was little more than the state bureaucracy's control over the productive apparatus.[25] The planning process was simply the instrument by which the surplus value produced by workers in state-owned enterprises was appropriated. A parasitical and self-serving "socialist bourgeoisie" had fortified its position with decisions that affected everyone, but its hostility to civil society prevented it from consulting anyone. Eastern European socialism was nothing more or less than the "maximization of the objective resources under the total control of the apparatus."[26] Even if terror had largely disappeared, then, the party-state still tried to atomize and control everything. Individuals had no power against it and were still unable to organize themselves. Paradoxically, the lessened role of terror only masked a more intrusive and powerful apparatus of coercion.

But a fundamental weakness was said to lurk at the heart of the whole socialist project. Echoing Hayek, some theorists began to look to the market because it seemed increasingly clear to them that no bureaucracy can respond sufficiently quickly to the enormous mass of signals generated by complex social orders. A perpetual shortage of consumer goods is the inevitable consequence of the attempt to "organize social production in principle from one administrative center, developing it according to the corporate power interest of this unified apparatus and subordinating it to the principle of the maximal extension of the material basis of the domination of the apparatus over society."[27] Turning Hegel on his head, the bureaucratic organization of civil society was now said to create permanent shortages that act as an effective and brutal "dictatorship over needs."[28]

Unable to break with its suspiciousness of civil society, some 1980s theorists suggested, the socialist state must drive to "disrupt all informal, spontaneous social connections and ties beyond the confines of the family."[29] Modern totalitarianism was now a particular variant on an all-too-familiar phenomenon: "political society means the primacy of the political state over the whole of societal life; society is an annex to the omnipotent state rather than a relatively independent entity."[30] Marxism's commitment to fuse state and civil society had been twisted into the stifling of civil society in the interests of a party-state apparatus whose separation from "the only authentic fountainhead of the relevant information: the individual and his autonomous associations" recalled Tocqueville.[31] The new totalitarianism renders individuals unable to articulate their needs, powerless to express themselves in an organized way, and helpless before a bureaucracy that enriches itself through exploitation of the workers, unnecessary shortages, and suffocating social control. Contrary to his fondest hopes, it was Tocqueville's *fears* about America that have been realized in Eastern Europe, where "there is an ongoing conflict between the state—claiming total power—and civil society. Society may have been shackled and no autonomous organization may be permitted, but its instinctual behavior stubbornly survives."[32] Freedom now requires liberal constitutionalism, the market, and Tocqueville to clear away the deadening, crushing, and empty conformity of "actual existing socialsm."[33]

"Instinct" is not a particularly valuable category for social analysis, but many of the theories of civil society that appeared in Eastern Europe during the 1980s were adaptations of earlier theories of totalitarianism. Some of them added important features of Tocqueville. Basing themselves on liberal constitutionalist principles, almost all agreed that the application of state power to shape civil society had to end.[34] Some thought that civil liberties and a revived civil society of intermediate associations could develop within the boundaries of "actual existing socialism." Others were more skeptical. All agreed that the time had come to transcend the fundamental difference between Western and Eastern Europe. "On the one hand we have the 'self-evident' freedom of individuals and social groups, limited only by the freedom of other groups; on the other, we see a central power not attached to any group or class, to some extent separate from society proper, responsible for the whole of society. This is the modern state."[35] All the theories that emerged from the period aimed at weakening the bureaucratized party-state and making it more directly accountable to the self-organized formations of "civil society."

The "Self-Limiting" Revolution

The intense antistatism that marked the early literature on civil society was a perfectly understandable reaction to the routinized and bureaucratic character of "actual existing socialism." But it also developed in conditions of weakness and initially refrained from challenging the fundamental structures of Eastern European life. By the late 1970s it was picturing civil society as "a sphere of autonomous, ostensibly non-political, social activity, which did not seek to challenge the state's control over the main levers of power and, indeed, obtained its status through a tacit contract with the authorities of the ruling party-state."[36] Such a view implied that these societies could no longer be described as totalitarian. If the state had really organized social life to the extent required by the category, *any* sort of autonomous activity would have been impossible—even if it was not directly political in character. The notion that the autonomous trade unions, new social movements, civic forums, human rights leagues, and other organs of a "socialist civil society" could reach an accommodation with the state implied that civil society could be theorized apart from direct state control and acknowledged that autonomous centers of power were developing in "mature" socialist societies.

Indeed, "totalitarianism's" usefulness had become increasingly problematic. By the late 1960s, two of the central claims theorists had made about it—that individual social relationships were atomized beyond repair and that autonomous political and social life was impossible—were under sustained attack. The simplistic notion that independent interests could not be organized in socialist societies, that the Communist Party was a monolithic apparatus of arbitrary violence and bureaucratic indifference, and that the state exercised total control over every aspect of social and individual life was gradually abandoned. It was succeeded by a distinctly pluralist model of the Soviet Union. Some scholars went so far as to reexamine elements of Stalinism and shed light on a surprising degree of nonstate and nonparty activity. "Civil society" was never dead in the Soviet Union on this account, even at the height of Stalinism. As "peaceful coexistence" replaced the unbridled hostility of the early cold war, other analysts insisted that the Soviet Union was becoming like other modern societies and demonstrated that an increasingly open political culture was developing a degree of independence from the Communist Party. The state was certainly more active and intrusive than in the West and the party still confined public affairs within fairly narrow boundaries, but private life had not been eliminated and networks of civic associations were developing relatively freely. Nikita Khrushchev's "goulash communism," increasing interest in market socialism, and tentative openings to what would become known as "Eurocommunism" both reflected and encouraged the differentiation of Soviet society and gave rise to Western analyses organized around relations of compromise and negotiation between centers of power that functioned with increasing independence from the party and the state. The uneasy coexistence between market reforms and orthodox political structures was said to be encouraging the sort of differentiation between economics and politics that characterized capitalist societies. The state was becoming less able to direct an increasingly complicated society and assert a single hierarchy of social goals. Intermediate organization and the clash of particular interests had come to socialism, courtesy of the complexity that accompanied its economic development and the differentiation that came with its turn toward the market.[37]

Elements of this analysis were extended to Eastern Europe as well. Some scholars argued that there was far more room for independent public activity in "actual existing" socialist societies than was generally supposed in the West and identified social forces that encouraged independent expression and organization. Education, urbanization, the spread of communications, foreign travel, and increasing wealth were creating centers of public and private power that enjoyed a measure of autonomy from the party-state. Important elements of official policy had the same effect. The general commitment to mass literacy and education, for example, stimulated the development of cultural and intellectual forms that were separate from—and tolerated by—official institutions. Independent expression was an unanticipated but not unwelcome byproduct of a genuine commitment to extend culture to the population as a whole.[38] On a more general level, some analysts thought that a satisfied socialist bureaucracy that had given up the project of transforming civil society was able to tolerate a greater measure of spontaneous activity than had been possible earlier.

One of the earliest suggestions that elements of a "socialist civil society" were developing treated the intelligentsia as a class in its own right and traced its use of the bureaucratized party-state to emerge as the representative of the general interest. Industrialization, wealth, urbanization, social peace, education, and other undoubted accomplishments had brought an end to the Soviet Union's incessant mobilizations and "campaign style of work." Socialism now meant the prosaic coordination of different bureaucracies—a task that rewarded the technocratic elements of this new ruling stratum. Earlier efforts to politicize all areas of life were no longer necessary, desirable, or possible. The original revolutionary urge to reconstruct the civil society Marx had described and create a "new man" had decayed, but another sort of civil society was seen in the Tocquevillean stirrings of independent associations. Socialism now meant the everyday, mundane, and decidedly nonrevolutionary work of organization and management. "In the post-Stalin era politics no longer comes in through the citizen's front door;

the doorbell-ringing agitator has given way to the television screen. The total politicization of daily life has come to an end, and the sanctity of private life has been restored. Working hours are for working, not politics, and in your free time you can do what you like."[39] On this reading, politics had retreated, the state's goals had become modest and unremarkable, and a variety of clubs and associations were springing up to fill the gap caused by the effective abandonment of an earlier commitment to transform civil society. Like his counterpart in Western societies, the citizen of bureaucratic socialism was profoundly privatized and depoliticized.

Events in Poland seemed to bear out a pluralist approach and to confirm earlier suspicions that a civil society of intermediate organizations was taking root. An energetic protest movement catalyzed earlier developments and concentrated them into Eastern Europe's first coherent theory of civil society. The earlier decision not to collectivize agriculture, the considerable power of the Roman Catholic Church, the wide influence of the intelligentsia, and the 1968 failure of the Prague Spring's effort to democratize socialist politics encouraged many intellectuals to turn their attention toward "society." A series of workers' demonstrations in 1970, the appearance of a human rights movement in the middle of the decade, and an increasingly effective alliance between disenchanted workers and dissident intellectuals led to a new strategy for an articulate and differentiated Polish opposition.[40]

Careful not to push things too far, the Polish opposition's spokespeople were anxious not to appear politically subversive. Instead of directly attacking state power, "the self-organization of society" sought to limit the party-state's reach outside its "proper" sphere. Organizers turned their attention to trade unions, student groups, cultural associations, workers' committees, *samizdat* publications, and the "flying university" as they sought to create an organized sphere of autonomous activity from below. A "self-limiting" movement tried to carve out a space for local activity but was careful not to challenge the supremacy of the Polish United Workers' Party or contest the socialist character of the economy. By the late 1970s, a variety of independent grass-roots organizations were working to transform the relationship between the state and "civil society."

A pronounced antistatism soon began to characterize much of the accompanying literature. Drawing on classical liberalism's awareness of the danger of concentrated and unaccountable political power, theories of civil society began to suggest that democracy was inherently opposed to the logic of the modern state. Some of its spokespeople doubtless imagined that the existing order and a "socialist civil society" could be accommodated, but they would soon be disabused of this hope. The dissident literature had taken shape as a protest against the arbitrariness and bureaucratization of everyday Polish life. It had been careful to avoid any suggestion that a renewed civil society would court the danger of restoring capitalism. But it was becoming difficult to maintain the fiction that the market and "civil society" could be considered in isolation from one another. "Civil society" soon came to mean something more than democratic self-organization.

Adam Michnik identified civil society with a "self-limiting" opposition and made the important suggestion that organizers focus their efforts on grounding authentic democratic activity in voluntary nonstate associations. Earlier political reform efforts tended to appeal to established centers of political power and accepted the party as the legitimate repository of political authority.[41] But the failure of these efforts required a new set of tactics, which now emphasized careful organizing from below and the creation of permanent sites of contestation. The opposition's goal was now "the rebirth of civic life in the difficult conditions of Poland." Democracy was said to require the self-organization and expansion of "civil society," and more than one theorist assumed that any such activity had to be oppositional. Poland would be marked by a more or less continuous conflict between the political regime and "society," a conflict that would bring political democracy to socialism.[42] Earlier appeals to the state had not worked; "the only policy for dissidents in Eastern Europe is an unceasing struggle for reforms, in favor of evolution which will extend civil liberties and guarantee a respect for human rights."[43] Civil society could serve as the seedbed for a constitutional revision of the socialist project. Invoking the Polish rebellion of 1956 and the Prague Spring's 1968 desire to organize "socialism with a human face," Michnik charted a pluralist strategy that owed as much to Tocqueville as to anyone and would prove very influential in the future course of events:

> What distinguishes the opposition today . . . is the conviction that such a program of evolution should be addressed to independent public opinion and not just to the totalitarian authorities. Instead of acting as a prompter to the government, telling it how to improve itself, this program should tell society how to act. As far as the government is concerned, it can have no clearer counsel than that provided by the social pressure from below.[44]

Almost all the participants in the Polish drama echoed Michnik's claim that democracy required defending "civil society" from the state. They tried to avoid charges of subversion by insisting that the voluntary organizations of which they spoke were independent of the market and did not imply a restoration of capitalism.[45] But the suggestion that civil society could be theorized as a nonstate and nonmarket public sphere proved increasingly problematic and it became unclear just what it consisted of. One syndicalist approach suggested that civil society comprised the "new social movements" that had arisen independently of the state, had no connection to the market, and could form the core of a "self-managing" society in the West as well as the East. Other participants adopted a classical Tocquevillean viewpoint and simply ignored the market. By the mid-1980s most of the movement's spokespeople were suggesting that the democratic opposition burrow into "society" to carve out a sphere of activity that would be protected from politics. But the earlier hopes that a reformed civil society could coexist with a single-party state and a socialist economy gradually faded. The temporary compromise between Solidarity and the government articulated in the 1980 Gdansk Agreement signified that "society" acknowledged the leading role of the Party and had decided not to seek political power. "For the first time," Michnik said, "organized authority was signing an accord with an organized society. The agreement marked the creation of labor unions independent of the state which vowed not to attempt to take over political power." But everyone knew that the Gdansk accords were temporary compromises between two antagonistic conceptions of civil society. The Church's resistance to official atheism, the villages' resistance to collectivization, and the intelligentsia's resistance to censorship had cleared the way for the workers to organize—for the moment, at least. "The essence of the spontaneously growing Independent and Self-governing Labor Union Solidarity lay in the restoration of social ties, self-organization aimed at guaranteeing the defense of labor, civil, and national rights. For the first time in the history of communist rule in Poland 'civil society' was being restored, and it was reaching a compromise with the state."[46] By the early 1980s the "self-limiting revolution of civil society against the state" had confined itself to limiting arbitrary state power and had settled into an unstable coexistence with a weakened but hostile political apparatus.[47]

Events in the Soviet Union seemed to confirm that a Tocquevillean civil society of autonomous organizations could grow in a socialist environment. Urbanization, the transformation of the countryside, widespread literacy and mass education, declining interest in politics, the slow growth of an "underground" economy, the development of "horizontal" forms of communication such as the automobile and the radio, and similar manifestations of a maturing social order led to a situation in which "the Communist party newspaper *Pravda* acknowledged the existence of more than 30,000 *neformaly,* grass-roots voluntary associations dedicated to various types of civic improvement."[48] A popular trend of thought identified Mikhail Gorbachev's political reforms as an eleventh-hour attempt to "uncork" the energy of a vibrant civil society that had somehow developed in the conditions of a command economy and a one-party state but was constrained by a conservative bureaucracy. Like his counterparts in Eastern Europe, Gorbachev seems to have regarded political democracy as the first step in a socialist renewal that was soon indistinguishable from classic social democracy. He knew that it had become impossible to stimulate the further development of Soviet civil society without significantly loosening political controls, for the weakened Soviet state was increasingly unable to direct social and political developments. A "revolution from above" was no longer possible, and Gorbachev seemed genuinely committed to some sort of "socialist pluralism" that would rest on market reforms and a "liberation of civil society." Buffeted by its own successes, hamstrung by its failures, and transformed by the evolution of electronically organized forces of production, Soviet society could no longer be organized on the basis of politically driven central planning. *Glasnost* could lead to *perestroika*; democracy in politics could bring democracy in civil society.[49]

No matter how promising some developments appeared, it was soon clear that the intense hostility to the state that characterized Eastern European conceptions of democracy and civil society was bound to open the door to the market. It proved impossible to think of a "socialist civil society" apart from the logic of capitalism. Civil liberties and constitutional protections are not inherently opposed to a planned economy and democratic supervision of the market, but the Eastern Europeans could not independently negotiate their way through the political and theoretical complexities of their immediate environment. In fairness to them, they were not alone. Whatever their intentions, their understanding of civil society soon proved incapable of coexisting with "actual existing socialism."

The Limits Are Reached

Their initial goal of a pluralist socialism led dissident spokespeople to describe their project as the simple "self-organization of society." But their commitment to a "self-limiting" process that would not directly challenge the prerogatives of the party-state faded as Eastern Europe's crisis intensified. An increasingly explicit denial that any social grouping can represent universal interests led Michnik to assert that in Poland "a stability founded upon an agreement with the will of the party has nothing to do with a democratic equilibrium which is the result of a continuously renewed compromise between the various elements of society."[50] His earlier call to turn away from the state was amplified in his suggestion that it was no longer a matter of forging a contract between a sovereign "society" and political authority, but "an agreement that society had to make with itself."[51] All over the region, civil society was explicitly identified with the opposition. It might be possible to negotiate a momentary compromise between it and increasingly illegitimate state, but the immediate task was to organize "an agreement of society with itself, independently of any agreement between society and state power."[52] This meant that "society" would have to organize and prioritize "its" demands in such areas as housing, health care, and education. Sooner or later these demands would be presented to the state, but for the moment civil society meant an independent network of communications, education, and information. Just how society would debate, prioritize, and represent "its" demands in the absence of political institutions or even a coherent theory of politics remained to be seen. For the moment it was clear that a civil society of voluntary organizations and social movements had to resist the state while stopping short of openly contesting it.[53]

A distinctly liberal political theory soon followed. Much of it arose in reaction to the ruling parties' demands that their "leading role" be respected. Echoing a criticism as old as the Russian Revolution, Vaclav Havel now equated socialism with empty sloganeering, the wooden extension of political categories into areas where they did not belong, and too little freedom from meddlesome politicians and their intrusive bureaucracies. The only proper task of the state, he said, is to defend the institutional bases of a depoliticized, independent, pluralist, and self-organizing civil society. Anything else is a mortal threat to personal autonomy and social health. This trend of thought, which had been implicit in the civil society literature from the very beginning, would soon consider how personal autonomy could be protected by political democracy, civil liberty, and the rule of law.[54]

Some theorists suggested that the artificial origin of Eastern European socialism explained their countries' distorted social structures. Their natural course of democratic capitalist development had been interrupted by World War II, and Yalta had imposed the USSR's state-led model on an environment to which it was ill-suited. The imperatives of world politics had held this artificial structure in place for a long time, but "society's internal dynamics more and more strain the limits of these institutions, which increasingly stifle economic growth, democratic impulses, and aspirations for personal autonomy."[55] The rest of Europe could no longer be ignored, and a healthy civil society required abandoning the Yalta settlement. If this required the dissolution of the Warsaw Pact and the unification of Europe, "antipolitics" would "put politics in its place and make sure it stays there, never overstepping its proper office of defending and refining the rules of the game of civil society. Antipolitics is the ethos of civil society, and civil society is the antithesis of military society."[56] Civil society's rebellion against socialism's hyperpolitics now assigned to the state the traditional liberal responsibility of establishing the rule of law and defending the institutions of market society. "Official quarters are gradually taking cognizance of reality in both economy and culture. They are also becoming aware of the real system of values, that of the market and of undirected popular opinion."[57]

If the market lay at the heart of civil society, then "antipolitics" generated a liberal theory of the state. "The state can be the protector of society and can serve to articulate its interests; indeed, those things are its business."[58] The only way to protect "society," safeguard individual autonomy, and control the party-state's tendency to politicize everything was to abandon Marxism and reassert the old liberal distinction between the state and society. "The state drags countless matters, questions, and decisions into politics that have no business there—private matters and technical questions with which, in the last analysis, the state has nothing to do."[59] Havel reported that the plight of an alternative rock-and-roll band led him to a more direct confrontation with the Czech regime, and other activists made the eminently reasonable point that a normal civil society requires that such areas as science, music, religion, and animal husbandry be freed from "the pathological bloat of the political state."[60] Not everything is amenable to political expression or solution. "I favor 'antipolitical politics,' that is, politics not as the technology of power and manipulation, of cybernetic rule over humans or as the art of the utilitarian, but politics as one of the ways of seeking and achieving meaningful lives, of protecting them and serving them," said Havel. "I favor politics as practical morality, as service to the truth, as essentially human and humanly measured care for our fellow humans."[61] A humanistic "antistatism" remained central to much of Eastern Europe's oppositional "civil society," but not all accounts of its potential were as vague as Havel's.

> Because politics has flooded nearly every nook and cranny of our lives, I
> would like to see the flood recede. We ought to depoliticize our lives, free

them from politics as from some contagious infection. We ought to free our simple everyday affairs from considerations of politics. I ask that the state do what it's supposed to do, and do it well. But it should not do things that are society's business, not the state's. So I would describe the democratic opposition as not a political but an antipolitical opposition, since its essential activity is to work for destatification.[62]

Consolidating an autonomous private sphere would require a set of property rights and a serious opening to the market. If the state's task is "defending and refining the rules of the game of civil society," it would be neutral in Hayek's liberal sense. Many areas of public and private life would now be left open, undecided, and unaddressed—but that meant that they would be determined by the market, increasingly seen as an impartial sphere of free choice, opportunity, and economic advance whose coercion could be ignored because it did not originate in politics. The formal abandonment of economic redistribution followed as a matter of course. "All those who want to replace formal democracy with so-called substantive democracy, and thereby reunify state and society in a totalizing way, surrender democracy as such."[63]

It was not long before civil society's antistatist ideology of spontaneous self-organization, privacy, interest, and self-actualizing activity explicitly embraced the market and the liberal state. Its early spokespeople had ignored economic matters and were never asked to explain how a "self-limiting" sphere could fail to end with the full-scale introduction of capitalism. By the end of the 1980s they dropped the pretensions. "Sociologists link the return of civil society to the growing interest in the marketization of the bankrupt communist economies," declared one analysis. If "civil society has been the counterpart of liberalism understood as a pluralist system where individuals organize themselves outside the orbit of statal domination," then perhaps Tocqueville and Smith were not so far apart after all.[64]

The Soviet system is, in part, a grand exercise in subordinating social relations to the human will. It is also testament to the futility of such an attempt. The exertions of the Soviet people themselves, whether encouraged, cajoled or bludgeoned by their rulers, have been enormous. Their results have not, on balance, been worth the costs. But there is a deeper point to be made. The very attempt to control all aspects of one's life, of which modern communism is an example, is doomed to failure. Social life is too complex; the methods we have for analyzing it are, at the finest levels, intrinsically distorting; the ways we have of intervening are too clumsy. In addition, individuals initiate social relations which then have a life of their own, in which individuals participate, but over which they have only limited control; the market is a prime—and in this case very relevant—example. Such social relations bring benefits as well as risks. To try to bend them to our wills tends to destroy whatever benefits they may have. The point of this classical liberal view . . . is that attempts such as the Soviet to master society and history are inevitably destructive and produce vastly more misery than they are promoted to eradicate.[65]

A "self-organizing" and "self-limiting" civil society separated from the state by property rights and the rule of law would inevitably be constituted by the market. Indeed, exchange relations were seen as just another sphere of civil society requiring benign protection from a limited constitutional state. "The term 'civil society' has a long history, but it has become prominent in the recent debates in Eastern Europe and the USSR over the future of socialist regimes. It is a way of connoting the separateness of certain social relations, especially those involving exchange, from those which characterize politics. Its users accept that social life is divided into separate spheres; its advocates accept that social life *ought* to be divided into separate spheres."[66] Command economies and one-party states disrupt the autonomy of these separate spheres so thoroughly that it becomes impossible to organize the pursuit of self-interest in the only sphere that really matters. Political democracy and capitalism were now one and the same:

> The point is that the success of political freedoms in the Soviet Union depends on the revival or reinvigoration of civil society—in effect, to create rival or countervailing powers to the power of the state—and that this in turn depends on the implementation of the right to private property and the restoration of the market, including the market in capital goods. There is no certainty about the links between private property and political freedoms; the former provides the necessary but not sufficient basis for the latter. The only certainty is that the attempt to destroy private property and the market is the prelude to the loss of political freedoms and the downgrading of living standards.[67]

Liberal theories of civil society have always held that the material foundation of freedom is private property and that civil society requires a legally protected system of individual property rights. It follows that the restoration of civil society in Eastern Europe "presupposes the transformation of collectivist property rights into private property rights, or the restoration of private property rights over basic resources."[68] But the restoration of market relations in Eastern Europe has required considerable activity by a highly interventionist state. Maybe the state is not such an inveterate enemy of liberty after all—provided that it nurtures the legal and material conditions for the development of markets and abandons the utopian dream of subjecting the economy to democratic supervision.

"Civil society" in communist systems was initially understood as an emerging sphere of autonomous association that required political and legal protection from a state before which it also stood as a democratic challenge. But it soon became clear that much more was implied than initially had been assumed. By the end of the 1980s events had outstripped the limitations of early projections. Now "the tasks assigned to civil society are substantially different: its role is to be constitutive and preservative of the liberal-democratic political systems and free-market economies that the new post-communist elites have so sonorously committed themselves to build."[69] Civil society is "the realm of society, lying outside the institutionalized political and administrative mechanisms of the state and the state-regulated part of the economy, where people carry on their publicly oriented social and economic activities. What makes it 'civil' is the fact that it is the locus where citizens may freely organize themselves into smaller or larger groups and associations at various levels in order to pressurize the formal bodies of state authority into adopting policies consonant with their perceived interests."[70] Tocqueville and Smith were happily reconciled.

As we have seen, the revival of interest in civil society originated in efforts by the dissident Eastern European intelligentsia to democratize "actual existing socialism." Understandably directing their efforts against the one-party state's monopoly of political activity, they paid relatively little attention to economic matters. But they were soon forced to confront the basic economic structures of a planned economy, and before long they discovered the market as a self-regulating sphere of individual opportunity and social welfare that could combat the dead hand of an inefficient, hypocritical, and self-serving state bureaucracy. In the end, their hopes that a "self-limiting" civil society could democratize communism without going over to capitalism could not transcend the limitations of their liberal content. Couching their appeals in terms of "democracy," the "public sphere," "pluralism," and the like, they failed to address the impact of the market and seem to have imagined that "civil society" could be reconstituted free of charge. A "self-governing" civil society with no professional political parties, autonomous political bodies, or institutionalized political life was a fantasy from the very beginning. The civic associations, student leagues, trade unions, and other voluntary groupings that played such a dramatic role in the late 1980s have been swept away; hopes of social, political, and economic renewal have dimmed; and economic inequality and social insecurity have accompanied the appropriation of the "self-limiting revolution" by traditional political formations. The links between liberal political theory and the capitalist market have been reasserted with a vengeance. Civil society could no more be theorized as an autonomous sphere in "actual existing socialism" than it can in actual existing capitalism.

Couched as it is in the liberal constitutionalist language of spontaneous voluntary organization, the new discourse of civil society is of only limited use in revealing what happened in Eastern Europe. It certainly illuminates some profound weaknesses of contemporary communism and sheds light on how mass movements were able to successfully confront the region's bureaucratized party-states. Even so, theories of civil society have fallen behind a social reality that they helped bring about but cannot satisfactorily explain. Understandably weary of the bureaucratized and empty public life that had come to characterize "actual existing socialism," Eastern Europeans had built these theories on a suspicion of state power and universal claims. But their elevation of autonomy, individual interest, and particularism serves to protect the economy from democratic scrutiny or supervision. It is not "civil society" that has been restored in Eastern Europe—it is *capitalism*.

The limitations of the civil society literature are not confined to Eastern Europe. The triumph of the right in England and the United States opened the way to an intensified attack on the welfare state, an increased reliance on markets, and a heightened level of social inequality. If civil society cannot solve the problems of communism, what does it have to say about the problems of its historic antagonist?

8

Civil Society and Capitalism

The Eastern European dissidents who deployed the language of civil society in their attack on the socialist state might be excused their failure to appreciate the looming danger of the capitalist market. Whatever combination of naiveté, desperation, and irresponsibility was at work, they had powerful antagonists to contend with, important allies to satisfy, and few indigenous sources of theoretical support or practical activity on which to draw. They may have honestly imagined that a resuscitated "civil society" could coexist with a generous set of social benefits, but the iron logic of the market's demands for austerity soon disabused them of their hopes.

Under the circumstances, it made sense that their civil society of liberal constitutionalism and intermediate associations had been aimed at the one-party bureaucratic state. "Actual existing socialism" had delivered an important measure of social welfare, but political democracy was quite another matter. This helps explain why the Eastern Europeans theorized civil society in liberal terms. Economic matters were mostly left aside, their unpleasant side effects to be addressed after the establishment of a "law-governed state" and the reunification of Europe. But there was a price to be paid, and the bill soon came due. The hope that an energized population would be able to defend its public sphere faded as both the market and the states that extended and protected it were revealed as arenas of compulsion, inequality, and exclusion. By the mid-1990s the once-heady discourse of civil society was beginning to fade in Eastern Europe.

No matter. Its enormous popularity in the United States cuts across the political spectrum and has become indispensable to a wide variety of public figures. In February 1998, Hillary Clinton asked the assembled bankers, industrialists, and politicians of the World Economic Forum to defend free markets, effective governments, and the intermediate associations of civil society that stand between them. Less than a month later, New York's Mayor Rudolph Giuliani announced his intention to make the city a "civil society" of people who temper their legendary surliness with good manners and public spirit. Banks, corporations, and governments are being asked to strengthen "micro-enterprises" in Africa, civic education projects in Bulgaria, and campaigns against littering, jaywalking, and car alarms in the Big Apple. Few observers cared to comment on how the First Lady's goals might be undermined by her husband's support for NAFTA, or how the Mayor's initiative could be reconciled with his plan to privatize the municipal hospital system. In one of the most thoroughly commercialized social orders in human history, civil society is supposed to limit the intrusive state, attenuate the ravages of the market, reinvigorate a moribund public sphere, rescue beleaguered families, and revitalize community life.

However recent this new American lexicon might appear, its foundations were laid by pluralist social science during the 1950s and 1960s. The suggestion that democracy requires more than formal political structures was aimed at revealing the sources of Western stability and articulating a credible alternative to communist "totalitarianism." Pluralism's central project was explaining how private interests can be organized and expressed without the destabilizing politics of social class. Private desires, the theorists of pluralism said, are "aggregated" by interest groups, voluntary associations, political parties, and parliaments and represented to appropriate governmental elites for adjudication and compromise. Intermediate bodies and overlapping forms of membership became a defining quality of "modernization" as intellectuals proclaimed "the end of ideology" and explained how citizen apathy could enable elites to lead mass societies in conditions of social reform and political stability. A consumer society without historic parallel was taking shape in the United States, and pluralism helped lower the temperature as it demonstrated how nonpolitical interests could serve social integration.

If contemporary theories of civil society are inspired by Tocqueville and the early pluralists, however, the environment in which they have developed is considerably more troubled and less celebratory than that of their forerunners. Massive deindustrialization, unprecedented inequality, and a pervasive sense of moral decline have led political leaders and intellectuals to ask more of civil society than ever before. Pluralism's ideology of citizen apathy, elite direction, and bureaucratic expertise has yielded to a quieter, less confident, and more local point of view. But "pluralism lite" has its blind side. Even if they are acutely aware of the dangers and opportunities of state power, contemporary theorists find it as difficult to take account of the market as did their predecessors.

Pluralist Foundations

Heavily influenced by economic models, American political science emerged from World War II focused on the individual actor as the only agent who can understand his interests and formulate a plan of action around them. In this scenario, the sum of individual decisions determined political activity. David Truman stood at the beginning of pluralist efforts to understand how interest groups shaped state activity in a period of heightened demands on political systems. "In all societies of any degree of complexity," he asserted, "the individual is less affected directly by the society as a whole than through various of its subdivisions, or groups." Understanding politics required an examination of the resulting mediations. Interest groups' impact on "the governmental process" depended on their formal structure, internal politics, quality of leadership, and sources of cohesion.[1]

Truman's emphasis on the process by which nongovernmental actors affect public affairs moved him away from the formal descriptions of institutions and structures that had characterized American political science. Individuals are driven to political activity by private concerns, which are "aggregated" by interest groups and presented to an open and permeable political system. Politics is about adjudicating disputes, and democracy requires a set of informal and legal procedures that guarantee access and equality. Power in civil society is widely distributed and extremely decentralized, and institutional neutrality is required if all interests are to receive a fair hearing. Periodic elections, a free press, and civil liberties enable different elites to present a variety of positions to political leaders and engage in open debate.

Truman's focus on individual interest and group behavior moved away from the broad, comprehensive concerns that have often animated political analysis. Like Tocqueville, pluralist theorists located stability in the interactions of the local, immediate, and small. They explicitly sought to replace the politics of social class with the bargaining of competitive interest groups, hoping to pose a credible alternative to the Left's tendency to embrace big political projects. If mass society threatened to create an empty space between individuals and the state, pluralism populated civil society with a multitude of interest groups that could tame popular passions and turn individual interest to the service of stability. "In developing a group interpretation of politics," Truman said, "we do not need to account for a totally inclusive interest, because one does not exist."[2] Public policy results from the interplay between interest group claims; access depends on their position in civil society, their internal organization, and the institutions toward which they direct their efforts. Understanding politics means understanding these complex interactions. "Whether we look at an individual citizen, at the executive secretary of a trade association, at a political party functionary, at a legislator, administrator, governor, or judge, we cannot describe his participation in the governmental institution, let alone account for it, except in terms of the interests with which he identifies himself and the groups with which he affiliates and with which he is confronted."[3]

Such an account relied on a market model to describe civil society and the state—but it was a market without Adam Smith's invisible hand. In its absence, Truman identified two regulatory devices that maintained political stability. The first was a complicated Madisonian structure of multiple memberships and overlapping loyalties. Class no longer provided a single center of gravity to individual and group interests, and the resulting dispersal weakened the force of any particular claim and limited the influence of any single group. The fact that people had a variety of often-competing interests spread public and private concerns over a wide area and made concentrated, focused activity difficult. Elites can operate relatively freely in such an environment because they will be only lightly restrained by civil society's diffuse network of interests.

But pluralism was not hostile to the state in principle, and Truman shared Madison's commitment to effective governance. If multiple affiliations and overlapping membership served stability, he warned, they could also result in paralysis. "We cannot account for an established American political system without the second crucial element in our conception of the political process, the concept of the unorganized interest, or potential group."[4] A widespread consensus underpins civil society's interest groups and the formal mechanisms of state. "These widely held but unorganized interests are what we have previously called the 'rules of the game'" and are guarded by elites; they can be summarized as adherence to the rule of law, respect for disagreement, an expectation that losers will not resort to violence after elections, and a modest social egalitarianism.[5] The turmoil of the 1960s and 1970s would drive consensual pluralism to the sidelines soon enough, but for the moment Truman was confident that he had discovered the two features of the American system's exceptional adaptability and stability:

> It is thus multiple memberships in potential groups based on widely held and accepted interests that serve as a balance wheel in a going political system

like that of the United States. . . . Without the notion of multiple memberships in potential groups it is literally impossible to account for the existence
of a viable polity such as that in the United States or to develop a coherent
conception of the political process. The strength of these widely held but
largely unorganized interests explains the vigor with which propagandists for
organized groups attempt to change other attitudes by invoking such interests. . . . In a relatively vigorous political system . . . these unorganized interests are dominant with sufficient frequency in the behavior of enough important segments of the society so that, despite ambiguity and other restrictions,
both the activity and the methods of organized interest groups are kept
within broad limits.[6]

Overlapping memberships and the "rules of the game" could cut across
many fault lines in civil society and discourage the sort of class conflict
whose divisive effects could be seen in Europe.[7] Tocqueville could tame
Marx. A "pathogenic" politics organized around class issues was always possible in the United States, but Truman echoed later pluralists' confidence
that disruption could be contained fairly easily. The "governmental process"
was stable and, like the market mechanisms on which it was modeled, it
tended toward equilibrium. Pluralist democracy required that elites compete, that they obey the rules of the game, and that voters be free to choose
among them. In an era of economic growth, political apathy, and ideological conformity, "the existence of the state, of the polity, depends on widespread, frequent recognition of and conformity to the claims of these unorganized interests and on activity condemning marked deviation from
them."[8] The cold war made it important to focus on fundamentals and understand how civil society could serve political stability.

> The strength of the unorganized "rules of the game" in the United States
> has been remarked by foreign observers from De Tocqueville to Myrdal. The
> latter, for example, speaks of them as being more "explicitly expressed" and
> "more widely understood and appreciated" in America than in other Western
> nations. The great political task now as in the past is to perpetuate a viable
> system by maintaining the conditions under which such widespread under-
> standing and appreciation can exist. These conditions are not threatened by
> the existence of a multiplicity of organized groups so long as the "rules of the
> game" remain meaningful guides to action, meaningful in the sense that ac-
> ceptance of them is associated with some minimal recognition of group
> claims. In the loss of such meanings lie the seeds of the whirlwind.[9]

Like Tocqueville, Truman looked to informal nonpolitical inclinations to
ensure responsiveness and safeguard unity in a complex polity. Political

equilibrium, economic expansion, and cold war were always pluralism's central concerns, and by the middle of the 1960s Gabriel Almond and Sidney Verba had imaginatively applied modern survey techniques to describe how "political culture" could fortify Truman's "rules of the game" and strengthen the already powerful tendency in American political science to attribute system effectiveness and regime stability to nonpolitical factors. Early pluralism's focus on interest groups testified to the newfound importance of sociology. Now an adapted anthropology was brought to bear. Democracy—still understood as a network of relations between elites and masses—required a determinate "political culture" whose roots could be found in "community life, social organization, and upbringing of children" in addition to the formal institutions of state.[10]

Three different amalgams of psychological dispositions and levels of political activity framed the analysis. The "parochial" culture of the undeveloped "third world" was marked by low levels of interest, activity, and allegiance, while communism's "subject" culture revealed high levels of political knowledge about governmental activity but was hobbled by a low sense of individual efficacy. Finally, the Anglo-American "participant" culture featured high levels of political interest, activity, and sense of individual influence. Echoing the concerns that were driving academic analysis and U.S. foreign policy, *The Civic Culture* recommended that the "modernizing" nation-states of Asia, Africa, and Latin America adopt a civil society that combined elements of all three. Economic progress and political development could best be managed by the open and flexible hybrid that had developed in England. Sharing pluralism's faith in the creative power of elites, Almond and Verba attributed the victory of British parliamentarism to modernizing aristocrats, merchants, and ministers whose political culture had enabled England to move away from royal absolutism without risking the disruptiveness of mass politics or sacrificing its plural civil society. Moderate and sensible England stood as a model to the world.

> What emerged was a third culture, neither traditional nor modern but partaking of both: a pluralistic culture based on communication and persuasion, a culture of consensus and diversity, a culture that permitted change but moderated it. This was the civic culture. With this civic culture already consolidated, the working classes could enter into politics and, in a process of trial and error, find the language in which to couch their demands and the means to make them effective. It was in this culture of diversity and consensualism, rationalism and traditionalism, that the structure of British democracy could develop: parliamentarism and representation, the aggregative po-

litical party and the responsible and neutral bureaucracy, the associational and bargaining interest groups, and the autonomous and neutral media of communication. English parliamentarism included the traditional and modern forces; the party system aggregated and combined them; the bureaucracy became responsible to the new political forces; and the political parties, interest groups, and neutral media of communication meshed continuously with the diffuse interest groupings of the community and with its primary communications networks.[11]

Political struggle, Chartism, Diggers and Levellers, Cromwell, strikes, bloody repression—all of these elements of British history were dwarfed by consensus and compromise in *The Civic Culture*. The media, bureaucracy, and state are neutral; class conflict disappears; and as soon as one learns the rules of the game one can become a productive citizen in a polity that gives political expression to all legitimate interests. Like many social scientists of the period, Almond and Verba shared Truman's worries that high levels of political activity might be politically destabilizing. This is why their composite "civic culture" combined participation with enough parochial and subject orientations to keep it within safe boundaries. "The nonparticipant, more traditional political orientations tend to limit the individual's commitment to politics and to make that commitment milder. In a sense, the subject and parochial orientations 'manage' or keep in place the participant political orientations," they observed. "The maintenance of these more traditional attitudes *and their fusion* with the participant orientations lead to a balanced political culture in which political activity, involvement, and rationality exist but are balanced by passivity, traditionality, and commitment to parochial values."[12] In a curious reversal of the classical understanding, democracy now required widespread apathy and nonparticipation.[13] The civic culture could pose an alternative to communism's dangerous political mobilization by limiting grand visions with local interests. Civil society's dense networks of associations increase citizens' political influence on the state, make them less vulnerable to mass demagoguery, and reduce the importance of politics by spreading interests over a wide public space. It is "the prime means by which the function of mediating between the individual and the state is performed" and "help him avoid the dilemma of being either a parochial, cut off from political influence, or an isolated and powerless individual, manipulated and mobilized by the mass institutions of politics and government."[14] Civil society makes possible the sort of moderate political activity that reconciles Tocquevillean localism with the large institutions of contemporary public life. Its members "are neither parochials, cut off from politics, nor intensely partisan in ways that might lead to political fragmentation. And this balance, as we have said, is needed for a successful democracy: there must be involvement in politics if there is to be the sort of participation necessary for democratic decision-making; yet the involvement must not be so intense as to endanger stability."[15] Civil society could provide a moderate anchor to public life in an unstable age.

> This is not to say that politics is unimportant in Britain and America. Respondents report that it plays a significant role in their lives, it is of interest to the populace, it is a topic of conversation. It is all these things frequently. . . . Yet politics is "kept in its place." The values associated with it are subordinate in significant respects to more general social values, and these more general social values act to temper political controversy within the two nations. In this way, again, we have a "managed" or "balanced" involvement in politics: an involvement that is kept from challenging the integration and stability of the political system.[16]

Like most liberal approaches to civil society, pluralism rested on interests generated outside politics. Almond and Verba's readiness to examine "political culture" introduced a more nuanced and subtle treatment than earlier attention to the individual determination of interest. "Primary affiliations," they asserted, "are important in the patterns of citizen influence—particularly if a diffuse set of social attitudes and interpersonal attitudes makes political matters less intense and divisive. Penetrated by primary group orientations and dispersed by a consensual political culture, public matters need not be driven by articulated principle and rational calculation."[17] Almond and Verba had learned the lesson of totalitarianism: too much politics is dangerous. It is best to think small, to be ready to compromise, and not to expect too much.

> In sum, the most striking characteristic of the civic culture . . . is its mixed quality. It is a mixture in the first place of parochial, subject, and citizen orientations. The orientation of the parochial to primary relationships, the passive political orientation of the subject, the activity of the citizen, all merge within the civic culture. The result is a set of political orientations that are managed or balanced. There is political activity, but not so much as to destroy governmental authority; there is involvement and commitment, but they are moderated; there is political cleavage, but it is held in check. Above all, the political orientations that make up the civic culture are closely related to general social and interpersonal orientations. Within the civic culture the norms of interpersonal relationships, of general trust and confidence in one's

social environment, penetrate political attitudes and temper them. The mixture of attitudes found in the civic culture . . . "fits" the democratic political system. It is, in a number of ways, particularly appropriate for the mixed political system that is democracy.[18]

Pluralism sought to explain how civil society's interest groups translate individual concerns into political terms and helped formulate public policy. It tried to demonstrate that they "articulate" and represent the desires of actors who enjoy equal opportunities to influence the positions of political elites. Multiple memberships and overlapping loyalties drive toward compromise and integration, and a moderate liberal democracy is best able to satisfy the broad range of interests generated in civil society without large-scale political disruption. Oriented toward regime stability and state legitimacy, pluralists were interested in intermediate associations if they could help elites lead and citizens approve. Government must be authoritative and responsible, and this required citizens who were influential and deferential. Civil society's intermediate associations were not a sphere of democratic action in their own right. They reinforced state legitimacy and helped it act in a Keynesian environment of cold war, economic growth, and moderate social reform.

Pluralism was perfectly adapted to the moderate politics of a contented postwar liberalism. Its organizing assumption was that private concerns of family, work, and consumption would absorb most citizens' energy. The fact that public matters were marginal and secondary served stability and elite autonomy. A consumerist "civic culture" reinforced social mobility, individual rights, moderation, regime effectiveness, and social order while holding participation in check and limiting the impact of ideology. In a period when American political science refused to theorize the state as a single coherent entity, pluralism's approval of a relatively uninformed and apathetic electorate was predicated on the view that voting was driven by local information and local interests.[19] Such an orientation made it difficult to explain why people would associate with one another for broad purposes at all.[20]

Social class disappeared from pluralist social science, even though it was clear that the interests that got organized, articulated, heard, and translated into policy were heavily influenced by economic considerations. But this was not easy for pluralist theorists to see. Pluralism's consumerist orientation toward politics—"who gets what, when and how"—located the source of individual preferences and interests outside the political system. Its claim that the masses are held in check by their ignorance, apathy, and deference turned out to be just as problematic as its assertion that elites are constrained by their internalized democratic values, the political system's institutions and periodic elections, and civil society's vigorous network of overlapping interest groups. Neither view would survive the revival of political life that characterized the late 1960s and early 1970s. The civil rights, anti-war, feminist, and other movements demonstrated that large numbers of people were perfectly capable of sustained democratic action, that elites were hostile as often as they were unreliable, and that existing political structures did not articulate all interests equally. Public life clearly added up to something more than the sum of individual interests, and many people were more than willing to act on the basis of big ideas. In many cases the obstacles to effective activity were hard to identify. But political affairs were clearly unfolding in a wider context than pluralism anticipated. As the period's "new social movements" developed, the operations of the economy became a central problem for theorists who were tempted to conceptualize civil society as an autonomous sphere.

The Commodified Public Sphere

Their effort to explain the crisis of the late 1960s led many Western intellectuals to the work of Antonio Gramsci. An early leader of the Italian Communist Party who was imprisoned for years by the fascists, Gramsci had tried to chart a new direction for the Left following the failure of the post–World War I revolutionary offensive. Gramsci wanted to know why European capitalism had survived a devastating world war, the Russian Revolution, a deep economic crisis, the defection of significant elements of the intelligentsia, and important proletarian uprisings. The notion of "hegemony" with which he is associated signaled a new focus on ideological and cultural matters that sparked an important superstructural theorization of civil society.

Gramsci began by tracing Leninism to the relatively undeveloped circumstances of Russian civil society. "In Russia," he observed, "the State was everything, civil society was primordial and gelatinous."[21] The relative openness and fluidity of the environment made possible a frontal attack on a state unprotected by strongly rooted social structures. The Russian autocracy was vulnerable because of its relative autonomy, and it followed that the class struggle in the East would be a "war of maneuver." But it was a mistake to assume that the Russian pattern of revolution would be repeated everywhere. The West had a far more complex and solid apparatus of bourgeois class rule, so a frontal attack on the state *à la Russe* was not possible. A long and difficult "war of position" would be necessary because the state and civil society were stronger and more articulated than had been the case in the first wave of revolution. In the West, said Gramsci, "there was a proper relation between State and civil society, and when the State trembled a sturdy structure of civil society was at once revealed."[22]

It followed that Western communists would not be served by a single-minded focus on the state. Gramsci's influential theory of hegemony suggested that the strong states and civil societies of Western Europe created different situations from those prevailing in the East. Since a powerful set of norms and institutions characterized bourgeois rule in advanced capitalist systems, Gramsci was convinced that Western Marxists had to pay serious attention to the culture and ideology that supported capitalism. Coercion was always important, but he believed that a hegemonic system of bourgeois rule had developed that enjoyed a high degree of support from all social classes. It followed that the tasks facing communists in the West were complex. "The massive structures of the modern democracies, both as State organizations, and as complexes of associations in civil society, constitute for the art of politics as it were the 'trenches' and the permanent fortifications of the front in the war of position; they merely render 'partial' the element of movement which before used to be 'the whole' of war, etc."[23]

Gramsci's account of the relation between the state and civil society was often unclear and contradictory, but he wanted to emphasize the role of ideology and accord it at least equal standing with state-organized coercion. A stratified consensual structure had arisen in advanced capitalist civil societies that was very fluid, flexible, and effective. Hegemony presupposed a certain measure of consent, incorporation, and collaboration. Institutions such as the family, property relations, and law interacted with the informal norms that governed marriage, work, and free time to produce a bourgeois civil society that organized a significant degree of consensus. None of this was new to Marxism, of course; Lenin had always insisted on the importance of ideological struggle and the mass parties of the Second and Third Internationals had developed such a complex array of labor institutions and social practices that it was possible to talk of "a state within the state." Their clubs, bars, newspapers, schools, publishing houses, comic books, camps, ethnic federations, and womens' groups certainly provided many sites from which to wage a counterhegemonic ideological struggle. Even if too much is often made of Gramsci's contribution to Marxism, he did understand that the course of events in Russia would not provide a universal template for Western communism. "The former had fallen at once, but unprecedented struggles had then ensued; in the case of the latter, the struggles would take place 'beforehand.' The question, therefore, was whether civil society resists before or after the attempt to seize power; where the latter takes place, etc."[24] The proletariat has to be prepared for a long war of position within the boundaries of capitalism, a struggle that would be similar to the bourgeoisie's protracted fight against medievalism.[25] Only after such a struggle was won could power be seized with the support of the population and socialism be built with the ease Marx had anticipated. If a still-untransformed civil society bedeviled Russia's communists after the relatively easy seizure of state power, Gramsci expected the more difficult early prospects for Western communists to put them in a much stronger position after their political victory.

Identifying civil society as the sphere in which hegemony is organized did not ignore the role of direct compulsion and domination. Gramsci simply wanted to highlight the importance of ideology and seems to have considered the state's task as combining hegemony and coercion, persuasion and force, consent and dictatorship. The state "in its integral meaning" was "dictatorship + hegemony," a formulation that illustrates his acute understanding of the importance of superstructural matters.[26] Consent was an indispensable element of bourgeois power in Europe, and Gramsci thought it essential that communists pay serious attention to the role of political democracy and a ramified civil society in organizing a stable pattern of bourgeois domination. Speaking in the elliptical language of the political prisoner, he asked his readers to consider civil society an aspect of bourgeois class rule. "If political science means science of the State, and the State is the entire complex of political and theoretical activities with which the ruling class not only justifies and maintains its dominance, but manages to win the active consent of those over whom it rules, then it is obvious that all the essential questions of sociology are nothing other than the questions of political science."[27] Direct force, domination, and the coercive institutions of "political society" are supplemented by the ideological hegemony the bourgeoisie exercises over national life through the schools, private associations, churches, and other institutions of its "civil society." Far from an autonomous sphere of voluntary association, then, Gramsci's civil society is as constituted by class power, market relations, and the commodity form as any other sphere of capitalist society.

Gramsci's interest in culture and ideology proved a prescient one. As interwar Europe lurched from crisis to crisis, more theorists began to wonder how it managed to survive. Max Horkheimer, Theodore Adorno, and their colleagues in the Frankfurt School turned their attention to the increasingly monpolistic, uniform, and dominant bourgeois culture that was developing with the technology of mass production and had become capable of structuring society as a whole.[28] All spontaneity was swallowed up by the market's ineluctable drive to arrange and package. Alternatives were erased by the triumph of a "culture industry" that presented a vast array of ideological commodities to passive consumers. If the proletariat had been unable to successfully resist fascism, Horkheimer and Adorno saw little hope in the aftermath of World War II. Written in 1948, their *Dialectic of Enlightenment* contended that the "normal" relationships between civil society and the state were being transformed because a structure of irresponsible and unaccountable bureaucratic power was acquiring the ability to weave all areas of public life into a seamless web of domination that was all the more powerful because it was so enthusiastically embraced.

The problem, they said, was that the Enlightenment had subverted its own emancipatory project. Its attack on myth and attempt to turn nature to the production of commodities had paralyzed the ability to imagine alternatives and identified freedom with a contented acceptance of the present. Modernity's progress had come with an enormous price. The triumph of the market and the commodification of everyday life turned instrumental rationality against all normative concerns, stimulated the triumph of bureaucratic forms of domination, and heralded the appearance of what Horkheimer and Adorno called the "totally administered society."

The Enlightenment had promised to free people from the dead hand of tradition, hierarchy, and superstition, but it ended up subordinating them to forces that stripped them of their capacity to make normative judgments—or even to realize that there were normative judgments to be made. A massive postwar consumer society stimulated the rapid growth of a conformist and profit-driven "culture industry" that sought the lowest common denominator for its products, hollowed everything out, penetrated every sphere of civil society, and eroded the ability to conceive of alternatives to the existing order. New forms of technology and novel methods of organizing production were transforming modern civilization, and powerful techniques of advertising were serving its mass markets. Everything these new social forces did was turned to the production and sale of commodities.

None of the old social classes—least of all the workers—could resist the logic of accumulation. Indeed, the new methods of social control were so effective because they relied on ideology. In an environment where everything could be bought and sold, ideology incorporated opposition and supplanted the direct application of coercive power to ensure conformity and strengthen domination. As the culture industry got more sophisticated, entertainment made oppression enjoyable precisely because it eliminated the cultural standards that used to supply a vantage-point for resistance. The totalizing logic of the commodity form found concrete expression in the organizing power of the culture industry.[29]

Horkheimer and Adorno extended Gramsci's work by focusing attention on the increasingly independent capacity of culture and ideology to organize civil society. Herbert Marcuse's *One Dimensional Man* brought their work to a new level in a powerful critique of civil society that enjoyed extraordinary influence during the tumultuous decade that followed its appearance in 1966. Advanced industrial society, it announced, has achieved new heights of integrating and absorbing the potential for resistance. Marcuse agreed with Horkheimer and Adorno that the project of turning nature to the production of commodities was the problem. "As the project unfolds, it shapes the entire universe of discourse and action, intellectual and material culture. In the medium of technology, culture, politics, and the economy merge into an omnipresent system which swallows up or repulses all alternatives. The productivity and growth potential of this system stabilize the society and contain technical progress within the framework of domination. Technological rationality has become political rationality."[30] Organized around the commodity form, instrumental reason, and bureaucracy, advanced industrial society systematically converts new technology from a tool of liberation into an instrument of domination.

Marcuse agreed with Horkheimer and Adorno that the culture industry was operating as an increasingly independent force. Its direct role in the commodification of life tends to flatten everything out because it seeks the lowest common denominator in an effort to sell as much as possible. Alternatives are integrated, potential sources of opposition are absorbed, and the emancipatory power of independent thought atrophies. Where earlier ages put civil liberties, speech, thought, reason, and conscience to subversive and liberating use, advanced industrial society uses them to refine the existing order. As alternatives vanish, nonconformity becomes increasingly hopeless and difficult. Technical means triumph over normative ends and reason now demands adaptation to oppression instead of a struggle against it. Just when domination, exploitation, and injustice have been intensified, Marcuse said, the culture industry makes resistance almost impossible because it renders it invisible. Anchored by advanced industrial society's enormous productivity and the ceaseless creation of artificial needs, a new sort of totalitarianism mocks pluralist democratic theory:

> By virtue of the way it has organized its technological base, contemporary industrial society tends to be totalitarian. For "totalitarian" is not only a terroristic political organization of society, but also a non-terroristic economic-technical coordination which operates through the manipulation of needs by vested interests. It thus precludes the emergence of an effective opposition against the whole. Not only a specific form of government or party rule makes for totalitarianism, but also a specific system of production and distribution which may well be compatible with a "pluralism" of parties, newspapers, "countervailing powers," etc.[31]

Marcuse thought that the new methods of social control are so powerful precisely because they operate at the level of consciousness. The culture industry engulfs the private and public spheres and subjects both to the same integrating and normalizing logic. No sphere is safe. Politics and culture become unified in a seamless web of numbing domination and entertaining oppression. "If mass communications blend together harmoniously, and often unnoticeably, art, politics, religion, and philosophy with commercials, they bring these realms of culture to their common denominator—the commodity form. The music of the soul is also the music of salesmanship. Exchange value, not truth value counts. On it centers the rationality of the status quo, and all alien rationality is bent to it."[32] Contemporary civil society's "happy consciousness" regards that which exists as that which must exist. In an environment where everything can be bought or sold, all certainties vanish with the ceaseless production of new fads and new scandals. Entertainment and conformity rule.

But all is not lost. Unlike Horkheimer and Adorno, for whom the Enlightenment's domination of nature and instrumental rationality culminated in Stalinism and Auschwitz, Marcuse discerned emancipatory possibilities in contemporary life. If the proletariat has been largely incorporated and is no longer the privileged agent of classical Marxism, "marginal groups" such as women, people of color, students, and the colonized can provide a critical perspective and subversive drive that could rescue the possibility of emancipation and revive the working class. Indeed, his ability to reclaim the liberating core of critical theory explains Marcuse's enormous popularity during the upheavals of the 1960s and 1970s.[33] At the same time, commodification had become such a powerful force that his concern about its effects were shared by much more cautious theorists.

Building on her earlier analysis of totalitarianism, Hannah Arendt tried to consider the effects of economic life on civil society. Alarmed by Nazism and communism, she shared a fear of mass political movements with many other intellectuals of her generation but was deeply worried by the hollowness of a postwar American politics that she feared was becoming identified with the most vulgar sort of commercialism. Ideological orthodoxy, mass communications, economic growth, the national security state, and a vast consumer society was accompanied by apathy, disengagement, and a celebration of domesticity. Some pluralists welcomed these developments and sought to incorporate them into a democratic theory that focused on elite responsiveness, but Arendt wanted to salvage the public sphere in an increasingly commodified and apolitical environment. She focused on the two distinctive attributes of "the human condition" that had been discovered in Athens.

The Greeks' distinction between the private and public, household and *polis*, constituted their first contribution to human freedom. This was supplemented by a second distinction between speech and action, the ways people disclose themselves to one another as they construct a common life. Both depend on plurality and multiplicity, but Arendt feared that the appearance of "society" was making it difficult for modern people to distinguish between what is properly private and what is legitimately public. The narrow issues the Greeks had relegated to the private realm have become inappropriate matters of common concern. "Society"—neither public nor private but a distorted amalgam of the two—represents the destructive and corrupting colonization of the public sphere by private concerns. "The disappearance of the gulf that the ancients had to cross daily to transcend the narrow realm of the household and 'rise' into the realm of politics is an essentially modern phenomenon."[34] The Greeks had called the household private because it was the sphere of necessity and need, but modernity's new hybrid realm lends private matters a false and misleading public significance.

> The emergence of society—the rise of housekeeping, its activities, problems, and organizational devices—from the shadowy interior of the household into the light of the public sphere, has not only blurred the old borderline between private and political, it has also changed almost beyond recognition the meaning of the two terms and their significance for the life of the

individual and the citizen. Not only would we not agree with the Greeks that a life spent in the privacy of "one's own" (*idion*), outside the world of the common, is "idiotic" by definition, or with the Romans to whom privacy offered but a temporary refuge from the business of the *res publica*; we call private today a sphere of intimacy whose beginnings we may be able to trace back to late Roman, though hardly to any period of Greek antiquity, but whose peculiar manifoldness and variety were certainly unknown to any period prior to the modern age.[35]

The victory of "society" has transformed the private sphere from a realm of necessity and unfreedom into a shelter for the individual and the intimate. Public life used to be constituted by speech and action precisely because it was freed from need and necessity, but "society" has driven its differences, pluralities, and multiplicities inward. The enrichment of the private is an impoverishment of the public, which atrophies when it ceases to make possible individual self-expression in the presence of others. Instead of characterizing people's life in public, "distinction and difference have become private matters of the individual."[36]

Echoing Burke, Arendt thought that society's ultimate victory is expressed in the bureaucratic state, the rule of nobody and the organizational expression of the "communistic fiction" that a single—or even a primary—interest can be discerned among the multitude of separate purposes, goals, and activities that constitutes any social organism. The problem is that politics has become polluted by material issues such as work, money, and welfare. The Greeks had consigned the morally deficient concerns of the "life process" to the private sphere, but mass society, commodification, Marxism, and the labor movement have brought them into public life. The state has become organized around the production and reproduction of wealth, and politics has lost its ennobling and humanizing distance from the material concerns of life. Based on everyday necessities and oriented toward the satisfaction of needs, commerce and labor have swallowed up the public sphere and emptied it of moral content. Living used to be the concern of the private sphere. Living *well*, on the other hand, concerned politics. But modern people live in "society" and can no longer make this essential distinction—or even understand why they should.

Public action can serve freedom only if it is made an end in itself, and this requires that the very category of "society" be contested. The state cannot take on the responsibility for social reproduction. Politics is more than civil liberties and constitutional rights; freedom is broader than the fulfillment of material desires; and public life cannot be a tool for protecting, adjusting, or reorganizing civil society. As troubled as she was by commodification, Arendt solved the problem of economics by declaring it inappropriate and irrelevant to politics. Her neo-Aristotelian sense of politics as leisurely self-revelation in a sphere of public action insulated from the contamination of economic affairs was an antimodern and elitist attempt to contain mass politics with the disinterestedness of public-minded aristocrats. Her idealized account of Greek life sought to preserve a public sphere where people freed from economic necessity could pursue excellence, honor, and recognition in speech and action. If the private sphere was the home of inequality, difference, and necessity, the *polis* recognized the equality of its members and made possible the purposive, deliberative construction of a common world. Arendt hoped that the lessons of Athens could provide modern people with a *point d'appui* in a mass society whose public life was increasingly colonized by economic concerns and private interests. In the end, she had little with which to counter the commodification of civil society except semi-aristocratic reminiscences.

Richard Sennett was far better able than Arendt to account for "the fall of public man" because he was less repelled by economic affairs than she was. He agreed that modernity places a unique value on private life, but he located the corruption of the public in an inappropriate and narcissistic drive for "intimacy" instead of the economic necessity that Arendt stressed. "In private we seek out not a principle but a reflection, that of what our psyches are, what is authentic in our feelings. We have tried to make the fact of being in private, alone with ourselves and with family and intimate friends, an end in itself." A commodified and self-absorbed civil society makes impossible that which it proclaims as the purpose of life. "Each person's self has become his principal burden; to know oneself has become an end, instead of a means through which one knows the world. And precisely because we are so self-absorbed, it is extremely difficult for us to arrive at a private principle, to give any clear account to ourselves or to others of what our personalities are. The reason is that, the more privatized the psyche, the less it is stimulated, and the more difficult it is for us to feel or express feeling."[37]

Even though its motive force is different, Sennett's "intimate society" is the product of the same breakdown of the public-private distinction that Arendt described. He was equally convinced that neither private nor public life was well served by their fusion. The lack of clear boundaries empties private life of its ability to nourish and saps the public sphere's capacity to address matters of common concern. The modern notion that the intimate is a matter of general public importance has given rise to a pervasively narcissistic culture that cannot articulate what is properly within the realm of the self—and, more importantly, what is outside it. Its debilitating self-absorption means that it cannot keep private what is genuinely private—a failure that renders it equally unable to appreciate what is public. Authenticity and self-disclosure cannot constitute a meaningful public life, said Sennett; to locate all meaning within the self spells the death of public life because it makes it difficult to work with strangers for common purposes. If knowing others and being known by them becomes the raison d'être of social life, it becomes impossible to understand the ancient truth that authentic public life depends on an important measure of anonymity.

> The obsession with persons at the expense of more impersonal social relations is like a filter which discolors our rational understanding of society; it obscures the continuing importance of class in advanced industrial societies; it leads us to believe community is an act of mutual self-disclosure and to undervalue the community relations of strangers, particularly those which occur in cities. Ironically, this psychological vision also inhibits the development of basic personality strengths, like respect for the privacy of others, or the comprehension that, because every self is in some measure a cabinet of horrors, civilized relations between selves can only proceed to the extent that nasty little secrets of desire, greed, or envy are kept locked up.[38]

The ancient notion of publicness implied meaningful contact with strangers and was always distinguished from the intimate, private sphere of family and friends. But the important moral content of a public life lived among strangers is lost as the pursuit of personal experience and feeling becomes the purpose of public as well as private life. "In an intimate society, all social phenomena, no matter how impersonal in structure, are converted into matters of personality in order to have a meaning."[39] Sennett's intimate society is characterized by the search for authenticity; the notion that social life must be organized around the search for openness and honesty; the narcissistic concern with the self; and the claim that isolation, loneliness, and alienation are the most important problems of modern life. They have a deeply harmful effect because they make it difficult to even think about changing existing conditions. The personal is not the political, he insisted. On the contrary, public life consists of strangers who cooperate in constructing the common good *without ceasing to be strangers*. The intimate society makes such a life impossible.

The reigning belief today is that closeness between persons is a moral good. The reigning aspiration today is to develop individual personality through experiences of closeness and warmth with others. The reigning myth today is that the evils of society can be understood as evils of impersonality, alienation, and coldness. The sum of these three is an ideology of intimacy: social relationships of all kind are real, believable, and authentic the closer they approach the inner psychological concerns of each person. This ideology transmutes political categories into psychological categories.[40]

Sennett revealed the bitter irony of an intimate society that makes civility impossible. People cannot develop relations with others when they are deemed insignificant precisely *because* they are impersonal. Contrary to its protestations, the intimate society is a rude society, for civility is "the activity which protects people from each other and yet allows them to enjoy each other's company."[41] Living with people does not require getting to "know" them or making sure that they "know" you. Confusing the two burdens others with oneself, falsely identifies sociability with self-centeredness, and substitutes intrusive selfishness for a genuine concern for the welfare of others. It creates people whose true incivility consists in their need for others only to the extent that they can talk about themselves. "Civility exists," Sennett observed, "when a person does not make himself a burden to others."[42]

Sennett's *The Fall of Public Man* is a remarkably prescient criticism of the currently fashionable notion that a civil society organized around community and intimacy necessarily provides a fit alternative to powerlessness, alienation, and loneliness. The logic of local defense against an invasive outside world ignores humanity's experience that people grow when they experience new things and new people. The intimate society is a symptom of the same disease it purports to cure. "Love of the ghetto, especially the middle-class ghetto, denies the person a chance to enrich his perceptions, his experience, and learn that most valuable of human lessons, the ability to call the established conditions of his life into question."[43] The defense of local interests will always invariably degenerate into a self-satisfied ideology of exclusion that denies the possibilities that come only when the autonomy of strangers is respected and prized. The deep meaning of social life is found when one joins with others in a common endeavor without having to "know" them. Civil society is not a tribe.

Horkheimer, Adorno, Arendt, and Sennett all worried that the commodification of civil society was making it impossible to defend public life from market forces. Each described the process differently, but their diagnoses of the disease were remarkably similar. The totalizing logic of the commodity form threatened to fuse public and private and thereby endanger democracy. In some respects, this has been the central problem of much modern political philosophy. No contemporary thinker has been more influential in trying to specify the public sphere as a series of mediations between civil society and the state than Jürgen Habermas, whose work represents critical theory's best effort to resolve the issues that engaged Arendt and Sennett.

Habermas was a student of Horkheimer and Adorno, and his great contribution to contemporary theories of civil society began with his historical account of the rise of a "discursive public sphere" that enabled people to talk about common concerns in conditions of freedom and equality. Conditioned by the development of capitalism and the early forms of commodity production, the liberal public sphere allowed the free exchange of views to construct public opinion and establish principles of legitimacy by limiting those who hold political power. "By 'the public sphere,'" he says, "we mean first of all a realm of our social life in which something approaching public opinion can be formed."[44] The free exchange of views and "public opinion" were intimately connected to the needs of merchants who sought public forums in which they could discuss their business affairs. Private economic matters assumed general significance as markets in commodities generated markets in news, and as information became essential to commerce. A press began to develop and was soon supplemented by coffee and tea houses, salons, playhouses, learned societies, and other venues organized around the free exchange of information.

The appearance of this "informational and discursive liberal public sphere" extended the private concerns of a developing bourgeois civil society into public affairs. Established political figures initially monopolized its relations of authority and administration, but it was not long before demands for autonomy were heard. As commodity production broke out of the household, control over the nascent public sphere was wrested from state authorities by a "critical reasoning" public of private businesspeople talking about common issues. "Citizens behave as a public body when they confer in an unrestricted fashion—that is, with the guarantee of freedom of assembly and association and the freedom to express and publish their opinions—about matters of general interest."[45] Protected from both the state and the market forces of civil society, the public sphere presupposed equality and freedom. It was the arena in which civil liberties and universal values could be expressed. It made it possible to exercise a democratic control over officeholders that was legally recognized and institutionally protected.

Society, now a private realm occupying a position in opposition to the state, stood on the one hand as if in clear contrast to the state. On the other hand, that society had become a concern of public interest to the degree that the production of life in the wake of the developing market economy had grown beyond the bounds of private domestic authority. *The bourgeois public sphere* could be understood as the sphere of private individuals assembled into a public body, which almost immediately laid claim to the officially regulated "intellectual newspapers" for use against the public authority itself. In these newspapers, and in moralistic and critical journals, they debated that public authority on the general rules of social intercourse in their fundamentally privatized yet publicly relevant sphere of labor and commodity exchange.[46]

"The bourgeois public sphere," Habermas continued, "may be conceived above all as the sphere of private people come together as a public; they soon claimed the public sphere regulated from above against the public authorities themselves, to engage themselves in a debate over the general rules governing relations in the basically privatized but publicly relevant sphere of commodity exchange and social labor. The medium of this political confrontation was peculiar and without historical precedent: people's use of their reason."[47] Tolerance and open-mindedness were essential for the development of capitalist social relations, and reason made it possible to constitute a liberal public sphere that did not depend on status or formal economic position. The free exchange of information encouraged a reading bourgeois public to criticize public authorities and civil society. "With the rise of a sphere of the social, over whose regulation public opinion battled with public power, the theme of the modern (in contrast to the ancient) public sphere shifted from the properly political tasks of a citizenry acting in common (i.e., administration of law as regards internal affairs and military survival as regards external affairs) to the more properly civic tasks of a society engaged in critical public debate (i.e., the protection of a commercial economy). The political task of the bourgeois public sphere was the regulation of civil society (in contradistinction to the *res publica*.)"[48] The liberal public sphere, then, assumed its mature shape when private individuals began communicating with one another as property owners who wanted to influence state policy and civil society in the name of their common interest. But the market's power soon made itself felt. Initially organized by reason, the public sphere was soon constituted by naked class interests that could no longer pretend to speak for society as a whole.

Echoing Horkheimer, Adorno, and Marcuse, Habermas has attributed the erosion of the public sphere's autonomy to the all-round commodification of modern life. The public sphere has been replaced by the pseudo-public and falsely private world of cultural consumption. An artificially produced consensus binds the individual to the existing order and undermines the possibility of understanding, independence, or resistance. Rational-critical debate has been replaced by passive watching, and the public sphere's free web of public communication has unraveled into isolated acts of individual reception.[49] The "public" can no longer critically reflect on public matters—it can only consume.

Public communication now tends toward what is acceptable to commerce because advertising and spectacle have transformed the public sphere from a neutral zone of debate to a servile manufacturer of conformity. Consensus is manufactured to serve consumption and imposed from above instead of coming from the discursive engagement of equals. "Publicity is generated from above, so to speak, in order to create an aura of good will for certain positions. Originally publicity guaranteed the connection between rational-critical public debate and the legislative foundation of domination, including the critical supervision of its exercise. Now it makes possible the peculiar ambivalence of a domination exercised through the domination of nonpublic opinion: it serves the manipulation *of* the public as much as legitimation *before* it. Critical publicity is supplanted by manipulated politics."[50] Unable to protect modernity from the commodity form, the public sphere can no longer bring reason to bear on political power.

The commodification of the public sphere stands behind the "legitimation crisis" of a political order that is unable to provide the rational justification for state power that it once could. Political leaders falsely appeal to a public that does not help shape policy but is manipulated to produce momentary support. The lengthy process of mutual consultation, enlightenment, and discussion that used to characterize the public sphere has withered, crushed between the demands of the state and the market requirements of civil society. Habermas deplores precisely what the pluralists celebrated.

> Competition between organized private interests invaded the public sphere. If the particular interests that as privatized interests were neutralized in the common denominator of class interest once permitted public discussion to attain a certain rationality and even effectiveness, it remains that today the display of competing interests has taken the place of such discussion. The consensus developed in rational-critical public debate has yielded to compromise fought out or simply imposed nonpublicly. The laws that come into existence in this way can no longer be vindicated as regards their elements of

"truth," even though in many cases the element of universality is preserved in them; for even the parliamentary public sphere—the place in which "truth" would have to present its credentials—has collapsed.[51]

Kant's hope that reason, debate, and publicity could provide principles for legitimate state power depended on the critical power of an informed public composed of free and equal individuals. For Habermas, the managed integration wielded by today's "staging agencies" are a mockery of a democratic public sphere. His effort to develop a "discourse ethic" for democratic politics is the direct result of the commodification of the public sphere. Still hoping that free and unrestrained communication can produce the best argument and protect the welfare of the whole from the divisive pull of particular interests, Habermas insists that discourse be open to all, respect be accorded to each, and arguments be supported by claims that can be universalized. Democracy is a set of procedures, and a discourse ethic can make it possible for private individuals to justify their claims rationally and to renounce self-interest in the face of superior arguments.

The time has come to extend Kant into civil society itself. Genuine public debate requires that political power be tamed and the market supervised. Classical liberalism focused on the need to restrain the state through publicity, but Habermas wants a wide array of institutions exposed to public scrutiny and democratic supervision. Private ownership is no longer a sufficient condition of autonomy. Interest groups, political parties, and other centers of power must reveal their internal organization, source of funds, investment decisions, and use of power. Faced with the relentlessly invasive logic of commodification, Habermas's hope that a discourse ethic can democratize everyday life has brought him closer to Tocqueville.

> This sphere of civil society has been rediscovered today in wholly new historical constellations. The expression "civil society" has in the meantime taken on a meaning different from that of the "bourgeois society" of the liberal tradition, which Hegel conceptualized as a "system of needs," that is, as a market system involving social labor and commodity exchange. What is meant by "civil society" today, in contrast to its usage in the Marxist tradition, no longer includes the economy as constituted by private law and steered through markets in labor, capital, and commodities. Rather, its institutional core comprises those nongovernmental and noneconomic connections and voluntary associations that anchor the communication structures of the public sphere in the society component of the lifeworld. Civil society is composed of those more or less spontaneously emergent associations, organizations, and movements that, attuned to how societal problems resonate in

the private life spheres, distill and transmit such reactions in amplified form to the public sphere. The core of civil society comprises a network of associations that institutionalizes problem-solving discourses of general interest inside the framework of organized public spheres. These "discursive designs" have an egalitarian, open form of organization that mirrors essential features of the kind of communication around which they crystallize and to which they lend continuity and permanence.[52]

For Habermas, the collapse of "actual existing socialism" demonstrates how difficult it is to steer complicated social orders. "Democratic movements emerging from civil society must give up holistic aspirations to a self-organizing society, aspirations that also undergirded Marxist ideas of social revolution. Civil society can directly transform only itself, and it can have at most an indirect effect on the self-transformation of the political system."[53] It is important not to expect too much from civil society in a time of reaction. At best, its private groups, voluntary organizations, and new social movements can help by placing issues on the public agenda; "in a perceived crisis situation, the *actors in civil society . . . can* assume a surprisingly active and momentous role."[54] Much of this depends on the strength of social movements and the receptiveness of the political system.

Habermas has correctly identified an important democratic potential of civil society. Many problems of contemporary public life, from civil rights to pollution, sexism, human rights, nuclear arms, and the like, were raised by the associations of civil society rather than through the still-untransformed mechanisms of state power. "Moving in from this outermost periphery, such issues force their way into newspapers and interested associations, clubs, professional organizations, academies, and universities. They find forums, citizen initiatives, and other platforms before they catalyze the growth of social movements and new subcultures. The latter can in turn dramatize contributions, presenting them so effectively that the mass media take up the matter. Only through their controversial presentation in the media do such topics reach the larger public and subsequently gain a place on the 'public agenda.'"[55] Wife-beating and sexual abuse might have been "family affairs" in an earlier period, but readjusting the lines between public and private has clearly—and appropriately—made them matters of politics and law.

Habermas wants integration and legitimacy by way of communication instead of domination, but it remains to be seen if the market's structural inequalities can sustain a public sphere from which relations of power and inequality are purged and within which all actors move in conditions of equality. Private rights, formal equality, and the rule of law are probably not enough to constitute a sphere of rational-critical discourse in an environment of pervasive material inequality. All communications are inevitably constrained, and there is no reason to expect that the better argument can prevail in civil societies that are so penetrated by the market. Habermas's approach is weakened by the same emphasis on "culture" and inattention to economics that vitiated the thrust of the Frankfurt School in general. Discourse ethics cannot constitute a democratic public life in an environment marked by political conflict, class struggle, violence, and the structural inequalities of capitalism. If civil society and the public sphere are thoroughly commercialized, it remains to be seen if they have any autonomous democratic potential.

Dreams of Renewal

Robert Bellah and his associates were convinced that American history furnished the answer to this dilemma because it demonstrated that individualistic categories cannot provide a sufficiently rich account of social life. People are not nearly as self-created as it seems. "We have never been, and still are not, a collection of private individuals who, except for a conscious contract to create a minimal government, have nothing in common. Our lives make sense in a thousand ways, most of which we are unaware of, because of traditions that are centuries, if not millennia, old. It is these traditions that help us to know that it does make a difference who we are and how we treat one another."[56]

Collective memory and selected traditions of "millennia" are not particularly trustworthy foundations for a theory of civil society, but it is easy to understand their attractiveness. Modern communitarians are trying to contend with the impact of a relentlessly totalizing economy and a leveling bureaucratic state—both of which constantly sweep away established customs and transform social connections. Communitarians' turn toward tradition and community marks a deeply conservative strain in their perfectly plausible recognition that "the commercial dynamism at the heart of the ideal of personal success . . . undermines community involvement. . . . The rules of the competitive market, not the practices of the town meeting or the fellowship of the church, are the real arbiters of living."[57] But Bellah knows that the answer does not lie in a romantic return to the past. The small-town virtues of a vanished era cannot provide democratic content to a modern civil society framed by mighty economic forces and a powerful state. But tradition can help. Perhaps "the biblical and republican traditions that the small town once embodied can be reappropriated in ways that respond to our present need" for a satisfying conception of community without falling into a reactionary and romantic nostalgia.[58] Can Tocqueville's insights about America be brought up to date?

Bellah worries that Americans' thinking is so shaped by the face-to-face relations of nineteenth-century small towns that they find it hard to identify contemporary society's invisible sources of power and domination. Much of this can be attributed to liberalism's lack of interest in coercion that lies outside politics, but an updated pluralism might fortify civil society. "A conception of society composed of widely different, but independent, groups might generate a language of the common good that could adjudicate between conflicting wants and interests, thus taking the pressure off the overstrained logic of individual rights. But such a conception would require coming to terms with the invisible complexity that Americans prefer to avoid."[59] A new "social ecology" might craft a communitarian and republican vision of commonality out of the discordant language of individual rights and private advantage. If individuals cannot live by exchange alone, Tocqueville's understanding that local interests can be combined with powerful traditions of voluntary association might anchor a civil society that attenuates the chaos of individual interest and the market. In the end, Bellah is back where so many contemporary theories of civil society begin: with republican ideals and civic culture.

So is Michael Sandel, who agrees with Bellah's critique of individualism but situates it in a Rousseauist and Tocquevillean discussion of American intellectual history. "Democracy's discontent," Sandel believes, is rooted in individualistic liberalism's failure to address the loss of self-government and erosion of community that mark contemporary American life. Because it cannot explain how individual interests can be formed or articulated apart from social life, its notion of an "unencumbered self" dissolves into empty formalism. Many things that we believe and practice do not originate in conscious individual choice but from our connections to the communities that shape our thinking. We are bound by many choices we never made, Sandel believes, and they often serve the interests of freedom. A public philosophy that can support self-government and strengthen community cannot rest on the fiction of autonomous individual choice and personal interest.

Like Bellah, Sandel looks backward and finds its source in an American vision of civil society that predates the "procedural republic" of contemporary life. Before the 1930s transition to Keynesianism's economic growth, mass consumption, and distributive justice, the reigning public philosophy in the United States rested on "the idea that liberty depends on sharing in self-government."[60] A tradition of civic republicanism required citizens who thought in wider terms than immediate self-interest. Such a tradition did not fully survive the twin pressure of modern commerce and the neutral state, but Sandel believes that its remnants offer a defense against anonymity and powerlessness. "The most promising alternative to the sovereign state is not a one-world community based on the solidarity of mankind, but a multiplicity of communities and political bodies—some more, some less extensive than nations—among which sovereignty is dispersed."[61] Sandel beats a familiar retreat to multiple local identities because he has little faith in comprehensive political action.

> If the nation cannot summon more than a minimal commonality, it is unlikely that the global community can do better, at least on its own. A more promising basis for democratic politics that reaches beyond nations is a revitalized civic life nourished in the more particular communities we inhabit. In the age of NAFTA, the politics of community matter more, not less. People will not pledge allegiance to vast and distant entities, whatever their importance, unless those institutions are somehow connected to political arrangements that reflect the identity of the participants.[62]

For Sandel, the institutions of civil society—schools, workplaces, churches and synagogues, trade unions, and social movements—are the new sites of democratic activity in a postmodern environment of multiple loyalties, identities, and selves. Dispersion, particularity and identity anchor a public philosophy that can address the loss of self-government and the erosion of community.[63] Less overtly hostile to politics than other theorists of civil society, communitarians want to protect the state's ability to nurture communities by protecting it from interest group bargaining. The frustrated "civic aspirations" that are roiling American politics can be addressed only by directly engaging the substantive moral concerns that used to animate the republican tradition. An affirmative state can advance a common good that is greater than pluralism's pull of private interest. In the end, Sandel's notion of civil society seeks to modify the large with the small and avoid a real consideration of politics and economics by conceiving civil society as a refuge from strangers.

Robert Putnam's important effort to explain the deep sources of democracy in northern Italy is less overtly moralistic than Sandel's work, but it also fails to engage the economic and political determinations of civil society. Like many pluralist and communitarian theorists, Putnam is interested in regime effectiveness and he draws on Tocqueville to discover that "the civic community is marked by an active, public-spirited citizenry, by egalitarian social relations, by a social fabric of trust and cooperation." His investigation reveals that effective political institutions depend on a developed civil society of intermediate associations and a civic culture. "Some regions of Italy," he reports, "are blessed with vibrant networks and norms of civic engagement, while others are cursed with vertically structured politics, a social life of fragmentation and isolation, and a culture of distrust. These differences in civic life turn out to play a key role in explaining institutional success."[64] Active participation in public affairs; widespread political equality; norms of solidarity, trust, and tolerance; and a thick structure of associations with multiple memberships correlate highly with one another and are consistently stronger in the industrialized north and center than in the more rural and undeveloped south. Northern Italians are active participants in public affairs, read the newspapers regularly, and vote often. They tend to be satisfied with local political bodies and leaders, have egalitarian and tolerant attitudes, are likely to be in labor unions, think and talk about public matters, and feel politically influential.

Putnam believes that a thousand years of decentralized government help explain the vitality of northern Italy's "civic community." The evolution of the region's medieval communes into commercial republics established a pattern of autonomous local institutions that supports today's highly developed civic life. The Church was just one institution among many, secular and lay associations were everywhere, a system of public finance was in place, public administration was well developed, independent schools were functioning, and political power was highly dispersed. The three foundations of mercantile capitalism—money, markets, and law—had a powerful effect in organizing northern life. In the south, on the contrary, a strong centralizing monarchy organized life from above, stifled local initiatives, and prevented the development of local traditions of civicness. Hierarchical social relations, an influential Church, and a powerful landed aristocracy also inhibited local self-government. The south's traditions of inequality and personal dependence persist to this day. Echoing both Tocqueville and Almond and Verba, Putnam found that "regions with many civic associations, many newspaper readers, many issue-oriented voters, and few patron-client networks seem to nourish more effective governments."[65]

These findings contradict an implicit communitarian assumption that civic life and republican norms will have greater effect in small, intimate communities with important premodern norms of universal solidarity than in modern, rational societies organized around the individual pursuit of self-interest. It is not true, Putnam suggests, that civic communities are atavisms that cannot survive modernity's large, impersonal bureaucratic structures. Fears of mass society notwithstanding, the most civic regions of Italy are also the most modern. "Modernization need not signal the demise of the civic community."[66] At the same time, Putnam knows that the north's complex civil society cannot be entirely explained on the basis of his relatively superficial reading of history. Like the pluralists, he falls back on a nonpolitical quality he calls "social capital"—that is, "features of social organizations, such as trust, norms, and networks, that can improve the efficiency of society by facilitating coordinated actions."[67] Northern Italians inherited social capital from the past that facilitates collective public action and enhances the effectiveness of local political bodies in the present. But Putnam's adaptation of the civic culture does not run very deep. If political or economic forces play any role in shaping his civil society, social capital is its operative principle. A healthy civil society is full of such nonpolitical civic associations as choral groups and soccer leagues. "This is one lesson gleaned from our research: *Social context and history profoundly condition the effectiveness of institutions.* Where the regional soil is fertile, the regions draw sustenance from regional traditions, but where the soil is poor, the new institutions are stunted. Effective and responsive institutions depend, in the language of civic humanism, on republican virtues and practices. Tocqueville was right: Democratic government is strengthened, not weakened, when it faces a vigorous civil society."[68]

If a tradition of "civicness" sustains Italian democracy, the same might be true of other polities. Bellah and Sandel articulate communitarian fears about a fraying American social order, and Putnam has tried to provide an explanation of the forces at work that does not rely on moralistic nostalgia. But the language of decline is the same, for he has extended his analysis of Italy to the United States and finds that "declining social capital" is threatening the foundations of American democracy. An earlier generation of social scientists was more than willing to demonstrate how apathy and disengagement freed elites and generated stability. Like Bellah, Sandel, and other communitarians, Putnam wants more participation.

Many students of the new democracies that have emerged over the past decade and a half have emphasized the importance of a strong and active civil society to the consolidation of democracy. Especially with regard to the post-communist countries, scholars and democratic activists alike have lamented the absence or obliteration of traditions of independent civic engagement and a widespread tendency toward passive reliance on the state. To those concerned with the weakness of civil societies in the developing or postcommunist world, the advanced Western democracies and above all the United States have typically been taken as models to be emulated. There is striking evidence, however, that the vibrancy of American civil society has notably declined over the past several decades.[69]

America's civil society is weakening, Putnam believes, because her social capital is declining. Despite higher levels of education, people are voting and participating in other political activities less than they used to. It is well known that they trust the government less than in earlier periods. But the decline is not limited to politics. Church attendance and church-related activity are down, labor unions have been shrinking, PTAs are less important than they used to be, membership in civic and fraternal organizations has dropped, and Americans are "bowling alone." Family bonds are loosening, and people socialize less with their neighbors than they used to. Even if organizations such as the Sierra Club and the American Association of Retired Persons have grown, the vast majority of their members are passive dues-payers who are unconnected to one another. Membership in support and self-help groups is up, but Putnam agrees with Sennett that such organizations do little more than enable people to talk about themselves in the presence of others. Total associational membership and activity in the United States has fallen "significantly" despite rising educational levels, an older population, and other factors that might be expected to reinforce the famous American propensity to associate.

Why? Increased mobility, suburbanization, the entry of large numbers of women into the workforce, heightened pressures of time and money, white flight, and other such factors do not explain the erosion of social capital and decline in civic engagement. Putnam found that older Americans tend to be more engaged and trusting than the young, but that they do not become so as they age. If we want to understand why social capital is declining, he concludes, we have to ask not how old people are, but when they were young. The data register "a powerful reduction in civic engagement among Americans who came of age in the decades after World War II, as well as some modest additional disengagement that affected all cohorts during the 1980s."[70] A "long civic generation" of people born before the 1930s has yielded to later generations that are significantly less involved. People are "bowling alone" because of something that happened in the 1940s and 1950s rather than in the 1960s and 1970s. Putnam thinks he knows the villain. The generation that watched a lot of television while it was young is the generation that is disengaged. Television's privatization, fragmentation, and demobilization are to blame for "the strange disappearance of civic America."

His focus on "social capital" signals Putnam's relative lack of interest in the political and economic roots of civic decline, something he shares with moralizing neo-Tocquevillean theories of civil society. But state activity has interacted with powerful economic trends to produce the very patterns of association and disengagement he illuminated. The penetration of southern Italy by the northern state after unification cannot be ignored if one wants to uncover the sources of southern backwardness, any more than the decline of American labor unions can be explained without understanding the influence of state "right to work" laws, the Taft-Hartley Act, and federal law permitting the hiring of "full-time replacement workers" in the event of strikes. Like many contemporary theorists of civil society, Putnam treats "social capital" as an informal set of norms that arises and declines in a sphere largely unaffected by the state or the market. For Tocqueville, a primordial disposition to associate spontaneously produced America's social capital. For Putnam, it is the result of a vaguely defined history. Such factors are no doubt important, but political, economic, religious, and other forces powerfully influenced the propensity to associate that Tocqueville discovered in the New World. The Second Great Awakening, periodic elections, newspapers, public schools, and a national post office all had an enormous impact on the formation of the voluntary organizations which impressed him and which operate as an independent sphere in so much contemporary theorizing. Many of the civic organizations that the prevailing consensus imagines were grass-roots responses to local conditions were actually organized and stimulated by the state. Wars, political parties, regulatory agencies, and other distinctly political phenomena helped form organizations such as the American Legion, the American Farm Bureau Federation, and the PTA. The assumption that some sort of autonomous local volunteerism is the lifeblood of a healthy democratic order ignores much of the historical record. "On the contrary," observes Theda Skocpol, "U.S. civic associations were encouraged by the American Revolution, the Civil War, the New Deal, and World Wars I and II; and until recently they were fostered by the institutional patterns of U.S. federalism, legislatures, competitive elections, and locally rooted political parties."[71] A long tradition of state activity has created, worked with, and strengthened the local and voluntary organizations that make up civil society. Federal money for social services is often channeled through local bodies such as Catholic Charities, the Red Cross, and the Salvation Army. The PTA and American Legion long pushed for social programs that were later incorporated in the program of a supposedly intrusive and leveling welfare state. AFDC, Social Security, and the GI Bill were organized after decades of pressure and relied on civil society's organizations to administer and expand them after they had been put in place.[72] "Civicness" and "social capital" cannot explain civil society apart from the influence of state-building, state strategy, and economic trends. Indeed, the sort of civil society Putnam describes might strengthen *any* regime's effectiveness; after all, northern Italy has seen monarchist, fascist, republican, socialist, and communist governments. Civil society may be linked to institutional capability in general rather than to any particular state formation, a possibility obscured by Putnam's failure to consider how it is constituted by politics and economics.[73]

As for the United States, Putnam's suggestion that the "long civic generation" of the 1950s and 1960s organized the voluntary organizations that make democracy work pays little attention to the *what kind* of organizations characterized the period. If this was the era of PTAs and bowling leagues, it was no less the period of White Citizens Councils and the Mafia. The presence of many organizations might be a sign of healthy civic life, but any nostalgia about a Golden Age of volunteerism should be tempered by a consideration of political and economic verities. After all, Putnam's healthy civil society was built on the systematic confinement of women in the home, the accompanying construction of a mass consumer culture, an institutionalized racial segregation throughout American society, McCarthyism, and a suffocating ideological uniformity—just to name a few of its elements. If American civil society is in as much trouble as Putnam suggests, the villain has to be more than television.

The Tocquevillean cries of alarm about the state that mark so many recent theories of civil society assume that an autonomous sphere of families, voluntary associations, religious organizations, and the like constitute the true grounding of democratic politics. But democracy is conditioned by considerably more than intimacy, localism, and moralism. Powerful states and invasive markets constitute and penetrate a civil society whose ability to mediate depends as much on the environment in which it sits as on its own intrinsic strength. Thinking small will not yield a theory of civil society that can do what its proponents would like. In the end, the important questions of contemporary democratic theory are political ones. So are the answers.

9

Civil Society and
Democratic Politics

Contemporary American thinking about civil society is thoroughly dominated by categories drawn from Tocqueville. Individual theorists may differ about where the family belongs or whether the Enlightenment has run its course, but almost all agree that a healthy democracy requires many voluntary associations and much local activity. At first glance, this seems to make eminent sense. Greater engagement, deeper commitment, more participation, and heightened solidarity seem desirable in any social order—particularly one plagued by cheapened politics and civic decline.

But a closer look might reveal why neo-Tocquevillean orthodoxy has become so attractive in a conservative period—and why some reservations might be in order. Contemporary thought is characterized by a pervasive skepticism of the state and of the possibilities afforded by broad political action. Now it is civil society that is supposed to revive communities, train effective citizens, build habits of respect and cooperation, provide a moral alternative to self-interest, limit intrusive bureaucracies, and reinvigorate the public sphere—all this in an environment of small government and local politics.[1] Indeed, a narrowed sense of public purpose and political possibility is central to contemporary public life and thought. For Colin Powell, who headed the President's Summit for America's Future, "a civil society is one whose members care about each other and about the well-being of the community as a whole." Tolerance, respect, and civility can be built by voluntary community service, for "we are helping the next generation of Americans to grow up to be good citizens, and we are reacquainting the present generation of Americans with the need to break down the barriers of race, class, and politics that divide us—which will help make us a more united and caring nation."[2] Good feelings, volunteerism, nostalgia, and community constitute civil society in an antipolitical period.

233

Superficial boosterism notwithstanding, Tocqueville's popularity is tied to the general pessimism of a conservative and unstable age. Three decades of deindustrialization and political reaction have come together in relentless attacks on the welfare state, static or declining standards of living for tens of millions of families, heightened levels of stress at work and home, unprecedented levels of cynicism about political institutions, and widespread contempt for public figures. Despite apparent economic prosperity and political tranquility, Americans are in a decidedly sour and uncivil frame of mind. Intellectual and political elites earnestly promote local commitments and good manners, and it is easy to agree that life would be better if more of us worked in soup kitchens and fewer of us wanted a gun after being cut off on the highway. But moralizing clichés and less television will not be enough to reverse the civic disengagement of contemporary life or convince a withdrawn citizenry that public affairs can be conducted without numbing levels of hypocrisy and vulgarity.

Tocqueville is not particularly helpful in these conditions. Categories derived from the face-to-face democracy of early nineteenth-century New England towns cannot furnish a credible model for public life in a highly commodified mass society marked by unprecedented levels of economic inequality. As important as they are, local voluntary activity and informal civic norms are too narrow to provide the broad and general orientation that the current environment urgently requires. But Tocqueville serves important purposes anyway, for his notion of civil society performs a normalizing function by making it difficult to see the economic roots of contemporary problems and blinding us to the political avenues for their resolution. He is not the only available thinker, after all. Civil society is a very old idea, and Tocqueville's is only one way of conceptualizing it. The two other strands of thought we have been charting—the premodern sense that civil society was the politically organized commonwealth and the second modern view that it is the sphere of necessity, production, class, property, and competition—can shed important light on an idea that has considerably more to offer than the restricted terms of current discourse make possible.

Part of the problem is that civil society is an unavoidably nebulous and elastic conception that does not easily lend itself to a great deal of precision. It is not enough to describe it as a mediating sphere of voluntary association supported by communitarian norms, for many organizations are destructive of civility and many local norms erode democracy. The Eastern Europeans understandably thought of it as a constitutional republic, but the liberal rule of law, formal equality, and civil liberties enjoy overwhelming popular support in the United States, and conceptualizing civil society in Polish terms cannot shed much light on the problems of advanced capitalist social orders. Civil society is also considerably broader than a Habermasian public sphere, since it is hard to base anything on the ideal of free discourse among equals in contemporary conditions.

How, then, should civil society be conceived? The most productive use of the term is to describe the social relations and structures that lie between the state and the market. Civil society delineates a sphere that is formally distinct from the body politic and state authority on one hand, and from the immediate pursuit of self-interest and the imperatives of the market on the other. Political activities, even when they are driven by the narrowest motives of individual gain, occur in an arena that addresses society's broadest questions. Economic activities, even when they take shape in the most cosmopolitan international arenas, are more narrow because they are frankly organized around the pursuit of advantage. Civil society can be found in the grey areas between these two spheres. Its voluntary associations, interest groups, and social movements always strive to maintain a measure of autonomy from the public affairs of politics and the private concerns of economics. At the same time, they are partially determined by the state and the market. Civil society is subject to the same contradictory imperatives of autonomy and determination that characterize all intermediate spheres.

Of course, a great deal of human activity takes place in civil society and one might easily think of it as the domain in which "everyday life" is lived. A powerful tendency to think of such activities as freely chosen drives a good deal of current thinking. Much of what we do seems to have an intrinsic rhythm and logic that appears to be independent of routine political affairs or the ups and downs of economic cycles. But superficial appearances often conceal important misconceptions. What civil society "is" can be grasped only by looking carefully at what its constituent structures do, how they are organized, and what political and economic forces are at work—no matter how strenuously some theorists try to describe it as an autonomous sphere of democratic activity. In this sense, civil society is really a heuristic device, a theoretical guide that can reveal important matters of social life but cannot be adequately described in and of itself. Simply understanding it as a nonmarket, nonstate sphere of voluntary public activity is not enough to help us make crucial distinctions between Robert Putnam's bowling leagues, soccer teams, and choral societies on the one hand, and Greenpeace, the National Organization for Women, and the Ku Klux Klan on the other. If a strengthened civil society is as central to democratic theory and practice as its admirers so evidently desire, more is needed than the Tocquevillean logic of local authenticity.

None of this is to deny the importance of the thrust toward autonomy that drives all organizations. This has often served democracy well, and even as it has long recognized that civil society was ultimately constituted by state power, liberal political theory still looks to intermediate groupings as a barrier to the thrust of central authority. But this formulation often obscures more than it reveals. Civil society can just as easily impede democracy as advance it, and the history of American segregation should give antistatist advocates of localism and community considerable pause. Nothing is automatic in political life, and it is important to avoid glib assumptions.

As is often the case, history and tradition can help us appreciate some of the complexities of civil society's connection to political affairs. Classical theorists conceptualized it as the state-organized counterpoint to particularism and guarantor of civilization, but the development of national markets and national states led liberals and Marxists alike to think of it in terms of individual interest. Its important role in limiting state power has been as important to the former as it has been problematic for the latter. Secured by the rule of law, legal equality, and civil liberties, a civil society founded on property rights and freedom of association played a central role in the development of liberal democratic theory. Tocqueville was certainly correct in recognizing that it could limit and diffuse state power, but his assumption of economic equality freed him from the necessity of examining its connection to the market. His contemporary followers do not have that luxury.

The two other traditions we have been following were not built on the parochialism, localism, and hostility to central authority that drive recent American thinking. The classical view of civil society identified it with the politically organized commonwealth and regarded state power as the indispensable guarantor of civilization's benefits. When the Greeks distinguished themselves from barbarians, they expressed their conviction that living in political communities made human life possible. They were not alone in this, for all precapitalist notions of civil society rested on a *political* distinction between civilization and savagery. No matter how important it was in the order of things, social life was made possible by public power. Plato's organic state, Aristotle's deliberative polity, Augustine's Christian Commonwealth, Aquinas's republic, Luther's sphere of obligation, Machiavelli's civic republic—none could be understood apart from state capacity. Plato fused political knowledge with power to organize his consolidated utopia; Aristotle's plural community was made possible by citizenship; Augustine's empire existed to protect the Church; Aquinas tried to infuse politics with the highest conceivable degree of Christian legitimacy; Luther called on the German princes to choose their subjects' religion; and Machiavelli knew that civilization rested on widely accepted republican principles. The classical tradition could not and did not develop an antistatist conception of civil society because it recognized that everyday life was made possible by organized political power.

The first branch of modern theory began to move away from the ancient identification of civil society with the commonwealth, but it retained an important role for political affairs and state activity. As markets began to dissolve long-established embedded economies, liberal thinkers sought to limit the thrust of central power but still assigned it protective and coordinating responsibilities with respect to a civil society of political liberty, economic growth, cultural development, and individual interests. In decisive contrast to a state of nature defined by antagonism and conflict, Hobbes's civil society—the everyday life of exchange, arts and letters, culture, and science—was made possible by the activity of a single point of sovereign power. Locke's crucial insight that human beings were naturally sociable and that the state was a conventional solution to the "inconveniences" of nature did not prevent him from seeing civil society as a politically protected sphere of individual rights and the rule of law that made possible a new regime of freedom and prosperity. Even Adam Smith, who came closest to identifying civil society with the market and leaned toward a starkly economic conception of human nature, reserved an essential role to the state.

If post-Hobbesian liberals accepted an important measure of state power, they also described civil society as a natural order. This is why Hegel's description of it as the sphere of selfishness, exploitation, and poverty was so important. Hegel looked to the state to overcome the chaotic destructiveness of modernity's "system of needs" because his civil society was an ensemble of social relations that stood in sharp distinction to political society. It was this understanding—and not, as often suggested, the dialectical method—that marked his contribution to Marx's view that civil society is a network of economic relations that has a decisive influence in shaping the state. Marx transformed the liberal distinction between economics and politics into a revolutionary doctrine by identifying civil society as the problem to be solved instead of the solution to be found. This is what made it possible for him to pose the relationship between civil society and the state as the central problematic of modern life.

It is no accident that liberalism and socialism, modernity's two great political traditions, share a similar understanding of civil society. Their profoundly important disagreements stem from what they want to do about it. Liberal thinkers crafted a coherent theory of the state because they sought to liberate civil society's market forces and social relations from medieval arbitrariness, while Marxism has always drawn its understanding of politics from ancient suspicions that unregulated markets could destroy the very possibility of civilized life.[3] Socialists seek to contain what liberals are disposed to liberate, but both children of the Enlightenment agree that civil society is largely constituted by state power and the social relations of the capitalist market.

Indeed, its political and economic determinations are crucial in any effort to understand what civil society "is." We have seen that attempts to explain regional differences in Italian "civicness" that fail to take state activity into account impute an internal coherence and autonomous logic to the category that neither theory nor the historical record supports. Political institutions have had a long history of recognizing and influencing *every* civil society's voluntary associations, interest groups, and social movements. The character of the legal system, national tax policy, administrative procedures, interference with membership practices that discriminate against women or racial minorities—all this, and a good deal more, has a palpable impact on the habits, norms, and organizations that stand between political institutions and the logic of the market. And state involvement in civil society goes considerably further than a series of interactions with an already-existing intermediate sphere. States often use civil society to further their own interests—whether they institutionalize the Hitler Youth, encourage the formation of veterans' organizations, establish a network of soccer leagues, or covertly assist a favored organization. *Any* civil society can be created, supported, manipulated, or repressed by *any* state, and it is profoundly misleading to try to conceptualize it apart from political power. The Eastern Europeans understandably theorized a sphere that would be independent of central authority, but this made them unable to grasp the danger that unrestrained market relations pose to intermediate formations. American thinking does not have to make the same mistake. Its shortsightedness can be better explained by its unthinking adoption of conservative ideological categories than by similarities between Poland and the United States. It is not enough to say that civil society serves democracy only if it sustains political opposition, for there are too many examples of state-supported associations that have served plurality, facilitated voluntary activity, and encouraged equality.

Having said that, it is equally essential to understand that civil society *does* often serve democracy by checking state power. The history of "actual existing socialism" furnishes many examples of how important a robust sphere of independent organizations can be, and the Mothers of the Plaza de Mayo need no lessons in how quickly an unaccountable state can turn criminally vicious. The student groups that brought down Suharto, American feminism, Amnesty International, and the Zapatistas have all performed admirable service in contesting the claims of central power and enriching the public sphere. As always, theory needs to be informed by solid analysis. Much depends on the nature of the state and the character of the associations, groups, and movements that populate civil society. People bowled, played soccer, and sang in choral groups in Jim Crow Mississippi and in New York City, but that does not mean that their civil societies were remotely similar. Everyday life was simply not the same in Nazi Germany as in Popular Front France, and if South Africans played rugby in conditions of apartheid it makes a world of difference that they now do so in conditions of freedom. The undoubted importance of voluntary activity and intermediate association cannot blind us to the overriding importance of broad and comprehensive *political* categories.

Neo-Tocquevilleanism's inherited prejudices make it difficult to grasp the implications of this elementary truth. Since it assumes that small units are structured more democratically than larger ones, it seems to follow that a society full of parochial self-governing bodies is likely to be relatively open and permeable. Local associations require high levels of debate and participation among people whose intertwined interests generate powerful motives for compromise and agreement. Disagreements can be addressed on the basis of common history, shared understandings, and collective interests. Democracy requires a measure of autonomy for such deliberations and is best served if external influences are kept to a minimum. Individuals know their own needs better than officials who may have more than one issue to think about and whose distance encourages arbitrariness. And, since local people have to live with the consequences of their actions, they have powerful reasons to exercise power responsibly.

There is much to recommend this view, but an important body of literature suggests that there may be more to these easy assumptions than meets the eye. Writing more than thirty years ago, Grant McConnell was not so eager to agree that local associations necessarily serve liberty because they limit the state. Instead, he suggested that the uncommon degree of power wielded by its private groups is American democracy's greatest problem rather than its most important strength. "Far from providing guarantees of liberty, equality, and concern for the public interest, organization of political life by small constituencies tends to enforce conformity, to discriminate in favor of elites, and to eliminate public values from effective political consideration," he suggested. The true importance of local organizations lies in "the guarantee of stability and the enforcement of order rather than in support for the central values of a liberal society."[4] *Private Power and American Democracy* is still a classic of modern political inquiry because its attack on pluralism's attachment to private intermediate associations calls into question the core position of almost all contemporary theories of civil society.

All organizations try to strengthen themselves, preserve their internal unity, and enhance their capacity for action, but McConnell found that local bodies do not have automatic safeguards against abuse just because they are local. They are subject to the same conflicting imperatives that drive all associations. Guarantees of individual rights, the presence of internal opposition, and formal limits on the power of leaders might strengthen internal democracy, but they must often yield to the requirements of organizational coherence and effectiveness.[5] McConnell anticipated Richard Sennett's critique of "intimacy" by suggesting that compulsion is easier to organize locally than in a more diverse, impersonal, and bureaucratized environment whose members do not "know" one another and are consequently harder to organize. "Impersonality is the guarantee of individual freedom characteristic of the large unit," he observed. "Impersonality means an avoidance of arbitrary official action, the following of prescribed procedure, conformance to established rules, and escape from bias whether for or against any individual."[6] Bureaucracy can limit arbitrariness and defend fair procedures and equal access as easily as it can stifle initiative and crush self-government. As always, much depends on the surrounding environment.

When he turned his attention to the wider implications of decentralization, McConnell found that local elites often used existing associations to buttress their own position.[7] Anticipating a dispute that still rages across much of the West, he discovered that "preemption"—the doctrine that public land should be opened to the use of those living near it—was little more than a rationale for private gain at public expense that exacerbated already-existing inequality. The repeated demands that federal management of public land be handed to the states—all made in the name of local autonomy, bringing government closer to communities, strengthening secondary organizations, and benefiting from authentic knowledge—ended up turning it over to local cattle ranchers, the largest and most powerful of whom always benefited the most. The same was true of other federal agencies. Transferring farm policy from the Department of Agriculture to local communities, for example, did not mean that rural poverty would be addressed. Quite the opposite: *devolution guaranteed that it would not be.* In general, McConnell found that the more local the group, the more homogeneous it was, the more exclusive was its policy, and the more it reflected the local distribution of power. Under such conditions, decentralization strengthens inequality.[8] More is required for democracy than local voluntary associations.

This "more" can only come from outside the logic of civil society. In a 1960s swipe at David Truman's claim that all interests worth representing will find a voice, McConnell observed that "farm workers, Negroes, and the urban poor have not been included in the system of 'pluralist' representation so celebrated in recent years. However much these groups may be regarded as 'potential interest groups,' the important fact is that political organization for their protection within the pluralist framework can scarcely be said to exist. Such protection as they have had has come from the centralized features of the political order—parties, the national government, and the presidency."[9] Martin Luther King, Jr., and Cesar Chavez were well aware of the powerful institutional obstacles that continue to obstruct the organization and recognition of "potential" interests. The movements they headed could not have challenged entrenched local power without the support of federal law, national officials, and comprehensive institutions. The only force capable of directing national attention and adequate resources to these problems, McConnell rightly found, was the Johnson *presidency.*

Private Power and American Democracy's core position stands in direct contradiction to the central assumptions of much contemporary democratic theory. Taken by itself, "civil society" can serve freedom or reinforce inequality. There is nothing inherent that drives it toward plurality, equality, or participation. Much depends on the character of the surrounding environment, and the presence or absence of strong central power to offset the influence of local associations is at least as important as the character of those bodies themselves. "Fortunately, not all of American politics is based on this array of small constituencies. The party system, the Presidency and the national government as a whole represent opposing tendencies. To a very great degree, policies serving the values of liberty and equality are the achievements of these institutions. Public values generally must depend upon the creation of a national constituency."[10] McConnell's critique of pluralism highlights a central problem for many contemporary theories of civil society: their failure to recognize that "autonomy is the means of preserving established power."[11]

Twenty years after *Private Power and American Democracy* was published, Jane Mansbridge's pathbreaking examination of a New England town meeting and an egalitarian workplace reinforced McConnell's reservations about the democratic capacity of local organizations. She found that the face-to-face structures that so impressed Tocqueville and are so important to contemporary theory work well when a measure of common interest is clear to all—but this also comes at the expense of democratic representation and decision-making. Local "unitary" democracies are often marked by a measure of economic equality, and this is what leads them to make decisions with a consensual process that accords equal respect to all views and minimizes the effects of disagreement and conflict. "Adversarial" systems, on the other hand, are organized around division and assume that democracy is about the management of contending purposes rather than the search for general interests. If unitary systems move through the presumption of a common good to consensus, adversarial ones move through the recognition of conflict to majority rule.

Stable democratic orders knit together elements of unitary and adversarial approaches, but Mansbridge found that this is not easy when civil society's local associations drive toward consensus. Indeed, her examination of a New England town meeting revealed that "unitary procedures occasionally mask actual conflicts of interests, to the detriment of citizens who are already at a disadvantage."[12] Public disagreement could disrupt customary social relations after town meetings were over, and this gave rise to a powerful disposition to informally arrange things beforehand and avoid hurt feelings. Those who were not known for holding strong views or having a direct stake in a given issue often found themselves cut out of important information and at a distinct disadvantage when the item came up for discussion and vote.[13] It was simply not true that everyone entered town meeting naked and equal and that deliberations were conducted without contamination from external sources of advantage. A group of influential individuals who already knew each other had considerable influence on the issues that were placed on the agenda and on the debates and discussions that followed. As dearly as Tocqueville admired it, Mansbridge found that the town meeting failed precisely because of what many theorists of civil society take to be its most democratic quality: its localism.

In this town meeting, as in many face-to-face democracies, the fears of making a fool of oneself, of losing control, of criticism, and of making enemies all contribute to the tension that arises in the settlement of disputes. The informal arrangements for the suppression of conflict that result tyrannize as well as protect. To preserve an atmosphere of agreement, the more powerful participants are likely to withhold information and to exert subtle pressures that often work ultimately to the disadvantage of the least powerful.

Such tyranny is not usually deliberate. Nor, although it generally works against the interests of the least powerful, is it always the tyranny of one stable group over another. . . . Participation in face-to-face democracies is not automatically therapeutic: it can make participants feel humiliated, frightened, and even more powerless than before. Joking, informality, avoiding public embarrassment, and downplaying disruptive issues help assuage these fears, but while setting an emotional tone conducive to democracy as friendship, these soothing measures further isolate the powerless.[14]

It was not just the desire to avoid open conflict that made it difficult to consider all points of view. Mansbridge also found a powerful tendency to assume that established residents and the wealthy were most capable of discovering and organizing the community's interest. These participants, who were overwhelmingly male, tended to be the ones who attended town meetings, were more effective public speakers, had more money, and held "better" jobs. Their views tended to shape the discussion and eventual decision—whether it was reached through "unitary" consensus or "adversarial" majority vote. In short, the very thing that Tocqueville admired about town meetings—their local and informal consensual norms—often worked against his expectation that they represent the best traditions of American republicanism. None of this is to deny that there was considerable give-and-take at town meetings or that many people freely debated whether a new pump truck for the fire department was more important than new teachers at the elementary school. The problems Mansbridge described were rooted in the nature of the small communities and local organizations that play such an important role in theories of civil society.[15] Even if they forge a higher degree of cohesion and increased commitment to a common interest, local democracies do not protect individuals equally or facilitate the distribution of power in situations where interests collide. Pretending that interests correspond when they do not only makes things worse. "The evidence," she reports, "points in two directions. The trappings of power appear to be more equally distributed between rich and poor in smaller units, suggesting that the interests of the poor should be more equally protected. But direct analysis of outcomes suggests that the interests of the poor are better protected in large units. I can only conclude that if one judges on adversary grounds, the claim that small units protect individual interests more equally than large ones has not been proven."[16]

There may be something inherent to the logic of localism and community that renders problematic the easy identity between a vibrant civil society and democracy. There is no question that intermediate associations, groups, and movements have often served democracy by restraining arbitrary and irresponsible state power. But civil society can support authoritarianism as easily as it can advance freedom. McConnell's structural critique and Mansbridge's analysis of participation strongly suggest that civil society cannot attenuate the pull of private interests any more than it can overcome the inequities that come from their pursuit. Voluntary associations and face-to-face structures can be important to citizens' lives even in modern conditions of large, divided societies, but their democratic potential depends on a variety of internal and external factors that are not given in "civil society" itself. It makes no sense to conceptualize these matters in moral terms. McConnell and Mansbridge demonstrated how civil society tends to reinforce already-existing distributions of power. It can also mitigate the effects of central authority, but it is not so clear that it can overcome the effects of structural economic inequity. In the best of circumstances, its intermediate associations are too weak to seriously contest the effects of inequality. In the worst of circumstances, they play an active role in strengthening them.

None of this is to denigrate the importance of civil society. Montesquieu, Tocqueville, the pluralists, and others correctly remind us to pay close attention to the nonpolitical structures and organizations that connect individuals to public life. But a measure of caution is required, particularly because unrestrained market forces have become the most active threat to political democracy and civil society in contemporary life. McConnell's and Mansbridge's warnings that intermediate association cannot automatically be theorized as a democratic sphere should alert us to the dangers of superficial analysis and easy assumptions—and they are not alone. Aided by an imaginative use of survey research, Sidney Verba, Kay Schlozman, and Henry Brady have shed a great deal of light on just how civil society affects political participation in times of accelerating economic inequality.

Voice and Equality's "civic voluntarism model" begins with a familiar proposition: the motivation and capacity to take an active part in public affairs are rooted in "the non-political institutions with which individuals are associated during the course of their lives."[17] Citizens acquire political resources, develop public orientations, and are recruited to politics in civil society's schools, families, jobs, voluntary associations and churches. But this does not guarantee equality, for differences in available resources dramatically affect the disposition to participate, skew the information that is communicated to political officials, distort public policy, and compromise the efforts of individuals and groups to defend their interests.[18]

Political participation in America has long been heavily biased toward the top.[19] From voting to writing letters, joining political organizations, giving money, and going to demonstrations, it is marked by significantly higher levels of inequality than most other forms of public activity. And one variable came through *Voice and Equality*: all the crucial forces that explain differences in political participation are generated by disparities in income. Verba's civil society is a sphere of economic inequality and privilege. It is thoroughly penetrated by class relations, and its unequal distribution of political resources is a function of economic life. "Political activity is firmly grounded in American social structure; that same social structure is also the prime source of the inequality in activity."[20] Few institutions are strong enough to offset the impact of income disparities, which are reinforced and multiplied by civil society itself.[21] It should not be particularly surprising that this is often invisible to a body of theory that generally fails to adequately address the impact of economic life. But it is not just contemporary thinkers who are at a loss to explain how class affects civil society. They are profoundly affected by a wide, familiar, and debilitating American infirmity:

> In comparison with other democracies, political conflict in America has traditionally been less deeply imbued with the rhetoric of class. In recent years, however, references to class seem to have become even less common in our political vocabulary than at any time since the New Deal, a circumstance that we could, speculatively, attribute to a number of developments over the past decade or two: the success of the Republican Party in defining itself as the party of the common folk; the erosion of the membership and power of labor unions; the emphasis upon multiculturalism; the declining appeal of Marxist social analysis as an intellectual tool; and changing occupational structures and the concomitant reduction in manufacturing employment. Nevertheless, the argument in this volume makes clear that, despite the absence of references to class in our political discourse, when it comes to political participation, class matters profoundly for American politics.[22]

Willful ignorance and well-meaning naiveté notwithstanding, a change is in the works. Economic inequality has become so glaring that new directions of analysis seem possible—but this requires a break with neo-Tocquevillean orthodoxy. In an extraordinary series of articles, the *New York Times*'s Sara Rimer investigated how "the downsizing of America" is eviscerating community life and eroding participation in the "heartland" areas that supply such grist to the conservative ideological mill.[23] Cities such as Dayton, Ohio, used to be full of stable industrial corporations that offered thousands of secure blue-collar jobs and anchored the rich community life celebrated by some of the more nostalgic theorists of civil society. But "the old era of making things and of job security" is giving way to "the new one of service and technology, takeovers, layoffs, and job insecurity." The effects on civil society have been profound. "Everything, seemingly, is in upheaval: not just the jobs and lives of tens of thousands of people, but also the big corporations, the banks, the schools, the religious and cultural institutions, the old relationships of politics and power, and, especially, people's expectations of security, stability, and a shared civic life."[24] There seems to be plenty of work, but the replacement of stable governmental and unionized manufacturing labor by nonunion, low-wage service and retail jobs has had a profoundly destructive impact on civil society. So has the wave of consolidation and centralization that has been transforming the country's economy.

> All workers may be replaceable. Not so volunteers. When one man, Vinnie Russo, left NCR in the turmoil after the takeover—he felt he had little choice, he said—and found a new job in Louisville, the eighty-five boys of Pack 530 lost their cubmaster; a new one has yet to sign on. With so many women working, it is harder to find people to help in the schools and libraries. Churches are losing members. So are service organizations; people say they cannot leave work for meetings, even if they last only an hour. In a town with a tradition of charity, the United Way has missed its $20 million goal by $1 million in each of the last two years.[25]

"Across Dayton," Rimer found, "scores of other people are too exhausted, or frustrated, or just too plain busy, to keep in touch. 'No one,' says Kathleen Stewart, 'has time to eat dinner together anymore.' Everywhere you go, you meet working mothers who used to stay home, people with two jobs who used to have one, high school students who have taken jobs to help out their families and prepare themselves for the future."[26] Perhaps the "unravelling of civic America" is due to changes in the nature of work rather than peoples' television habits or their individualism.

It must have something to do with the lack of work as well. Sociologist William Julius Wilson has spent many years investigating the impact of deindustrialization and the isolation of minority communities on urban social structure. When jobs disappear, he reports, so does civic life.[27] Cities were once centers of industrial production, and stable blue-collar jobs anchored the church organizations, little leagues, block associations, and other institutions of a vibrant civil society. But three decades of economic hollowing out and catastrophic unemployment have created an entirely new urban reality. "A neighborhood in which people are poor but employed is different from a neighborhood in which people are poor and jobless. Many of today's problems in the inner-city neighborhoods—crime, family dissolution, welfare—are fundamentally a consequence of the disappearance of work." Civil society is impossible in such an environment, for reliable community life depends on the habits, discipline, and schedules required for productive involvement with the outside world. "Neighborhoods plagued by high levels of joblessness are more likely to experience low levels of social organization; the two go hand in hand. High rates of joblessness trigger other neighborhood problems that undermine social organization, ranging from crime, gang violence and drug trafficking to family breakups. And as these controls weaken, the social processes that regulate behavior change."[28] Wilson's findings reinforce the ominous implications of *Voice and Equality*'s conclusion and remind us how important it is to consider economic matters when we assess civil society's role in democratic politics:

> We stated at the outset that meaningful democratic participation requires that the voices of citizens in politics be clear, loud, and equal: clear so that public officials know what citizens want and need, loud so that officials have an incentive to pay attention to what they hear, and equal so that the democratic ideal of equal responsiveness to the preferences and interests of all is not violated. Our analysis of voluntary activity in American politics suggests that the public's voice is often loud, sometimes clear, but rarely equal.[29]

The ways in which civil society is affected by economic inequality has particularly important implications for the United States, since our recent history has been marked by widening material disparities and the largest transfer of wealth from the poor to the rich in human history. In a country where the top 1 percent of the population has enjoyed two-thirds of recent increases in wealth, nearly half the families have lower real incomes today than in 1973. Surely these two phenomena are related. Surely they help explain disparities in the ability to organize and resulting differences in political power. The problem is not new, nor is it likely to go away. Social inequality has reached historic levels, and this makes it particularly important to reexamine the assumptions about civil society that guide contemporary thinking. Tocqueville's orientation toward a self-organizing, self-policing, and self-limiting sphere of voluntary associations never paid much attention to the political ramifications of economic developments. But contemporary America is very different from the society he visited a century and a half ago, and more is required for a theory of civil society than lamentations about bad manners, nostalgia for vanished communities, and faith in a historic disposition to associate. Democracy certainly requires a vibrant civil society that encourages local voluntary activity and keeps the state accountable. But it also requires public supervision of the market, and this necessitates sustained public action, vigorous state activity, and broad political thought. As important as voluntary associations are, it is more than a little ironic that theories of civil society have become hegemonic in what is now the most unequal industrialized society on earth.[30]

It is also no accident that accelerating inequality is proceeding hand in hand with a historically unprecedented concentration and centralization of economic power and private wealth. "Not since a wave of industrial takeovers created the great oil, steel and auto companies at the beginning of the century has corporate America been reshaped by a sweep of merger activity as broad as the one taking place today," the *New York Times* recently reported. "Last year alone, a record $1 trillion in mergers involved American companies, a pace almost unrivaled in business history."[31] Enormous centers of consolidated power cannot fail to have a decisive effect on local activity, but moralistic approaches make it difficult to see the connections between broad economic trends and everyday life. The economy is not just another sphere of association like a book group, bowling league, or block association. It is an extraordinarily powerful set of social relations whose imperatives are penetrating and organizing ever-wider areas of public and private life. No conceivable combination of PTAs, soup kitchens, choral societies, or Girl Scout troops can resist it. It is no longer possible to theorize civil society as a site of democratic activity and counterpoise it to an inherently coercive state without considering how capitalism's structural inequities constitute everyday life.

Coercion, exclusion, and inequality can be as constitutive of any civil society as self-determination, inclusion, and freedom. Nothing is written in stone or is true by definition; a "robust" civil society can serve all sorts of purposes, and the presence or absence of bowling leagues proves nothing by itself. Organizations of lung cancer survivors are not the same as the American Tobacco Institute; the White Citizens Council was different from the Student Non-Violent Coordinating Committee; and it makes no theoretical or political sense to lump the Christian Coalition together with the American Civil Liberties Union. Qualitative distinctions and political choices must be made.

More is involved here than the limits of positive thinking. Aristotle warned that Plato's effort to impose a unitary notion of the common good on a differentiated social order risks a suffocating conformity that can destroy the very possibility of a common life. It is well to pay attention to this ancient advice. The tendency to moralize about social problems is as old an American "habit of the heart" as Robert Bellah's primordial traditions of civic republicanism, but it is not particularly helpful when trying to account for the decline of civicness and political participation. There is something deeply authoritarian about the marriage of a discourse of moral decay and a vision of a virtuous civil society that changes citizens from carriers of rights to bearers of duties. Surely overworked families are at least as credible an explanation for civic decline as watching a lot of television.[32] Surely a more assertive labor movement that made a little trouble from time to time would do more to reinvigorate civil society than moralizing reproaches about individualism and laments about the bad habits of the poor. Promoting "common purpose" through a discourse of values can only reinforce the mistaken notion that social decay is a moral problem first and foremost and that a civic culture of correct orientations is its solution.

In the end, reviving civil society requires the breadth of thought and action that only politics and an orientation toward the state can provide. It is simply not true that public purposes derive their strength from being anchored to personal, local, and immediate experience. Abstract principles and broad political ideals have always driven history's most important movements for justice, equality, and democracy. They still matter, all the more so in an age that has precious little of either in its public life. This requires a willingness to recognize that the social totality shaping civil society is a sphere of inequality and conflict—and that maybe revitalizing civil society requires heightened levels of political struggle over state policy rather than good manners and "civil discourse."

There are encouraging signs that this important lesson has not been lost, and it is noteworthy that the most significant come from outside the United States. The French educational system is backed by a single national tax that is levied and collected in Paris. Funding and curricular standards are applied equally across the country, and the population's profound attachment to revolutionary universalism and egalitarianism is amply demonstrated by the readiness with which hundreds of thousands of citizens took to the streets to beat back recent attacks on the system. American financing of education through property taxes, on the contrary, built as it is on the localism that Tocqueville so admired, guarantees that the quality of childrens' education is directly dependent on the value of their parents' homes. The dreadful inequalities that result sap community vitality, erode democracy, and make a mockery of civil society.[33]

Tocqueville thought that the French could learn something important about democracy from the Americans. Now history has come full circle. Momentary success has generated theoretical crisis, and communism's collapse demands that assumptions be reexamined. One of the most prominent defenders of "open societies," George Soros has spent a lot of time and money supporting civil society against concentrated state power. But now he is worried. In an influential article in the *Atlantic Monthly*, he expressed his fear that uncontrolled markets have penetrated so deeply into social life that "the untrammeled intensification of laissez-faire capitalism and the spread of market values into all areas of life is endangering our open and democratic society. The main enemy of the open society, I believe, is no longer the communist but the capitalist threat."[34] Soros knows what he is talking about. Deepening inequality and gigantic concentrations of private power pose the most important danger to democracy and civil society alike. Political, economic, and social affairs are as mutually dependent today as they always have been—no matter what claims are made about the autonomous logic of different spheres. Extending democracy to the economy, the state, *and* civil society is the central challenge of contemporary life. As always, this requires comprehensive political activity and theory that must begin with the redistribution of wealth. After all is said and done, France has something to teach America. It is time to learn the lessons.

Notes

NOTES TO CHAPTER 1

1. Thucydides, *The Peloponnesian War* (Baltimore: Penguin, 1967), 118–9.
2. Ibid., 120.
3. Plato, *The Republic*, trans. Francis MacDonald Cornford (New York: Oxford University Press, 1977), 24.
4. Ibid., 37.
5. Ibid., 163.
6. Ibid., 143.
7. Ibid., 59–63, 87.
8. Ibid., 112.
9. Ibid., 163–4.
10. Ibid., 270.
11. Ibid., 333–7.
12. Ibid., 110.
13. Ibid., 104.
14. Ibid., 109.
15. Ibid., 234.
16. Aristotle, *The Politics*, trans. and ed. Ernest Barker (New York: Oxford University Press, 1965), 1.
17. Ibid., 4–5.
18. Ibid., 6.
19. Ibid., 6–7.
20. See, e.g., ibid., 10.
21. Ibid., 16–7.
22. Ibid., 19, 23.
23. See Karl Polanyi, *The Great Transformation: The Political and Economic Origins of Our Time* (Boston: Beacon Press, 1957).
24. Aristotle, *The Politics*, 24–5.
25. Ibid., 26–7.
26. Ibid., 28.
27. Ibid., 41.
28. Ibid., 40–1.

29. Ibid., 41.

30. Ibid., 49.

31. Ibid., 51.

32. Ibid., 92.

33. Ibid., 93.

34. Ibid., 111.

35. Ibid., 112.

36. Ibid., 115.

37. Ibid., 178.

38. Ibid., 180–1.

39. Ibid., 181.

40. Ibid., 228.

41. Aristotle, *The Nichomachean Ethics*, trans. Martin Ostwald (Indianapolis: Bobbs-Merrill, 1962), 232.

42. Seneca, "On Tranquility," in Moses Hadas, ed., *Essential Works of Stoicism* (New York: Bantam, 1961), 79.

43. Marcus Aurelius, *Meditations*, trans. Maxwell Staniforth (New York: Penguin, 1964), 65.

44. Ibid., 45, 66, 99.

45. Ibid., 101.

46. Cicero, *The Republic*, trans. Walter Keyes (Cambridge: Cambridge University Press, 1988), 65.

47. Ibid., 15, 67.

48. Ibid., 23.

49. Ibid., 49.

50. Cicero, "On Duties," in *Selected Works*, trans. Michael Grant (Baltimore: Penguin, 1965), 167.

51. Ibid., 166–7.

52. Ibid., 168.

53. Cicero, *Republic*, 169.

54. Ibid., 181–3.

55. Ibid., 77.

NOTES TO CHAPTER 2

1. Saint Augustine, *The City of God*, trans. Marcus Dods (New York: Random House, 1950), 159.

2. Ibid., 477.

3. Ibid., 482–3, 484–7, 502–4.

4. Ibid., 692–3.

5. Ibid., 63.

6. Ibid., 699.

7. Ibid., 112–3.

8. Ibid., 481–2.

9. Ibid., 410.

10. Ibid., 21.

11. Ibid., 693–4.

12. Ibid., 694–5.

13. Ibid., 698–99.

14. Arthur Lovejoy, *The Great Chain of Being* (Cambridge: Cambridge University Press, 1936).

15. Otto Gierke, *Political Theories of the Middle Age*, trans. Frederick William Maitland (Cambridge: Harvard University Press, 1987).

16. See Susan Reynolds, *Kingdoms and Communities in Western Europe, 900–1300* (Oxford: Oxford University Press, 1984).

17. See Ernst Kantorowicz, *The King's Two Bodies: A Study in Medieval Political Theology* (Princeton: Princeton University Press, 1957), chap. 5, for an excellent account of the development of an organic theory of medieval church and state corporatism.

18. Ernst Troeltsch, *The Social Teaching of the Christian Churches* (New York: Harper & Brothers, 1960), 1:201.

19. Thomas Aquinas, "Commentary on the Politics," in Ralph Lerner and Muhsin Mahdi, eds., *Medieval Political Philosophy* (Ithaca: Cornell University Press, 1963), 299.

20. Ibid., 300.

21. Ibid., 311.

22. Thomas Aquinas, "On Kingship," in Dino Bigongiari, ed., *The Political Ideas of St. Thomas Aquinas* (New York: Hafner, 1953), 175–9.

23. Ibid., 176.

24. Dante Alighieri, *On World-Government*, trans. Herbert Schneider (Indianapolis: Bobbs-Merrill, 1949), 9–10.

25. Ibid., 20.

26. Ibid., 68.

27. Ibid., 52–80, 71–3.

28. Ibid., 79.

29. Ibid., 20.

30. Ibid., 6.

31. Ibid., 77–80.

32. Giles of Rome, "On Ecclesiastical Power," in Lerner and Mahdi, eds., *Medieval Political Philosophy*, 392.

33. Ibid., 396.

34. John of Paris, "On Kingly and Papal Power," in Lerner and Mahdi, eds., *Medieval Political Philosophy*, 411–2.

35. Ibid., 413.

36. Marsilius of Padua, "The Defender of the Peace," in Lerner and Mahdi, eds., *Medieval Political Philosophy*, 445–6.

37. Ibid., 449.

38. Ibid., 449–50.

39. Ibid., 479.

40. Ibid., 478.

NOTES TO CHAPTER 3

1. Johan. Huizinga, *The Waning of the Middle Ages* (New York: Doubleday, 1954).

2. See Maurice Dobb, *Studies in the Development of Capitalism* (New York: International Publishers, 1947).

3. Jacob Burkhardt, *The Civilization of the Renaissance in Italy* (New York: Harper & Brothers, 1958), 1:22.

4. Niccolò Machiavelli, *The Prince*, trans. George Bull (New York: Penguin, 1961), 97.

5. Ibid., 54.

6. Ibid., 70.

7. Ibid., 123.

8. Niccolò Machiavelli, *The Discourses*, trans. Leslie J. Walker, ed. Bernard Crick (New York: Penguin, 1970), 97.

9. Ibid., 113.

10. See J. G. A. Pocock, *The Machiavellian Moment: Florentine Political Thought and the Atlantic Republican Tradition* (Princeton: Princeton University Press, 1975), for an important elaboration of this theme.

11. Machiavelli, *Discourses*, 111.

12. Ibid., 334–9.

13. Ibid., 123. See also the famous chapter 25 of *The Prince*, where Machiavelli compares fortune to a raging river against which agility and adaptability are the most important political virtues.

14. Ibid., 201.

15. Ibid.

16. Ibid., 202–3.

17. Ibid., 203.

18. Ibid., 475.

19. Ibid., 385–90.

20. Ibid., 112.

21. Ibid., 275.

22. Martin Luther, "The Freedom of a Christian," in *Martin Luther: Selections from His Writings*, ed. John Dillenberger (New York: Doubleday, 1962), 55.

23. Ibid., 61–2.

24. Martin Luther, "The Pagan Servitude of the Church," in *Selections*, 304.

25. Luther, "Freedom of a Christian," 64.

26. Ibid., 72.

27. Martin Luther, "An Appeal to the Ruling Class of German Nationality as to the Amelioration of the State of Christendom," in *Selections*, 403–85.

28. Ibid., 409.

29. Ibid., 411.

30. Ibid., 412.

31. Ibid., 414.

32. Ibid., 416.

33. Ibid., 434–83, passim.

34. Ibid., 483.

35. Ibid., 440–1.

36. Martin Luther, "Friendly Admonition to Peace concerning the Twelve Articles of the Swabian Peasants," in Hans J. Hillerbrand, ed., *The Protestant Reformation* (New York: Harper & Row, 1968), 83.

37. Luther, "Freedom of a Christian," 78.

38. Ibid., 78–9.

39. Martin Luther, "Secular Authority: To What Extent It Should Be Obeyed," in Hillerbrand, ed., *The Protestant Reformation*, 369.

40. Ibid., 371.

41. Ibid., 370.

42. Ibid., 375.

43. Ibid., 374–5.

44. Ibid., 383.

45. Ibid., 385.

46. Ibid.

47. Ibid., 387.

48. Thomas Hobbes, *Leviathan*, ed. C. B. Macpherson (New York: Penguin, 1985), 150.

49. See the famous debate between Michael Oakeshott (introduction to *Leviathan* by Thomas Hobbes [Oxford: Blackwell, 1946]) and C. B. Macpherson (*The Political Theory of Possessive Individualism* [Oxford: Oxford University Press, 1962]).

50. Hobbes, *Leviathan*, 161.

51. Ibid., 183.

52. Ibid., 185.

53. Ibid., 186.

54. Ibid., 190. Unless otherwise noted, all emphases are Hobbes's.

55. Ibid., 202.

56. Ibid., 227.

57. Ibid., 187–8.

58. Ibid., 227.

59. Ibid., chap. xxii.
60. Ibid., 264.
61. Ibid.
62. Ibid., 365–6.
63. Ibid.
64. Ibid., 314, 317.

NOTES TO CHAPTER 4

1. John Locke, "Second Treatise on Government," in *Two Treatises on Government*, ed. Peter Laslett (New York: Cambridge University Press, 1960), para. 25, p. 286. Unless otherwise noted, all emphases are Locke's.
2. Ibid., 280.
3. Ibid., 271.
4. Ibid., 274.
5. Ibid., 268.
6. Ibid., 350.
7. Ibid., 381.
8. Ibid., 289.
9. Ibid., 350–1.
10. Ibid., 324.
11. Ibid., 350–1.
12. The best treatment of this is still Karl Polanyi's masterpiece, *The Great Transformation: The Political and Economic Origins of Our Time* (Boston: Beacon Press, 1957).
13. Peter Gay, *The Enlightenment: An Interpretation* (New York: Norton, 1966–69), 1:17.
14. Ibid., 1:3, and 2:5–6.
15. See Ernst Cassirer, *The Philosophy of the Enlightenment* (Princeton: Princeton University Press, 1951).
16. See Peter Gay, *The Enlightenment: An Interpretation*, 2:437–47, for an informative discussion of Beccaria.
17. See Adam Seligman, *The Idea of Civil Society* (New York: Free Press, 1992), 25–36.
18. Adam Ferguson, *An Essay on the History of Civil Society* (New Brunswick, NJ: Transaction Publishers, 1995), 205.
19. Ibid., 31.
20. Ibid., 32.
21. Ibid., 51.
22. Ibid., 39–40.
23. Ibid., 56–7.

24. Ibid., 54.

25. Ibid., 18–9.

26. Ibid., 96.

27. Ibid., 98.

28. Ibid., 122.

29. Ibid.

30. Ibid., 123.

31. Ibid., 237.

32. Ibid., 218.

33. Ibid., 219–20.

34. Ibid., 222.

35. Ibid., 161–2.

36. Ibid., 49.

37. See Eric Hobsbawm's classic, *The Age of Revolution: 1789–1848* (New York: New American Library, 1962), chap. 1.

38. See Peter Gay, *The Enlightenment: An Interpretation*, 2:344–68.

39. Adam Smith, *An Inquiry into the Nature and Causes of the Wealth of Nations*, ed. Kathryn Sutherland (Oxford: Oxford University Press, 1993), 11.

40. Ibid., 13.

41. Ibid., 11.

42. Ibid., 18.

43. Ibid., 9.

44. Ibid., 36.

45. Ibid., 120–1.

46. Ibid., 21.

47. Ibid., 22.

48. Ibid., 203–4.

49. See Albert Hirschman, *The Passions and the Interests: Political Arguments for Capitalism before Its Triumph* (Princeton: Princeton University Press, 1977).

50. Smith, *Wealth of Nations*, 225.

51. Ibid., 289.

52. Ibid., 291–2.

53. Ibid., 391.

54. Ibid., 407–8

55. Ibid., 413.

56. Ibid.

57. Ibid., 190.

58. Ibid., 260.

59. Ibid., 204–5.

60. Ibid., 459.

61. Ibid., 429–30.

62. Ibid., 430.

NOTES TO CHAPTER 5

1. Immanuel Kant, "Idea for a Universal History with a Cosmopolitan Purpose," in *Political Writings*, ed. Hans Reiss, trans. H. B. Nisbet (Cambridge: Cambridge University Press, 1991), 41–53. Unless otherwise noted, all subsequent references to Kant will be to this volume.

2. See Immanuel Kant, *Critique of Practical Reason*, trans. Lewis White Beck (New York: Macmillan, 1993).

3. Immanuel Kant, "An Answer to the Question: What Is Enlightenment?" 54. All emphases are Kant's.

4. Kant, *Critique of Practical Reason*, 30.

5. Ibid., 30–59.

6. Kant, "What Is Enlightenment?" 55.

7. Ibid.

8. Immanuel Kant, "A Renewed Attempt to Answer the Question: Is the Human Race Continually Improving?" 177–90.

9. Immanuel Kant, "Idea for a Universal History with a Cosmopolitan Purpose," 44.

10. Immanuel Kant, "On the Common Saying: 'This May Be True in Theory, but It Does Not Apply in Practice,'" 73.

11. Kant, "Idea for a Universal History," 46.

12. Kant, "On the Common Saying: 'This May Be True in Theory,'" 75.

13. Ibid., 75–6.

14. Ibid., 74.

15. See Leonard Krieger, *The German Idea of Freedom* (Boston: Beacon Press, 1957).

16. Kant, "Idea for a Universal History," 45.

17. Ibid., 75–6.

18. See two of the great histories of the French Revolution: Georges Lefebvre, *The French Revolution* (New York: Columbia University Press, 1964), vol. 2, trans. John Hall and James Friguglietti; and Albert Soboul, *The French Revolution 1787–1799* (New York: Vintage, 1975).

19. G. W. F. Hegel, *The Philosophy of Right*, trans. T. M. Knox (Oxford: Oxford University Press, 1967), preface, 5.

20. Ibid., 30.

21. Ibid., 134.

22. Ibid., 109.

23. G. W. F. Hegel, *The Philosophy of History*, trans. J. Sibree (New York: Dover, 1956), 42.

24. Hegel, *Philosophy of Right*, 41–2, 45–6.

25. Ibid., 122.

26. Ibid., 122–3.

27. Ibid., 123.

28. Ibid., 129–30.

29. Ibid., 122–3.

30. Ibid.

31. Ibid., 124–5.

32. Ibid., 276.

33. Ibid., 148.

34. Ibid., 123.

35. Ibid., 269.

36. Ibid., 150.

37. Ibid., 277–8.

38. Ibid., 150.

39. Ibid., 130.

40. Ibid., 155.

41. Ibid., 71.

42. Hegel, *Philosophy of History*, 24–5.

43. Hegel, *Philosophy of Right*, 156.

44. Ibid., 164–74.

45. Ibid., 147.

46. Ibid., 279.

47. Ibid., 147.

48. Ibid., 160–1.

49. Ibid., 161.

50. Ibid., 160–1.

51. Ibid., 109.

52. Ibid., 191.

53. There are many discussions of "the social question" in nineteenth-century European socialism. See, e.g., George Lichtheim, *The Origins of Socialism* (New York: Praeger, 1969); and Eric Hobsbawm, *The Age of Revolution: 1789–1848* (New York: New American Library, 1962).

54. See John Ehrenberg, *The Dictatorship of the Proletariat: Marxism's Theory of Socialist Democracy* (New York: Routledge, 1992), chaps. 1 and 2.

55. Karl Marx, "Comments on the Latest Prussian Censorship Instructions," in Karl Marx and Frederick Engels, *Collected Works* (New York: International Publishers, 1975–), 1:109, 120, 131. All subsequent references will be to this edition.

56. Karl Marx, "Contribution to the Critique of Hegel's Philosophy of Law," 3:8.

57. Ibid., 3:48. All emphases are Marx's.

58. Karl Marx, "On the Jewish Question," 3:155.

59. Ibid., 3:160.

60. Ibid., 3:163.

61. Ibid., 3:152.

62. Ibid., 3:164.

63. Ibid., 3:166.

64. Ibid., 3:167.

65. Ibid., 3:164.

66. Karl Marx, "Contribution to the Critique of Hegel's Philosophy of Law: Introduction," 3:184.

67. Ibid.

68. Ibid., 3:186.

69. Ibid.

70. Karl Marx, "Economic and Philosophical Manuscripts of 1844," 3:280.

71. Karl Marx and Frederick Engels, "The German Ideology," 5:50.

72. Karl Marx, "Theses on Feuerbach," 5:8.

73. Karl Marx, "The Poverty of Philosophy," 6:212.

74. Karl Marx, "Preface to 'A Contribution to the Critique of Political Economy,'" 29:262.

75. Karl Marx, "Economic Manuscripts of 1857–58 (First Version of *Capital*) or *Grundrisse*," 28:26–36, 29:29–31.

76. Karl Marx, "Capital," 35:8.

77. Ibid., 35:45.

78. Ibid., 35:83–4.

79. Ibid., 35:186.

80. Marx and Engels, "The German Ideology," 5:46–7.

81. Ibid., 5:90.

82. Karl Marx and Frederick Engels, "Communist Manifesto," 6:504.

83. Ibid., 505.

84. Ibid., 6:514.

85. Karl Marx, "Critical Marginal Notes on the Article 'The King of Prussia and Social Reform. By a Prussian,'" 3:206.

86. Marx and Engels, "Communist Manifesto," 6:505–6.

NOTES TO CHAPTER 6

1. Baron de Montesquieu, *The Spirit of the Laws*, trans. and ed. Anne M. Cohler, Basia Carolyn Miller, and Harold Samuel Stone (Cambridge: Cambridge University Press, 1989), 18.

2. Ibid., 17–8.

3. Ibid., 72–4.

4. Ibid., 72.

5. Ibid., 73.

6. Ibid., 74.

7. Ibid., 73.

8. Ibid., 18.

9. Ibid., 75.

10. Ibid., 131.

11. Ibid., 155.

12. Ibid., 160.

13. Ibid., 187.

14. Ibid., 19.

15. Ibid., 337–56.

16. Jean-Jacques Rousseau, "Discourse on the Origin and Foundation of Inequality among Men," in *The First and Second Discourses*, ed. Roger Masters, trans. Roger Masters and Judith Masters (New York: St. Martin's Press, 1964), 137.

17. Ibid., 95.

18. Ibid., 133.

19. Jean-Jacques Rousseau, *On the Social Contract*, trans. Judith Masters, ed. Roger Masters (New York: St. Martin's Press, 1978), 52.

20. Ibid.

21. Ibid., 55–6.

22. Ibid., 53.

23. Ibid., 67.

24. Ibid., 53.

25. Ibid., 53–4. The emphases are Rousseau's.

26. Ibid., 84–5.

27. Ibid., 102. The emphasis is Rousseau's.

28. Ibid., 61.

29. Ibid.

30. Ibid., 66.

31. Ibid., 71.

32. Rousseau, "Discourse on the Origin and Foundation of Inequality," 50–1.

33. Rousseau, *On the Social Contract*, 62.

34. Edmund Burke, *Reflections on the Revolution in France*, ed. H. D. Mahoney (New York: Macmillan, 1955).

35. Ibid., 23.

36. Ibid., 40.

37. Ibid., 37.

38. Ibid.

39. Ibid., 42, 55.

40. Ibid., 87.

41. Ibid., 109.

42. Ibid., 215–6.

43. Ibid., 242–3.

44. Ibid., 243.

45. Alexis de Tocqueville, *Democracy in America* (New York: Random House, 1990), 1:3.

46. Ibid.
47. Ibid., 1:70.
48. Ibid., 1:39.
49. Ibid., 1:40.
50. Ibid., 1:61.
51. Ibid., 1:67.
52. Ibid., 1:68.
53. Ibid., 1:90.
54. Ibid., 1:81.
55. Ibid., 1:191.
56. Ibid., 2:108–9.
57. Ibid., 2:106.
58. Ibid., 1:90–1.
59. Ibid., 1:194.
60. Ibid., 1:195.
61. Ibid., 1:140.
62. Ibid., 1:256.
63. Ibid., 1:22.
64. Ibid., 1:99.
65. Ibid., 1:103.
66. Ibid., 1:104.
67. Ibid., 1:108.
68. Ibid., 1:109.
69. Ibid., 1:110.
70. Ibid.
71. Ibid., 1:304.
72. Ibid., 1:324.
73. Ibid., 1:329.
74. Ibid., 2:245–6.
75. There is an extensive historical literature concerning economic equality during the Age of Jackson. A good place to begin is Edward Pessen, "The Egalitarian Myth and the American Social Reality: Wealth, Mobility, and Equality in the 'Era of the Common Man,'" *American Historical Review* 70, no. 4 (October 1971): 989–1031, and *Jacksonian America: Society, Personality, and Politics* (Homewood, IL: Dorsey Press, 1978). Both works contain valuable bibliographical information on both sides of the debate about American equality.

NOTES TO CHAPTER 7

1. V. I. Lenin, "Newspaper Report of a 'Report on the Tasks of Soviet Power' delivered at the meeting of the Petrograd Soviet of Workers' and Soldiers' Deputies,

October 25, 1917," in *Collected Works* (Moscow: Progress Publishers, 1960–72), 26:240.

2. See John Ehrenberg, *The Dictatorship of the Proletariat: Marxism's Theory of Socialist* Democracy (New York: Routledge, 1992), for a further development of these themes.

3. Ibid., chaps. 7 and 8.

4. Friedrich Hayek, *The Road to Serfdom* (Chicago: University of Chicago Press, 1944), vii.

5. Ibid., 36.

6. Ibid., 48–9.

7. Ibid., 59.

8. Ibid., 75.

9. See Karl Polanyi, *The Great Transformation: The Political and Economic Origins of Our Time* (Boston: Beacon Press, 1957); and Sheldon Wolin, *Politics and Vision: Continuity and Innovation in Western Political Thought* (Boston: Little, Brown, 1960), chap. 9.

10. Hayek, *Road to Serfdom*, 106.

11. Ibid., 206.

12. Carl Friedrich and Zbigniew Brzezinski, *Totalitarian Dictatorship and Autocracy* (Cambridge: Harvard University Press, 1965).

13. Ibid., 161.

14. Ibid., 22.

15. Ibid., 229.

16. Ibid., 279.

17. Hannah Arendt, *The Origins of Totalitarianism* (Cleveland: Meridian, 1966).

18. Ibid., 318.

19. Ibid., 419.

20. Ibid., 311.

21. Ibid., 315.

22. Ibid., 475.

23. Ibid.

24. Jacques Rupnik, "Totalitarianism Revisited," in John Keane, ed., *Civil Society and the State: New European Perspectives* (London: Verso, 1988), 272. See Agnes Heller, "An Imaginary Preface to the 1984 Edition of Hannah Arendt's 'The Origins of Totalitarianism,'" in Reiner Schurmann, ed., *The Public Realm: Essays on Discursive Types in Political Philosophy* (Albany: SUNY Press, 1989), 256.

25. Ferenc Feher, Agnes Heller, and Gyorgy Markus, *Dictatorship over Needs* (New York: St. Martin's Press, 1983).

26. Ibid., 68.

27. Ibid., 88–9.

28. Ibid., 89.

29. Ibid., 76.

30. Ibid., 253.

31. Ibid., 254.

32. Mihaly Vajda, "East-Central European Perspectives," in Keane, ed., *Civil Society and the State*, 340.

33. See Vaclav Havel, "The Power of the Powerless," in *Open Letters* (New York: Knopf, 1991), 125–214.

34. See Vaclav Havel, "Politics and Conscience," in *Open Letters*, 249–71.

35. Vajda, "East-Central European Perspectives," 342.

36. Robert Miller, "Civil Society in Communist Systems: An Introduction," in Robert Miller, ed., *The Development of Civil Society in Communist Systems* (North Sydney: Allen & Unwin, 1992), 5–6.

37. See, among others, the work of E. H. Carr, Sheila Fitzpatrick, Jerry Hough, and Alec Nove.

38. See Jeremy Goldfarb, "Social Bases of Independent Public Expression in Communist Societies," *American Journal of Sociology* 83, no. 4 (1978): 920–39.

39. Georg Konrad and Ivan Szelenyi, *The Intellectuals on the Road to Class Power*, trans. Andrew Arato and Richard Allen (New York: Harcourt Brace Jovanovich, 1979), 199–200.

40. See Daniel Singer, *The Road to Gdansk* (New York: Monthly Review Press, 1981).

41. Adam Michnik, "The New Evolutionism," *Survey*, Summer–Autumn 1976, 269.

42. Ibid., 271, 274.

43. Ibid., 273.

44. Ibid., 274

45. Andrew Arato, "Civil Society against the State: Poland 1980–81," *Telos* 47 (Spring 1981): 23–47.

46. Adam Michnik, *Letters from Prison and Other Essays*, trans. Maya Katynski (Berkeley: University of California Press, 1985), 124.

47. Andrew Arato, "Empire vs. Civil Society: Poland 1981–82," *Telos* 50 (Winter 1981–82): 19–48.

48. S. Frederick Starr, "Soviet Union: A Civil Society," *Foreign Affairs*, Spring 1988, 26–41.

49. Gail Lapidus, "State and Society: Toward the Emergence of Civil Society in the Soviet Union," in Seweryn Bialer, ed., *Politics, Society, and Nationality inside Gorbachev's Russia* (Boulder, CO: Westview, 1989).

50. Adam Michnik, "What We Want to Do and What We Can Do," *Telos* 47 (1981): 75. See also Mihaly Vajda, *The State and Socialism: Political Essays* (New York: St. Martin's Press, 1981).

51. Michnik, "What We Want to Do," 73.

52. Ibid.

53. Three excellent examples of this line of thinking are U.S. Helsinki Watch Committee, *Reinventing Civil Society: Poland's Quiet Revolution* (New York: U.S. Helsinki Watch Committee, 1986); Robert Miller, ed., *Poland in the Eighties: Social Revolution against "Real Socialism"* (Canberra: Australian National University, 1984); and Vladimir Tismaneanu, ed., *In Search of Civil Society: Independent Peace Movements in the Soviet Bloc* (New York: Routledge, 1990).

54. Havel, "The Power of the Powerless."

55. Georg Konrad, *Antipolitics* (New York: Harcourt Brace Jovanovich, 1984), 67.

56. Ibid., 92.

57. Ibid., 167.

58. Ibid., 160.

59. Ibid., 228.

60. Vaclav Havel, *Disturbing the Peace* (New York: Knopf, 1990), 125ff.; and Havel, *Antipolitics*, 229.

61. Havel, "Politics and Conscience," 269.

62. Havel, *Antipolitics*, 229.

63. Agnes Heller, "On Formal Democracy," in Keane, ed., *Civil Society and the State*, 131.

64. Vladimir Tismaneanu, "Against Socialist Militarism: The Independent Peace Movement in the German Democratic Republic," in Tismaneanu, ed., *In Search of Civil Society*, 182.

65. Chandran Kukathas, David Lovell, and Wiliam Maley, eds., introduction to *The Transition from Communism: State and Civil Society in the USSR* (Melbourne: Longman Cheshire, 1991), 2–3.

66. Ibid., 6.

67. Ibid., 12.

68. Laszlo Csapo, "The Implosion of Collectivist Societies," in Kukathas, Lovell, and Malley, eds., *Transition from Communism*, 171–2.

69. Miller, "Civil Society in Communist Systems," 8.

70. Ibid. See also T. H. Rigby, "The USSR: End of a Long, Dark Night," in Miller, ed., *Development of Civil Societies*, 14.

NOTES TO CHAPTER 8

1. David Truman, *The Governmental Process* (New York: Knopf, 1951), viii–ix, 15

2. Ibid., 51.

3. Ibid., 502.

4. Ibid., 510–1.

5. Ibid., 512.

6. Ibid., 514.

7. Ibid., 521–2.

8. Ibid., 515.

9. Ibid., 524.

10. Gabriel Almond and Sidney Verba, *The Civic Culture* (Boston: Little, Brown, 1965), ix.

11. Ibid., 6.

12. Ibid., 30.

13. Peter Bachrach's *The Theory of Democratic Elitism* (Boston: Little, Brown, 1967) is still a classic criticism of this perspective.

14. Almond and Verba, *The Civic Culture*, 245.

15. Ibid., 240.

16. Ibid., 241–2.

17. Ibid., 339.

18. Ibid., 360.

19. See Philip Converse, Warren Miller, and Ronald Stokes, *The American Voter* (New York: Wiley, 1960), for an example of this tendency.

20. See V. O. Key, *Public Opinion and American Democracy* (New York: Knopf, 1961).

21. Antonio Gramsci, *Selections from the Prison Notebooks*, ed. and trans. Quentin Hoare and Geoffrey Nowell Smith (New York: International Publishers, 1971), 238.

22. Ibid.

23. Ibid., 243.

24. Ibid., 236.

25. Ibid., 5–23, 133.

26. Ibid., 239. See also 262, 271.

27. Ibid., 244.

28. Max Horkheimer, "The Culture Industry: Enlightenment as Mass Deception," in Max Horkheimer and Theodore Adorno, *Dialectic of Enlightenment* (New York: Continuum, 1995), 120–67.

29. See Neil Postman, *Amusing Ourselves to Death* (New York: Viking, 1986).

30. Herbert Marcuse, *One Dimensional Man* (Boston: Beacon Press, 1966), xvi.

31. Ibid., 3.

32. Ibid., 57.

33. Stephen Eric Bronner, *Of Critical Theory and Its Theorists* (Cambridge: Blackwell, 1994).

34. Hannah Arendt, *The Human Condition* (Chicago: University of Chicago Press, 1958), 33.

35. Ibid., 38.

36. Ibid., 41.

37. Richard Sennett, *The Fall of Public Man: On the Social Psychology of Capitalism* (New York: Random House, 1978), 4.

38. Ibid., 4–5.

39. Ibid., 219.

40. Ibid., 259.

41. Ibid., 264.

42. Ibid., 269.

43. Ibid., 295.

44. Jürgen Habermas, "The Public Sphere: An Encyclopedia Article," in Stephen Eric Bronner and Douglas McKay Kellner, eds., *Critical Theory and Society: A Reader* (New York: Routledge, 1989), 136.

45. Ibid.

46. Ibid., 138–9.

47. Jürgen Habermas, *The Structural Transformation of the Public Sphere: An Inquiry into a Category of Bourgeois Society*, trans. Thomas Burger (Cambridge: MIT Press, 1989), 27.

48. Ibid., 52.

49. Ibid., 168.

50. Ibid., 177–8.

51. Ibid., 179–80.

52. Jürgen Habermas, *Between Facts and Norms: Contributions to a Discourse Theory of Law and Democracy*, trans. William Rehng (Cambridge: MIT Press, 1996), 366–7.

53. Ibid., 372.

54. Ibid., 380.

55. Ibid., 381.

56. Robert Bellah et al., *Habits of the Heart: Individualism and Commitment in American Life* (Berkeley: University of California Press, 1985), 282.

57. Ibid., 251.

58. Ibid., 283.

59. Ibid., 285.

60. Ibid., 5.

61. Ibid., 345.

62. Ibid., 346.

63. Ibid., 350. See Jean Bethke Elshtain, *Democracy on Trial* (New York: Basic Books, 1995), for a slightly different interpretation.

64. Robert Putnam, *Making Democracy Work: Civic Traditions in Modern Italy* (Princeton: Princeton University Press, 1993), 15.

65. Ibid., 99.

66. Ibid., 115.

67. Ibid., 167.

68. Ibid., 182.

69. Robert Putnam, "Bowling Alone: America's Declining Social Capital," *Journal of Democracy* 6, no. 1 (January 1995): 65.

70. Robert Putnam, "The Strange Disappearance of Civic America," *American Prospect* 24 (Winter 1996): 45.

71. Ibid., 24.

72. See Theda Skocpol, "Unravelling from Above," *American Prospect* 25 (March–April 1996): 17–20.

73. See Sidney Tarrow, "Making Social Science Work across Space and Time: Reflections on Robert Putnam's *Making Democracy Work*," *American Political Science Review* 90 (June 1996): 389–97.

NOTES TO CHAPTER 9

1. In addition to the literature cited in earlier chapters, see Benjamin Barber, *Jihad vs. McWorld: How Globalism and Tribalism Are Reshaping the World* (New York: Ballantine Books, 1996); Jean Bethke Elshtain, *Democracy on Trial* (New York: Basic Books, 1995); Francis Fukuyama, *Trust: The Social Virtues and the Creation of Prosperity* (New York: Free Press, 1995); Ernest Gellner, *Conditions of Liberty: Civil Society and Its Rivals* (New York: Penguin, 1994); and Adam Seligman, *The Idea of Civil Society* (New York: Free Press, 1992) and *The Problem of Trust* (Princeton: Princeton University Press, 1997).

2. Colin L. Powell, "Recreating the Civil Society—One Child at a Time," *Brookings Review* 15, no. 4 (Fall 1997): 2, 3.

3. See Karl Polanyi, *The Great Transformation: The Political and Economic Origins of Our Time* (Boston: Beacon Press, 1957).

4. Grant McConnell, *Private Power and American Democracy* (New York: Knopf, 1966), 6.

5. See Grant McConnell, "The Spirit of Private Government," *American Political Science Review* 52, no. 3 (September 1958): 754–70.

6. McConnell, *Private Power and American Democracy*, 107.

7. Ibid., 154.

8. Ibid., 349.

9. Ibid.

10. Ibid., 8.

11. Ibid., 294.

12. Jane Mansbridge, *Beyond Adversary Democracy* (Chicago: University of Chicago Press, 1983), 35.

13. Ibid., 68–70.

14. Ibid., 70–71.

15. Ibid., 118.

16. Ibid., 280–1.

17. Sidney Verba, Kay Lehman Schlozman, and Henry E. Brady, *Voice and Equality: Civic Voluntarism in American Politics* (Cambridge: Harvard University Press, 1995), 3.

18. Ibid., 10–2.

19. Ibid., 11.

20. Ibid., 512.

21. Ibid., 521–2.

22. Ibid., 532–3.

23. Sara Rimer, "The Fraying of Community," in *The Downsizing of America* (New York: Times Books, 1997), 111–38.

24. Ibid., 113.

25. Ibid.

26. Ibid., 127.

27. William Julius Wilson, "When Work Disappears," *New York Times Magazine*, August 18, 1996. See also his *The Truly Disadvantaged* (Chicago: University of Chicago Press, 1987).

28. Wilson, "When Work Disappears," 28.

29. Verba, Schlozman, and Brady, *Voice and Equality*, 509.

30. Edward Wolff, *Top Heavy: The Increasing Inequality of Wealth in America and What Can Be Done about It* (New York: New Press, 1995). See also *New York Times*, June 22 and August 16, 1992; and Gary Wills, "It's His Party," *New York Times Magazine*, August 11, 1996.

31. *New York Times*, January 19, 1998.

32. See Theda Skocpol, "Unravelling from Above," *American Prospect* 25 (March–April 1996): 20–5.

33. See Jonathan Kozol, *Savage Inequalities* (New York: Crown, 1991).

34. George Soros, "The Capitalist Threat," *Atlantic Monthly*, February 1997, 45.

Bibliography

ARTICLES

Anderson, Perry. "The Antinomies of Antonio Gramsci." *New Left Review* 100 (November 1976–January 1977): 5–78.

Arato, Andrew. "Civil Society against the State: Poland 1980–81." *Telos* 47 (Spring 1981): 23–47.

———. "Empire vs. Civil Society: Poland 1981–82. *Telos* 50 (Winter 1981–82): 19–48

———. "Revolution, Civil Society and Democracy." *Praxis International* 10, nos. 1–2 (April–July 1990): 24–38.

Benhabib, Seyla. "The 'Logic' of Civil Society: A Reconsideration of Hegel and Marx." *Philosophy and Social Criticism* 8, no. 2 (1981): 151–66.

Berman, Sheri. "Civil Society and the Collapse of the Weimar Republic." *World Politics* 49 (April 1997): 401–29.

Booth, William James. "On the Idea of the Moral Economy." *American Political Science Review* 88, no. 3 (September 1994): 653–67.

Bozoki, Andras, and Miklos Sukosd. "Civil Society and Populism in the Eastern European Democratic Transitions." *Praxis International* 13, no. 3 (October 1992): 224–41.

Bronner, Stephen Eric. "The Great Divide: The Enlightenment and Its Critics." *New Politics*, Spring 1995, 65–86.

"Civil Society." Special issue, *Brookings Review* 15, no. 4 (Fall 1997).

Cohen, Jean, and Andrew Arato. "Social Movements, Civil Society, and the Problem of Sovereignty." *Praxis International* 4, no. 3 (1984): 266–83.

Cohen, Joshua, and Joel Rogers. "Secondary Associations and Democratic Governance." *Politics and Society* 20, no. 4 (December 1992): 393–472.

Commager, Henry Steele. "Tocqueville's Mistake." *Harper's*, August 1984, 70–4.

Gleason, Abbott. "'Totalitarianism' in 1984." *Russian Review* 43 (1984): 145–59.

Goldfarb, Jeremy. "Social Bases of Independent Public Expression in Communist Societies." *American Journal of Sociology* 83, no. 4 (1978): 920–39.

Hankiss, Elemer. "The 'Second Society': Is There an Alternative Social Model Emerging in Contemporary Hungary?" *Social Research* 55, nos. 1–2 (Spring–Summer 1988): 13–42.

Hunt, Geoffrey. "Gramsci, Civil Society and Bureaucracy." *Praxis International* 6, no. 2 (1986): 206–19.

Kumar, Krishnan. "The Revolutions of 1989: Socialism, Capitalism, and Democracy." *Theory and Society* 21 (1992): 309–56.

———. "Civil Society: An Inquiry into the Usefulness of an Historical Term." *British Journal of Sociology* 44, no. 3 (September 1993): 375–95.

McConnell, Grant. "The Spirit of Private Government." *American Political Science Review* 52, no. 3 (September 1958): 754–70.

Michnik, Adam. "The New Evolutionism." *Survey*, Summer–Autumn 1976, 267–77.

———. "What We Want to Do and What We Can Do." *Telos* 47 (1981): 66–87.

Miller, Robert. "Theoretical and Ideological Issues of Reform in Socialist Systems: Some Yugoslav and Soviet Examples." *Soviet Studies* 41, no. 3 (July 1989): 430–48.

Norris, Pippa. "Does Television Erode Social Capital? A Reply to Putnam." *PS* 29, no. 3 (September 1996): 474–80.

Pessen, Edward. "The Egalitarian Myth and the American Social Reality: Wealth, Mobility, and Equality in the 'Era of the Common Man.'" *American Historical Review* 70, no. 4 (October 1971): 989–1031.

Pierson, Christopher. "New Theories of State and Civil Society: Recent Developments in Post-Marxist Analysis of the State." *Sociology* 18, no. 4 (November 1984): 563–71.

Powell, Colin L. "Recreating the Civil Society—One Child at a Time." *Brookings Review* 15, no. 4 (Fall 1997): 2, 3.

Putnam, Robert. "Bowling Alone: America's Declining Social Capital." *Journal of Democracy* 6, no. 1 (January 1995): 65–78.

———. "The Strange Disappearance of Civic America." *American Prospect* 24 (Winter 1996): 34–48.

Rau, Zbigniew. "Some Thoughts on Civil Society in Eastern Europe and the Lockean Contractarian Approach." *Political Studies* 35 (1987): 573–92.

Schudson, Michael. "What If Civic Life Didn't Die?" *American Prospect* 25 (March–April 1996): 17–20.

Skocpol, Theda. "A Society without a 'State'? Political Organization, Social Conflict, and Welfare Provision in the United States." *Journal of Public Policy* 7 (October–December 1987): 349–71.

———. "Unravelling from Above." *American Prospect* 25 (March–April 1996): 20–25.

Soros, George. "The Capitalist Threat." *Atlantic Monthly*, February 1997, 45–58.

Starr, S. Frederick. "Soviet Union: A Civil Society." *Foreign Affairs*, Spring 1988, 26–41.

Swain, Nigel. "Hungary's Socialist Project in Crisis." *New Left Review* 176 (1989): 3–29.

Tarrow, Sidney. "Making Social Science Work across Space and Time: A Critical Reflection on Robert Putnam's *Making Democracy Work.*" *American Political Science Review* 90 (June 1996): 389–97.

Taylor, Charles. "Modes of Civil Society." *Public Culture* 3, no. 1 (Fall 1990): 95–118.

Walzer, Michael. "The Idea of Civil Society." *Dissent*, Spring 1991, 293–304.

Wartenberg, Thomas E. "Poverty and Class Structure in Hegel's Theory of Civil Society." *Philosophy and Social Criticism* 8, no. 2 (1981): 169–82.

Wills, Gary. "It's His Party." *New York Times Magazine*, August 11, 1996.

Wilson, William Julius. "When Work Disappears." *New York Times Magazine*, August 18, 1996.

Wood, Ellen Meiksins. "The Uses and Abuses of 'Civil Society.'" *Socialist Register 1990*, 60–84.

———. "From Opportunity to Imperative: The History of the Market." *Monthly Review* 46 (1994): 14–40.

Wood, Neal. "The Economic Dimensions of Cicero's Political Thought: Property and State." *Canadian Journal of Political Science* 16, no. 4 (December 1985): 739–56.

BOOKS

Almond, Gabriel, and Sidney Verba. *The Civic Culture.* Boston: Little, Brown, 1965.

Anderson, Perry. *Considerations on Western Marxism.* London: Verso, 1979.

Arendt, Hannah. *The Human Condition.* Chicago: University of Chicago Press, 1958.

———. *The Origins of Totalitarianism.* Cleveland: Meridian, 1966.

Aristotle. *The Nichomachean Ethics*, trans. Martin Ostwald. Indianapolis: Bobbs-Merrill, 1962.

———. *The Politics*, trans. and ed. Ernest Barker. New York: Oxford University Press, 1965.

Augustine, Saint. *The City of God*, trans. Marcus Dods. New York: Random House, 1950.

Aurelius, Marcus. *Meditations*, trans. Maxwell Staniforth. New York: Penguin, 1964.

Avineri, Shlomo. *The Social and Political Thought of Karl Marx.* London: Cambridge University Press, 1968.

———. *Hegel's Theory of the Modern State.* Cambridge: Cambridge University Press, 1972.

Bachrach, Peter. *The Theory of Democratic Elitism.* Boston: Little, Brown, 1967.

Barber, Benjamin. *Jihad vs. McWorld: How Globalism and Tribalism Are Reshaping the World.* New York: Ballantine Books, 1996.

Barker, Ernest. *Principles of Social and Political Theory.* New York: Oxford University Press, 1961.

Bellah, Robert, et al. *Habits of the Heart: Individualism and Commitment in American Life.* Berkeley: University of California Press, 1985.

Berlin, Isaiah. *Four Essays on Liberty.* London: Oxford University Press, 1977.

Bialer, Seweryn, ed. *Politics, Society, and Nationality inside Gorbachev's Russia.* Boulder, CO: Westview, 1989.

Bigongiari, Dino, ed. *The Political Ideas of St. Thomas Aquinas.* New York: Hafner, 1953.

Blackburn, Robin, ed. *After the Fall: The Failure of Communism and the Future of Socialism.* London: Verso, 1991.

Bronner, Stephen Eric. *Of Critical Theory and Its Theorists.* Cambridge: Blackwell, 1994.

Bronner, Stephen Eric, and Douglas McKay Kellner, eds. *Critical Theory and Society: A Reader.* New York: Routledge, 1989.

Bryson, Gladys. *Man and Society: The Scottish Inquiry of the Eighteenth Century.* Princeton: Princeton University Press, 1945.

Burke, Edmund. *Reflections on the Revolution in France,* ed. H. D. Mahoney. New York: Macmillan, 1955.

Burkhardt, Jacob. *The Civilization of the Renaissance in Italy.* 2 vols. New York: Harper & Brothers, 1958.

Calhoun, Craig, ed. *Habermas and the Public Sphere.* Cambridge: MIT Press, 1994.

Cassirer, Ernst. *The Philosophy of the Enlightenment.* Princeton: Princeton University Press, 1951.

Cicero. *Selected Works,* trans. Michael Grant. Baltimore: Penguin, 1965.

———. *The Republic,* trans. Walter Keyes. Cambridge: Cambridge University Press, 1988.

Cohen, Jean. *Class and Civil Society: The Limits of Marxian Critical Theory.* Amherst: University of Massachusetts Press, 1982.

Cohen, Jean, and Andrew Arato. *Civil Society and Political Theory.* Cambridge: MIT Press, 1992.

Colletti, Lucio. *From Rousseau to Lenin: Studies in Ideology and Society.* New York: Monthly Review Press, 1972.

Converse, Philip, Warren Miller, and Ronald Stokes. *The American Voter.* New York: Wiley, 1960.

Dante Alighieri. *On World-Government,* trans. Herbert Schneider. Indianapolis: Bobbs-Merrill, 1949.

Dobb, Maurice. *Studies in the Development of Capitalism.* New York: International Publishers, 1947.

Ehrenberg, John. *The Dictatorship of the Proletariat: Marxism's Theory of Socialist Democracy.* New York: Routledge, 1992.

Elshtain, Jean Bethke. *Democracy on Trial.* New York: Basic Books, 1995.

Feher, Ferenc, Agnes Heller, and Gyorgy Marcus. *Dictatorship over Needs*. New York: St. Martin's Press, 1983.

Ferguson, Adam. *An Essay on the History of Civil Society*. New Brunswick, NJ: Transaction Publishers, 1995.

Friedrich, Carl, and Zbigniew Brzezinski. *Totalitarian Dictatorship and Autocracy*. Cambridge: Harvard University Press, 1965.

Fukuyama, Francis. *Trust: The Social Virtues and the Creation of Prosperity*. New York: Free Press, 1995.

Gay, Peter. *The Enlightenment: An Interpretation*, 2 vols. New York: Norton, 1966–69.

Gellner, Ernest. *Conditions of Liberty: Civil Society and Its Rivals*. New York: Penguin, 1994.

Gierke, Otto. *Political Theories of the Middle Age*, trans. Frederick William Maitland. Cambridge: Harvard University Press, 1987.

Gorz, Andre. *Farewell to the Working Class: An Essay on Post-Industrial Socialism*. Boston: South End Press, 1982.

———. *Critique of Economic Reason*, trans. Gillian Handyside and Chris Turner. London: Verso, 1989.

Gouldner, Alvin. *The Two Marxisms: Contradictions and Anomalies in the Development of Theory*. New York: Seabury, 1980.

Gramsci, Antonio. *Selections from the Prison Notebooks*, ed. and trans. Quentin Hoare and Geoffrey Nowell Smith. New York: International Publishers, 1971.

Habermas, Jürgen. *The Structural Transformation of the Public Sphere: An Inquiry into a Category of Bourgeois Society*, trans. Thomas Burger. Cambridge: MIT Press, 1989.

———. *Between Facts and Norms: Contributions to a Discourse Theory of Law and Democracy*, trans. William Rehng. Cambridge: MIT Press, 1996.

Hadas, Moses, ed. *Essential Works of Stoicism*. New York: Bantam, 1961.

Hall, Stuart, and Martin Jacques, eds. *New Times: The Changing Face of Politics in the 1990s*. London: Lawrence & Wishart, 1989.

Hann, C. M., ed. *Market Economy and Civil Society in Hungary*. London: Frank Cass, 1990.

Havel, Vaclav. *Disturbing the Peace*. New York: Knopf, 1990.

———. *Open Letters*. New York: Knopf, 1991.

Hayek, Friedrich. *The Road to Serfdom*. Chicago: University of Chicago Press, 1944.

Hegel, G. W. F. *The Philosophy of History*, trans. J. Sibree. New York: Dover, 1956.

———. *The Phenomenology of Mind*, trans. J. B. Baillie. New York: Harper & Row, 1967.

———. *The Philosophy of Right*, trans. T. M. Knox. Oxford: Oxford University Press, 1967.

Hillerbrand, Hans J., ed. *The Protestant Reformation*. New York: Harper & Row, 1968.

Hirschman, Albert. *The Passions and the Interests: Political Arguments for Capitalism before Its Triumph*. Princeton: Princeton University Press, 1977.

Hobbes, Thomas. *Leviathan*, ed. C. B. Macpherson. New York: Penguin, 1985.

Hobsbawm, Eric. *The Age of Revolution: 1789–1848*. New York: New American Library, 1962.

Hont, I., and M. Ignatieff, eds. *Wealth and Virtue: The Shaping of Political Economy in the Scottish Enlightenment*. New York: Cambridge University Press, 1983.

Horkheimer, Max, and Theodore Adorno. *Dialectic of Enlightenment*. New York: Continuum, 1995.

Huizinga, Johan. *The Waning of the Middle Ages*. New York: Doubleday, 1954.

Kant, Immanuel. *Political Writings*, ed. Hans Reiss, trans. H. B. Nisbet. Cambridge: Cambridge University Press, 1991.

———. *Critique of Practical Reason*, trans. Lewis White Beck. New York: Macmillan, 1993.

Kantorowicz, Ernst. *The King's Two Bodies: A Study in Medieval Political Theology*. Princeton: Princeton University Press, 1957.

Kaufmann, Franz-Xaver, Giandomenico Majone, and Vincent Ostrom, eds. *Guidance, Control, and Evaluation in the Public Sector*. Berlin: Walter de Gruyter, 1986.

Keane, John. *Democracy and Civil Society*. London: Verso, 1988.

———, ed. *Civil Society and the State: New European Perspectives*. London: Verso, 1988.

Key, V. O. *Public Opinion and American Democracy*. New York: Knopf, 1961.

Kolakowski, Leszek, and Stuart Hampshire, eds. *The Socialist Idea: A Reappraisal*. New York: Basic Books, 1974.

Konrad, Georg. *Antipolitics*. New York: Harcourt Brace Jovanovich, 1984.

Konrad, Georg, and Ivan Szelenyi. *The Intellectuals on the Road to Class Power*, trans. Andrew Arato and Richard Allen. New York: Harcourt Brace Jovanovich, 1979.

Kozol, Jonathan. *Savage Inequalities*. New York: Crown, 1991.

Krieger, Leonard. *The German Idea of Freedom*. Boston: Beacon Press, 1957.

Kukathas, Chandran, David Lovell, and William Maley, eds. *The Transition from Communism: State and Civil Society in the USSR*. Melbourne: Longman Cheshire, 1991.

Lefebvre, Georges. *The French Revolution*, vol. 2, trans. John Hall and James Friguglietti. New York: Columbia University Press, 1964.

Lenin, V. I. *Collected Works*. Moscow: Progress Publishers, 1960–72.

Lerner, Ralph, and Muhsin Mahdi, eds. *Medieval Political Philosophy*. Ithaca: Cornell University Press, 1963.

Lichtheim, George. *The Origins of Socialism*. New York: Praeger, 1969.

Locke, John. *Two Treatises on Government*, ed. Peter Laslett. New York: Cambridge University Press, 1960.

Lovejoy, Arthur. *The Great Chain of Being*. Cambridge: Cambridge University Press, 1936.

Luther, Martin. *Martin Luther: Selections from His Writings*, ed. John Dillenberger. New York: Doubleday, 1962.

Machiavelli, Niccolò. *The Prince*, trans. George Bull. New York: Penguin, 1961.

———. *The Discourses*, trans. Leslie J. Walker, ed. Bernard Crick. New York: Penguin, 1970.

Macpherson, C. B. *The Political Theory of Possessive Individualism*. Oxford: Oxford University Press, 1962.

Maier, Charles. *Changing Boundaries of the Political*. Cambridge: Harvard University Press, 1987.

Mansbridge, Jane. *Beyond Adversary Democracy*. Chicago: University of Chicago Press, 1983.

Marcuse, Herbert. *Reason and Revolution: Hegel and the Rise of Social Theory*. Boston: Beacon Press, 1960.

———. *One Dimensional Man*. Boston: Beacon Press, 1966.

Marx, Karl, and Frederick Engels. *Collected Works*, 50 vols. New York: International Publishers, 1975–.

McConnell, Grant. *Private Power and American Democracy*. New York: Knopf, 1966.

McCoy, Charles and John Playford, eds. *Apolitical Politics: A Critique of Behaviorism*. New York: Thomas Crowell, 1967.

Michnik, Adam. *Letters from Prison and Other Essays*, trans. Maya Katynski. Berkeley: University of California Press, 1985.

Miller, Robert, ed. *Poland in the Eighties: Social Revolution against "Real Socialism."* Canberra: Australian National University, 1984.

———. *The Development of Civil Society in Communist Systems*. North Sydney: Allen & Unwin, 1992.

Montesquieu, Baron de. *The Spirit of the Laws*, trans. and ed. Anne M. Cohler, Basia Carolyn Miller, and Harold Samuel Stone. Cambridge: Cambridge University Press, 1989.

Mouffe, Chantal, ed. *Gramsci and Marxist Theory*. London: Routledge and Kegan Paul, 1979.

Nove, Alec. *An Economic History of the USSR 1917–91*. London: Penguin, 1992.

Parenti, Michael. *Democracy for the Few*. New York: St. Martin's Press, 1995.

Pelczynski, Z. A., ed. *The State and Civil Society: Studies in Hegel's Political Philosophy*. Cambridge: Cambridge University Press, 1984.

Pessen, Edward. *Jacksonian America: Society, Personality, and Politics*. Homewood, IL: Dorsey Press, 1978.

Plato. *The Republic*, trans. Francis MacDonald Cornford. New York: Oxford University Press, 1977.

————. *The Last Days of Socrates*, trans. Hugh Tredennick. New York: Penguin, 1985.

Pocock, J. G. A. *The Machiavellian Moment: Florentine Political Thought and the Atlantic Republican Tradition.* Princeton: Princeton University Press, 1975.

Polanyi, Karl. *The Great Transformation: The Political and Economic Origins of Our Time.* Boston: Beacon Press, 1957.

Postman, Neil. *Amusing Ourselves to Death.* New York: Viking, 1986.

Putnam, Robert. *Making Democracy Work: Civic Traditions in Modern Italy.* Princeton: Princeton University Press, 1993.

Reynolds, Susan. *Kingdoms and Communities in Western Europe, 900–1300.* Oxford: Oxford University Press, 1984.

Riedel, Manfred. *Between Tradition and Revolution: The Hegelian Transformation of Political Philosophy.* Cambridge: Cambridge University Press, 1984.

Rimer, Sara. *The Downsizing of America.* New York: Times Books, 1997.

Ritter, Joachim. *Hegel and the French Revolution*, trans. Richard Dien Winfield. Cambridge: MIT Press, 1982.

Rousseau, Jean-Jacques. *The First and Second Discourses*, trans. Roger Masters and Judith Masters. New York: St. Martin's Press, 1964.

————. *On the Social Contract*, trans. Judith Masters, ed. Roger Masters. New York: St. Martin's Press, 1978.

Sandel, Michael. *Democracy's Discontent: America in Search of a Public Philosophy.* Cambridge: Harvard University Press, 1996.

Schneider, Louis, ed. *The Scottish Moralists on Human Nature and Society.* Chicago: University of Chicago Press, 1967.

Schor, Juliet. *The Overworked American: The Unexpected Decline of Leisure.* New York: Basic Books, 1993.

Schurmann, Reiner, ed. *The Public Realm: Essays on Discursive Types in Political Philosophy.* Albany: SUNY Press, 1989.

Seligman, Adam. *The Idea of Civil Society.* New York: Free Press, 1992.

————. *The Problem of Trust.* Princeton: Princeton University Press, 1997.

Sennett, Richard. *The Fall of Public Man: On the Social Psychology of Capitalism.* New York: Random House, 1978.

Singer, Daniel. *The Road to Gdansk.* New York: Monthly Review Press, 1981.

Smith, Adam. *An Inquiry into the Nature and Causes of the Wealth of Nations*, ed. Kathryn Sutherland. Oxford: Oxford University Press, 1993.

Soboul, Albert. *The French Revolution 1787–1799.* New York: Vintage, 1975.

Thucydides. *The Peloponnesian War.* Baltimore: Penguin, 1967.

Tismaneanu, Vladimir, ed. *In Search of Civil Society: Independent Peace Movements in the Soviet Bloc.* New York: Routledge, 1990.

————. *Reinventing Politics: Eastern Europe from Stalin to Havel.* New York: Free Press, 1993.

Tocqueville, Alexis de. *Democracy in America*, 2 vols. New York: Random House, 1990.

Tokes, Rudolf L., ed. *Opposition in Eastern Europe*. Baltimore: Johns Hopkins University Press, 1979.

Troeltsch, Ernst. *The Social Teaching of the Christian Churches*. New York: Harper & Brothers, 1960.

Truman, David. *The Governmental Process*. New York: Knopf, 1951.

U.S. Helsinki Watch Committee. *Reinventing Civil Society: Poland's Quiet Revolution*. New York: U.S. Helsinki Watch Committee, 1986.

———. *Toward Civil Society: Independent Initiatives in Czechslovakia*. New York: Human Rights Watch, 1989.

Vajda, Mihaly. *The State and Socialism: Political Essays*. New York: St. Martin's Press, 1981.

Verba, Sidney, Kay Lehman Schlozman, and Henry E. Brady. *Voice and Equality: Civic Voluntarism in American Politics*. Cambridge: Harvard University Press, 1995.

Walzer, Michael. *The Revolution of the Saints*. New York: Atheneum, 1965.

———. *Spheres of Justice: A Defense of Pluralism and Equality*. New York: Basic Books, 1983.

Weber, Max. *The Protestant Ethic and the Spirit of Capitalism*. New York: Scribner's, 1958.

Wilson, William Julius. *The Truly Disadvantaged*. Chicago: University of Chicago Press, 1987.

Wolff, Edward. *Top Heavy: The Increasing Inequality of Wealth in America and What Can Be Done about It*. New York: New Press, 1995.

Wolin, Sheldon. *Politics and Vision: Continuity and Innovation in Western Political Thought*. Boston: Little, Brown, 1960.

Wood, Ellen Meiksins. *The Retreat from Class: A New "True" Socialism*. London: Verso, 1986.

———. *Democracy against Capitalism*. Cambridge: Cambridge University Press, 1995.

Wood, Neal. *Cicero's Social and Political Thought*. Berkeley: University of California Press, 1988.

Zeitlin, Irving. *Liberty, Equality, and Revolution in Alexis de Tocqueville*. Boston: Little, Brown, 1971.

Zetterman, Marvin. *Tocqueville and the Problem of Democracy*. Stanford: Stanford University Press, 1967.

Index

About the Author

John Ehrenberg grew up in the Bronx and attended DeWitt Clinton High School, Dartmouth College, and Stanford University. Active in the civil rights, antiwar, and other movements of the late 1960s and 1970s, he has been teaching political science at the Brooklyn Campus of Long Island University since 1980. He has written extensively about Marxism, democratic thought, and the history of political theory.